SPORT
OF A
LIFETIME

*Enduring Personal Stories
From Tennis*

JUDY AYDELOTT

SPORT
OF A
LIFETIME

Enduring Personal Stories
From Tennis

"Sport of a Lifetime" is published by New Chapter Press (www.NewChapterMedia.com) and distributed by the IPG (www.IPGBook.com) © Judy Aydelott, 2017

ISBN: 978-1937559649

For more information on this title or New Chapter Press contact: Randy Walker, Managing Partner, New Chapter Press, 1175 York Ave, Suite #3s, New York, NY 10065 Rwalker@NewChapterMedia.com

Photo credits are as follows: INTRODUCTION (Courtesy of Judy and Gordon Aydelott), FRED KOVALESKI (Judy Aydelott), GEORGE and LETTY BRIA (Courtesy of George and Letty Bria), GARDNAR MULLOY (Judy Aydelott and Univ. of Miami Sports Hall of Fame), TONY FRANCO (Courtesy of Tony Franco), DAVID DINKINS (Judy Aydelott), HENRY TIBERIO (Judy Aydelott), KATRINA ADAMS (Courtesy of Northwestern University and the USTA), DONNA FLOYD FALES (Judy Aydelott), BETTY EISENSTEIN (Judy Aydelott), FRAN MEEK (Judy Aydelott), JOHN POWLESS (Judy Aydelott), ROLF THUNG (Judy Aydelott), JIM NELSON (Courtesy of Bill Nelson), JOHN JAMES (Judy Aydelott), HARLAN STONE and JONATHAN BATES (Judy Aydelott), CHRIS and BILL DRAKE (Judy Aydelott), MAS and SUSAN KIMBALL (Judy Aydelott), THE SAW MILL BOYS (Judy Aydelott), BERNICE MYERS (Judy Aydelott), JULIE VERRONE (Judy Aydelott), DAN WSZOLEK (Judy Aydelott), TOM BRUNKOW (Judy Aydelott), TOMMIE WALKER (Judy Aydelott), CHUCK NIEMETH (Judy Aydelott), GREG TEBBE (Courtesy of Greg Tebbe), ROB LABRIOLA (Courtesy of Rob Labriola), JOHN NEWCOMBE (Judy Aydelott), ROY EMERSON (Judy Aydelott), OWEN DAVIDSON (Judy Aydelott), JUDY and GORDON AYDELOTT (Courtesy of Judy and Gordon Aydelott), JIMMY BIGGS and GORDON AYDELOTT (Courtesy of Gordon Aydelott)

Contents

"While getting old is unavoidable,
being old is something you don't have
to surrender to"
— Wise words of a friend, Chuck Griffith

INTRODUCTION

My tennis partner Deb and I were playing an interclub tennis match five years ago on a July day boasting a temperature and humidity of 95. The match ended after a three-hour struggle with us losing in the third-set tiebreaker. But the match was well fought, and I was not as disappointed as you might think. I was happy to be a part of the process.

As we approached the net to shake hands, Mary Pat, one of our opponents, asked Deb, "How come you keep calling Judy 'Mom?'"

"Because she is my Mom!" Deb replied.

"Nooo," said Mary Pat hesitating before adding, "You're kidding."

Lisa, her partner, added, "Are you really her Mom? Her birth mom?"

I nodded with a smile, and was pleased that they thought me youthful.

"How do you stay in such good shape?"

"Well, I exercise, have good health and play lots of tennis."

We went back to talking about key points in the match as we gobbled up some fruit and lemonade.

But Mary Pat changed the subject, and said, "You know, Judy, you should write a book."

"No way."

"No. Really. You should. We've got all these baby boomers entering retirement age but wanting to stay active, and certainly everybody is aware of the obesity epidemic. This could play right into that. And look at all the celebrities today who are in or are pushing their 70's - Paul McCartney, Mick Jagger, Barbra Streisand. You could call their publicists for an interview."

I thought that idea was preposterous. How in the world would I, an unknown, get such an interview? I soon forgot the book idea. Until...

A few months later, I was at a men's and women's New England 70-and-over tennis tournament at the Essex County Club in Gloucester, Massachusetts, famous for having hosted women's national tournaments before the Open Era. My husband, Gordon, was playing doubles with Walt Beatty, and I played with his wife, Anne. The men were more successful than Anne and I, but we were just glad to be out there playing and enjoying ourselves.

While watching all the players, men and women at least in their seventies, I began to give the book idea some more thought. Tennis did keep us feeling young! The men and women were fit, with sculpted legs and muscled arms. The camaraderie among the players who met for drinks and dinner in the evening was contagious as old 'war' stories were told of past matches against one another. Laughter and good will filled the air.

Tennis friends could be a good starting point to delve into stories of good health and happiness as the years pile up.

Not long after, in July 2014, I went with Gordon to the Atlantic Coast Cup championship as he was playing in the 65-and-over category.

Gordon and Judy Aydelott

The Atlantic Coast Cup championships, a competition among four USTA sections from the East Coast - New England, Eastern, Middle Atlantic and Middle States - are held every summer in age categories from the 45s through the 75s. Each team selects a captain who organizes his team. In the 45 to 65 age categories, the teams consist of three singles players and four doubles teams; in the 75-and-above category, the teams consist of two singles players and three doubles teams, who compete over a two day period. Each team hosts the event on a rotating basis and often two teams from each section will participate, for instance, one team of 65 and over, the other team playing in the 75s.

In July, 2014, the 65s and 75s were playing on grass at the Essex County Club in Gloucester, obviously a popular venue. I decided this would be a good time to see whether I could interview players and come up with some good life stories and reasons why senior tennis was good for your well-being.

The first day of the matches was rainy, but fortunately a nearby indoor facility was made available. The chance to play on the coveted grass was not an option that day, but the indoor hard courts were fine. Armed with a pen, legal pad and a big smile, I watched the men gathering in clusters, chatting with teammates and friends on other teams, searching in their tennis bags for head bands, wrist bands, knee braces and other assorted necessities while they waited for their court assignments. I didn't see anyone I recognized, except Dan Wszolek.

"Dan, how are you? I haven't seen you since you played a couple years ago at Sleepy Hollow. How's your tennis?" I asked.

"About the same. Still lousy strokes, but I get to the ball, which drives my opponents mad," he answered with a grin.

Then he added, "What's the legal pad for? Working on a case?"

Dan knew I was a lawyer.

"No. Actually I want to interview you players to find out how you got into the game of tennis and what keeps you playing in your senior years. How would you like to be my first victim?"

"Sure."

Dan was full of stories, and you can read them in Chapter 21.

While I was meeting with Dan, several gentlemen stopped by, curious, and asked, "Are you a reporter?"

"No. Actually, I'm working on a project to learn more about senior tennis players and why they love the game." I didn't say I was writing a book, as I thought that would be presumptuous though that was my hope.

"Oh. Well, after my next match, I'm available," offered one of the players.

And that's how it went. The players were more than willing to be interviewed. I went through a couple of legal pads and probably twelve to fourteen interviews. Some stories didn't make the cut for the book, but the others, I think, added depth, humor and insight into seniors still playing tennis and why.

From there, I was on a roll. Gordon and I have been playing tennis for many years, know a lot of players and know of a lot of players. I probably interviewed 60 or 70, some more extensively than others, but all with stories to tell. Only one person, Fred Kovaleski, a former spy with the CIA, turned me down - for good reasons - but he had second thoughts and gave me one of the best accounts of his life and his tennis I think you'll find fascinating. Others whom I didn't know - Katrina Adams, the President of the U.S. Tennis Association, former New York City Mayor David Dinkins, who was responsible for keeping the U.S. Open in New York City, 102-year-old Gardnar Mulloy, John Newcombe, Roy Emerson and Owen Davidson – all world champions in their day - graciously let me learn of their backgrounds and careers.

Please join me on my journey.

—Judy Aydelott

CHAPTER 1:

FRED KOVALESKI

On a rainy New York City day the sidewalks were a sea of umbrellas obscuring the faces of the commuters. Annoying puddles had to be avoided, but that didn't bother me a bit. I was excited to meet with Fred Kovaleski, one of the top senior players for decades whose life stories are humorous, adventuresome, compelling and heartwarming all - the stuff of a good movie.

I found his apartment building, got into the elevator, pressed '10' and as the door opened, Fred greeted me with a big smile and a kiss on my cheek. He led me into a living room filled with treasures from all over the world - silver pieces, beautifully carved furniture and contemporary art on all the walls, white sofas with colorful pillows and family photographs everywhere.

"This is all Manya's doing," explained Fred as we surveyed the surroundings.

"I'm sure. It looks like her - warm, sunny, elegant," I added.

I first heard of Fred and his wife, Manya, during a Men's Century Doubles Tournament played some years ago at The Saw Mill Club in Mt. Kisco, New York.

In excited whispers, spectators were saying, "Fred Kovaleski is playing… and his beautiful Russian wife, Manya, is here."

The Century Tournament at Saw Mill has been going on for years. Each doubles team must equal 100 years in age. Fred, then 67, was playing with Cliff Adler, a former Harvard varsity tennis player and top Eastern competitor. The team was seeded No. 1 and did not disappoint, winning in the final. The year was 1990. As I watched, I remember being impressed with Fred's strong, muscular legs, his quick feet, scorching forehand and blistering serve. Manya, I missed and didn't meet until an Atlantic Coast Cup Tournament in New England many years later.

Fred was born on October 8, 1924, the fourth son - a daughter came later - of Polish immigrants in Hamtramck, Michigan, a Polish enclave almost completely surrounded by Detroit. His hero was his older brother, Charles, who was accepted by the U.S. Naval Academy by virtue of the Open Examination, a rare feat, and not by Congressional appointment. Charles joined the Air Wing, trained at Pensacola, Florida and served on the USS Yorktown as a Company Commander. Tragically, he was killed during a mission in the Pacific.

Handball was the big sport in Fred's elementary school, the Polaski Polish Grammar School. His gym teacher, Jean Hoxie, was impressed with Fred's athleticism when, in the third grade, he won the school handball championship.

"Mrs. Hoxie - I always called her Mrs. Hoxie till the day she died - said to me 'You're a good athlete. Would you like to learn how to play tennis?' I didn't even know what tennis was. She said, 'Ask your Dad to buy a racquet. It'll cost $10, and I'll take care of the rest.' So I asked my father. He said, '$10 for a racquet? Go learn how to play baseball.'

Fred Kovaleski

"Mrs. Hoxie was undeterred. She said, 'I'll find an old racquet.' She did. She painted a line the height of a tennis net on the gym wall, painted three boxes - one to the left, one straight ahead and one to the right - gave me some basic instructions and a big garbage can of old balls. 'Aim your shots and your serves at those three squares,' and I was on my way."

Fred paused for a moment as tears came to his eyes. "Mrs. Hoxie made me what I am today. She was great, and I get sentimental whenever I think of her. She didn't just teach me how to play tennis. She taught me how to present myself in public. 'How do you do, Mrs. Jones?' How to eat properly with good table manners. She taught me about the business world and political figures. And she opened doors for me making it possible to go to college, and she set me on a path that I would never have dreamed of."

I asked, "Did she think of you as her surrogate son?"

"I didn't think of it at the time, but yes, she did. She didn't have any children of her own."

After a pause in the questioning, I asked, "How was your tennis coming along?"

"Pretty well. When I was 12, Mrs. Hoxie decided to enter me in a 15-and-under tournament in Detroit. She's the one who entered me in the tournaments, who drove me to the tournaments and who paid the entry fees. Well, to everyone's surprise, I won the tournament. That really got Mrs. Hoxie started. She continued to coach me throughout junior high and then when I got to high school, she became the coach of the Hamtramck High School tennis team."

"She took care of everything, didn't she?"

Fred smiled with a nod.

"She proved she deserved it too. Our varsity team won the Detroit Interscholastic Championship for the first time ever.

"When I was 17, Mrs. Hoxie wanted me to compete against men, not juniors, and entered me in the Tri-State Championship in Cincinnati, Ohio. I was entered in the singles draw, but Mrs. Hoxie wanted me in the doubles draw too. She asked the club host, 'Do you have anyone around here who can play doubles?' His answer was 'Not really any good enough to play in this tournament. But we've got a South American Indian fellow here. He's 19 and not entered in the doubles.' 'Great, put him and Fred down as a team,' responded Mrs. Hoxie.

"I met the South American. He didn't speak English except 'Hey, Baby' to attract the young women, and 'Me forehand; you backhand.' That was fine with me since I liked playing the backhand side. There was no talk during play, but I kept score. We get to the finals, and our opponents are Billy Talbert and the Argentinian Davis Cupper Alejo Russell. They were well-known players and were expected to win. Well we win, and Mrs. Hoxie goes 'ape!'"

"So. Who was your partner?"

"Pancho Segura!" exclaimed Fred with a big grin. "This was before he became known, but he was good! He was bow-legged from rickets that he contracted as a kid, but could he run!"

Fred took a breath before launching into another story.

"I was starting my senior year in high school, and Mrs. Hoxie wanted me out of Hamtramck. 'I want you out of Hamtramck and I want you out of Michigan for college.' Somehow she knew the William & Mary tennis coach Sharoy Umbeck, an intellectual and head of the Sociology Department."

Umbeck agreed that Fred was a safe risk, and said, "Maybe we can get your boy a scholarship."

Fred graduated from high school in June, 1942, played on the U.S. Junior Davis Cup team against Canada during the summer, and, in September, he started as a freshman at William & Mary in Williamsburg, Virginia. He couldn't believe how beautiful the campus was, but his stay was short-lived. Fred turned 18 in October, 1942, and he immediately enlisted in the Army.

"I'm going to be a hot shot paratrooper," he explained. "I liked their boots! And I liked that the paratroopers were all volunteers so there wouldn't be any backsliders. They all wanted to be jumping out of planes.

"My grades weren't very good. I think I had a D average, but fortunately I was called up in March, 1943 before they could flunk me out.

"I was sent to Fort Benning, Georgia for basic training. I got my boots, and we began to learn how to jump out of planes, safely, under all conditions. After basic, I joined the 11th Airborne Division stationed on islands in the Pacific.

"Our first landing was New Guinea, but there was no fighting there. Our next stop was the Philippines where we had three combat jumps on the Island of Luzon. Luzon is the largest island in the archipelago, and Manila is its major city. An internment camp was located on the island, and our mission was to free the 2,100 internees, all civilian families and many of them Americans. Six hundred paratroopers jumped from countless planes onto the camp, and after securing it, we marched the internees to a body of water, Lacuna del Bay. The territory we covered was controlled by the Japanese, so we couldn't continue to march them on land. Small water craft met us at the bay, and we got the internees to an abandoned prison, the New Bilobid Prison. Our generals were very considerate and moved all 2,100 into prison cells, took advantage of the dining hall and gave all of us paratroopers two and three-day passes to spend time with the people we had just rescued.

"You've never seen a more grateful group. I stayed in touch with 11 or 12 of them for years."

Fred gathered himself for a moment before he went on.

"The next jump was Appari, up in the northern part of Luzon. The 1st Cavalry was pushing the Japanese up north. The Japanese were in retreat, and it was our job, as the General said, 'to squeeze them from behind.' Fortunately, we accomplished our mission.

"I was discharged in February, 1946 and glad to be alive. I had seen some awful stuff -- guys getting shot, guys getting killed. Being in the Philippines, in particular at that time, people had been displaced by the warfare. Homes in the cities were destroyed and families tried to find new homes in the country.

"The Japanese were very cruel to the local population and they didn't hesitate to execute people. People were wandering hopelessly, begging for a handout. And you saw little children begging. So sad. And you saw women sitting on street corners with a child who was disfigured with a leg off or something.

"Most of us - young guys from the US - had never seen anything like this. It made an indelible impact - the ruthlessness of the Japanese. Then we come in as the liberators. We were well supplied - plenty of food, chocolates, cigarettes. Kids would climb up the palm trees and cut down coconuts to give us in exchange for food and candy. We'd hand them out fairly liberally because we were never short of food. But more important, Chesterfield and Lucky Strike cigarettes were pure gold to them. We'd get little packs of four cigarettes with our rations and give them out to those begging.

"I returned to William & Mary, now on the G.I. Bill, with a new attitude about college. All of us who had returned from the war had matured. I figured this is my only chance, and I can't just fiddle around. I took my courses seriously and became a student!"

"But did you find time to get back on the tennis courts?" I asked.

"Oh yes. Coach Umbeck was grateful to have a team again, and he welcomed us with a new intensity. I played No. 1 on the varsity, and our No. 2 player was Tut Bartzen who, after graduation in 1949, went on to win the National Clay Courts in Lake Forest, Illinois four times."

"In 1947 and 1948, William & Mary won the NCAAs and you won the singles. What happened in 1949?" I asked.

"I lost in the finals to Vic Seixas of the University of North Carolina in five long sets. That was a tough loss."

I reminded him that Seixas was ranked as high as No. 3 in the world and won all four Grand Slam tournaments in either singles or doubles.

"Yes. He was good."

The phone rang, and Fred went into the bedroom to answer it. It was Serge, his son, finalizing plans for dinner that night. While Fred was out of the room, I examined all the photos and found one that I loved of Fred and his very beautiful wife Manya.

I showed it to Fred, and again, tears came to his eyes.

"We had a great marriage. Really good. Sixty years."

Manya passed away in January 2014, and Fred still struggled with his loss.

Getting back on course, I asked, "What happened after you graduated from William & Mary?"

"I played in tournaments all summer. Then Mrs. Hoxie got me a job back in Michigan but after two months, she said 'This is the pits!' I agreed. So we had some serious discussions about playing in Europe, and, in particular, Wimbledon. Mrs. Hoxie paid for everything. 'Maybe I can get you invited to play in some other tournaments as well. And she did. I played in Dusseldorf, where I beat Jack Harper, an Aussie, in the finals. With that win, I was invited to play in Antwerp, Brussels, Pakistan and India. A lot of these tournaments were warm ups to Wimbledon. Expenses were paid and I was given $100 just to play! No prize money though - just a lot of nice trophies.

"This was 1950, and I qualified to play at Wimbledon and got as far as the round of sixteen. That was a thrill. And then because I did as well as I did, I was invited to play in Hong Kong and the Philippines. In the Philippines, I was treated like a rock star. A newspaper reporter did some research and learned that I had been a paratrooper in the Philippines and had been a part of liberating the internment camp. I was on the radio and featured in the newspapers.

"The American ambassador and an American businessman, Chuck Parsons, a good friend of the ambassador's, came to see me play in the finals. The businessman brought his beautiful Czech-born wife with him, and I fell in love right then and there. Not really," confided Fred, "but she was gorgeous!"

"Now it's getting to be March, 1951, and I leave the Philippines to go to Egypt at a very opportune time. The Egyptian International Championship was being played at the Gezira Sporting Club in Cairo. The Sporting Club, a very upscale, stunning facility with well-manicured courts, had a policy of inviting all the foreign ambassadors to become members of the club, a very smart move. I was playing Fausto Gardini, an Italian Davis Cupper, in the finals. The American ambassador and his deputy, Joseph Sparks, were in the audience. I lost to Fausto in five long sets, 11-9 in the fifth. I had him 4-1 in the fifth but hit an easy overhead close to the net a bit wide. That changed the game's momentum. And I had beaten Fausto in Switzerland. I couldn't get that out of my mind."

Tennis players never forget those game-changing moments when they lose focus, and the momentum shifts - even 65 years later.

"Anyway, after the match Mr. Sparks came over to talk to me, and our personalities clicked immediately. He asked me to tea at the Embassy, and I accepted.

"Getting down to business, he asked 'I know you've got a great life now, but are you going to play tennis all your life?'"

"I'm loving it."

"'I can see that. But if you ever think about giving it up, give me a call. You speak Polish and Russian. You were a government major at William & Mary. I think you would be a good candidate for the foreign service. If you decide to stop playing tennis, let me know.'"

"I told him I would. My next stop on the tour was the Monte Carlo Championship, where I lost in the finals. Soon after, a USLTA [United States Lawn Tennis Association] official who was at the matches said that if I stayed out of the United States any longer I'd be considered a pro. That wasn't good news back then, as few players could make a living as a pro, so I returned to the U.S. That's when I realized that I was loving tennis and travelling, but I wasn't making any money, and this really wasn't a good career path. So, much sooner than I expected, I wrote a letter to Mr. Sparks and told him I was interested in his proposal.

"He sent me copies of letters he had sent to, it seemed to me, every State Department Under Secretary in Europe and South America, but soon I was meeting guys in coffee shops and hotel lobbies with last names like Smith, Jones, and Brown. They didn't seem to be State Department personnel. One of them finally said, 'Listen, you may have a future outside the State Department. Why don't we introduce you to this gentleman - I was never told his name.

"I was invited to this gentleman's home in Bethesda, Maryland, offered a drink, and he said, 'You know, you have an interesting background. You're fluent in Polish and Russian. You majored in Government at William & Mary, and you're a tennis player known around the world.' I didn't learn until later that this gentleman had been contacting people I knew in the past - friends and my family in Hamtramck. And I didn't understand at the time where he was going with these comments.

"Finally, he said, 'You're a likely candidate for the CIA.'"

"I asked 'What's the CIA?'"

"'It's a secret organization.'"

"'I thought, 'All right! Tell me more.'"

During World War II, the Office of Strategic Services was formed, but when the war ended, the Central Intelligence Agency was established to take its place in 1949. In 1951, when Fred was being considered as a potential officer in this secret organization, few people knew of its existence.

"I had no money; I had no job, and I was intrigued by the prospects. Actually, I couldn't wait to start."

"But didn't you think about the danger?" I asked.

"When you're that young in your early twenties, everything is a great adventure. Fear just doesn't figure into the equation. To me it was glamorous, and I needed a job.

"Shortly after the meeting with the gentleman from Maryland I get a phone call to go to a certain address on C Street in D.C. It's an office building where I'm given a polygraph. I didn't know a polygraph from a phonograph. But I passed the test. Then I'm asked about my military service which must have been acceptable to the interrogators.

"I'm hired in 1951, and training began at Camp Peary, ironically, outside of Williamsburg where I had spent my college years.

"The recruits are told right up front, 'We do spy work. It's our job.' The six-week course involved learning how to recruit other spies, how to detect whether you're being followed, how to follow others, how to blow up buildings, how to write letters using invisible ink and how to tap phones."

Intrigued, I asked, "How do you use invisible ink?"

Fred explained, "You write a regular letter with sufficient space between the lines to add later, in invisible ink, the message you want to convey. The ink is not detectable without an infrared lamp. It really works."

Fred continued as I listened, transfixed.

I was 'Ted King.' Everyone had pseudonyms, and you never knew each other's real names. One of my very good friends at Camp Peary - we double-dated and saw each other socially - later became the Station Chief at Khartoum, Sudan where we crossed paths again.

"My first assignment after Camp Peary is Washington D.C. where I get more training - physical training - and training in the use of Morse code, short wave radios and other spying apparatus. I become an officer in the SR 4 - Soviet Russia 4. As an officer I'm privy to top secret information regardless of the source.

"I first worked with Russian defectors who were being sent back to the Soviet Union to spy for the U.S. We stayed in a safe house in Virginia, and being fluent in Russian I was asked to debrief them. They had enlisted in the Soviet Army, and after three years wanted out. I taught them the necessary skills: Morse code, shortwave radio, invisible ink, etc. When they were ready, we equipped them with radio transmitters, survival gear and an agenda of what information we wanted them to give us. They then went to the West Coast where they were picked up by a U.S. submarine that took them through the Pacific to Siberia. Then they were on their own."

"How did they do?"

Fred paused thoughtfully.

"Unfortunately, they didn't do well. We were able to stay in contact with them for three months and then communication ceased. We knew what that meant - they were caught."

"What was your next adventure?" I asked.

"After six months or so in D.C., I was sent to Aden in the Middle East, then a British colony and now a part of Yemen. The CIA was convinced that the government was Communist-infiltrated. The station chief wanted me to penetrate the unions and report on the leaders and their activities. We communicated through letters written with invisible ink.

"This is where my cover as a tennis player came in handy. I'm playing tennis, mostly with the British and having fun while investigating and learning that a top accountant was active in the Communist party, who became a useful source for me. He worked in the Pepsi office, believe it or not. I have to talk to him about his business. I learn that he is a member of the Communist Party – he turned out to be a useful resource for the CIA.

"In my tennis role, I meet a member of the British government, Arthur Charles, at a party at the U.S. Consulate, who is a good tennis player himself. We played a few times, but our matches were cut short. He was murdered by Adenese revolutionaries.

"Nobody was safe."

I commented, "Probably not even you."

But Fred didn't comment on his own precarious situation.

"No. Aden was in turmoil, and the revolutionaries were fearless. They wanted their freedom from the British and put bombs in the market places and restaurants. These guys in the center of Aden would set off a bomb and create havoc, just like today.

"Next, I was sent to Cairo."

At this point, the phone rang bringing us back to the present. Fred's good friend and current doubles partner Hugh Stewart was calling about his computer being wiped out. One of today's "disasters," but a far cry from the mayhem of the Middle East in the early 1950's.

When he returned, Fred continued, "The assignment in Cairo was to get a telephone tap on the Soviet embassy and to translate the conversations. I had an 'in' with an Egyptian who was familiar with the Cairo telephone system. Peter Niblo, a CIA officer and former member of the Los Angeles Police Department, was an electronics expert who knew how to tap phones. Peter, dressed in a Muslim robe and turban, lifted a manhole cover, and with my Egyptian friend went underground and found where the phone lines were. The tap worked, and I translated thousands of conversations."

"Fred, didn't you go back to D.C. to work with a Russian defector?"

"In early 1954, yes, I was transferred back to Washington. A Lt. Colonel with the KGB had had a sudden, unplanned recall to Russia from Tokyo, where he had been stationed for many years. Such a recall of a Soviet spy means the spy was under surveillance, did something the KGB did not approve of, and certain imprisonment or execution awaited him upon his return to Russia. The night before he was to fly back to Moscow, he telephoned an American woman, a teacher with the U.S. Army who had been teaching him English with the Army's permission, hoping the teacher could get some information from and about him. The Lt. Colonel had become friendly with the teacher, and apparently, he trusted her. He said he had to get out of Tokyo at once.

"His next 24 hours were harrowing. It was late January, and a violent snowstorm blanketed Tokyo. He was to be met by a black Chevrolet sedan at a specific location near the Tokyo train station. He arrived early and waited…and waited. There was no American car, and the Lt. Colonel feared that his superiors would know of his intended escape and send someone to kill him. Finally, after many long minutes, he saw the black Chevrolet sedan, jumped in and was rushed to the airport where a C-47 was waiting. But the snowstorm was unrelenting and prevented the plane's departure. The Lt. Colonel knew that every second counted and that the Soviets would be on his tail. Finally at 3 a.m., the storm lessened, the plane took off and delivered the Colonel to Okinawa where he spent a month being debriefed.

"Following that, he was taken to a safe house in Maryland for more debriefing. The CIA knew that Lt. Colonel Yuri Rastvorov was a very valuable defector, having supervised three dozen foreign agents in Japan for 11 years and having become the second in command at the Soviet mission there. He was to be handled very carefully. This is where I came into the picture.

"I knew the gentleman as 'Dipper 19' - he knew me as 'Ted.' Dipper 19 loved tennis and played quite well. His English was poor. We were a good fit because I played tennis and spoke Russian. I lived with Dipper 19 for six months in the safe house, which was well stocked with food and drink and lots of vodka. There were some nights when we got nicely loaded.

"The Soviet section of the CIA spent seven to eight hour days of intense debriefing with Dipper 19. I was the 'good cop' who befriended him, played tennis with him and gained additional information.

"Dipper 19 was an enormous resource. He was able to identify literally hundreds of Soviet spies, those he knew personally or from photographs. Later we determined that the Soviets changed a lot of personnel in Southeast Asia as a result of the information given to us by Dipper 19.

"Dipper 19 and I actually became very good friends. One day he said to me, 'What do you think I am? A monk?' He needed a woman. I told him I'd pass the information on to the CIA. In short order, the CIA found a motel, and three rooms right next to each other near our safe house. At 4 a.m. the motel rooms were stocked with snacks and drinks. Security occupied room #1, Dipper 19 occupied Room #2 and Security occupied Room #3. Security was well-armed. The night was a success, Dipper 19 was refreshed and the debriefing continued.

"Several years later, I got a letter from a 'Martin Simon' who had seen a photograph of me in USLTA magazine, when I won the 45-and-over championship in Sydney, and I was identified as 'Fred Kovaleski.' Martin Simon wrote that he had known a 'Ted' who looked exactly like the man in the photo, and referred to an incident while driving on a road in Maryland and that if Fred Kovaleski knew of the incident which he didn't describe, he would be his friend 'Ted.'"

Fred remembered the incident well. He wrote back to Martin.

"'Martin,' then Dipper 19, and I had had a night on the town in D.C. and the driver, a security guy, was driving us back to the safe house around midnight. Martin is seated in the front next to the driver; I'm in the back. While on a dark country road, a calf wanders onto the roadway. The driver couldn't avoid it and wounds it, perhaps fatally. A young girl from a nearby farmhouse hears the commotion and comes out yelling, 'That's my prize-winning calf.' In the meantime, the driver says to Martin, 'Head for the woods.' The driver calls headquarters immediately to alert them to call off the local police who had been contacted by the girl's family. When the police arrived, the driver explained 'This is a government affair.' The local police seemed satisfied and left. Once the area was cleared, I found Martin in the bushes. Martin came back, and we got to the safe house without incident. The next day there was nothing in the newspapers. Absolutely nothing which was a relief to the CIA, as Martin was a high ranking defector who knew a lot and would likely be assassinated if the Soviets figured out where he was.

"I wrote Martin. He was overjoyed, and when I was back living in Manhattan a few years later, he visited. Actually we got together a couple of times. Yuri's life had its ups and downs. He lived lavishly, drank too much, had fits of depression and paranoia, was married and divorced with two children, but continued to play tennis and seemed resigned to being 'Martin Simon.' He died in 2004."

"How would you characterize Yuri's life as Martin Simon?"

"Let me tell you, he lived a very privileged life. He married a girl from Minneapolis who came from a very wealthy family. She - Hope - was employed by the CIA in D.C. as a staff officer working on secret plans and papers.

"Through his work with the CIA, Martin met Hope at a party. One thing led to another, and they were married and had two beautiful daughters - really good looking girls. And Hope inherited a beautiful property in Maryland, so he really got lucky. But, Martin and Hope divorced after some years. I think his drinking and extravagant life style got to Hope. He was very robust, outspoken - a joyous guy who liked to have a good time. That eventually got to her.

"Martin continued on as a consultant because he could identify so many Soviet agents. In one case, when we were trying to recruit a Soviet KGB officer, Martin was sent to Austria where he was used by us to try to recruit him. He was very useful to us for many years.

"After working with Dipper 19, were you sent back to Cairo?"

"Yes. We were broken up into divisions - Europe, the Middle East and elsewhere - to analyze reports coming in from around the world. I was to work with Pete Niblo again, the highly trained electronics guy from the LAPD, on the tapped Soviet phone conversations. He knew how to tap into the telephone lines. We were able to identify a lot of Soviet operatives who were traveling as private individuals, such as an economist or a professor or some other profession or cover. They would come in and try to recruit sympathizers, working against us. They were attempting to recruit Egyptian sympathizers.

"Many of the Soviet operatives who became familiar to us through the tapes were also members of the Sporting Club. My mission was to recruit them, but they were difficult to penetrate. Security was extremely high, and their commitment to their cause was deep. They were impressed that I spoke Russian, but as an American - and a tennis player at that - they were suspicious. I was able, though, to give names to the CIA of operatives who were meeting with certain Egyptians. 'Joseph is meeting with Ahmed in the tearoom,' I'd tell them. I was then to surveil them and find out from my 'vetted' Egyptian friends who 'Ahmed' was. It was complicated…."

"I can imagine. And dangerous too. You were putting yourself in a very vulnerable position."

"True. All of us CIA officers were not under official cover, I mean, we were not a part of the embassy which had diplomatic cover. If something happened to me, I'd disappear. The Agency would have no inclination to claim I was a part of the CIA.

"As this intrigue was going on, the U.S. Embassy in Cairo got a call from the Consulate in Alexandria. 'We have a guy who is a Russian and he wants to defect, but we can't communicate with him.' The Embassy says, 'No problem. We can handle that. We have a Russian speaker, but we'd first like to establish his bonefides. He may be a plant.'

"My role then was to discuss certain questions with the Embassy and send them to the potential defector in Russian. After this exchange, we decided he was a legitimate defector. The plan then was for me to travel up to Alexandria to meet with our CIA paramilitary team, bring the defector to the Cairo Embassy, where he would be protected with immunity, and then send him off in one of our military aircraft to Frankfurt for further interrogation.

"Getting up to Alexandria was no problem, but getting back with a defector would be. I met with the paramilitary team leader. 'Here's the plan. We'll leave at midnight with three cars. The road should be empty then, but we are crossing the Sahara, so you never know what could happen. One paramilitary unit, fully armed, is in the first car; the second paramilitary unit, also fully armed, is in the third car. You, fully armed, and the defector will be in the middle car. We have to get through two checkpoints, and there will be no speed limit. This isn't a casual drive. We'll be going at top speed. Any questions?' I replied, 'No.'

"I knew the exact mileage - 220 kilometers from Alexandria to Cairo. We get in our formation and take off. Fifteen minutes later, at 12:15 a.m., we reach the first checkpoint. The Egyptian guard is in a wooden kiosk, fortunately half asleep. He waves us on without incident. The journey continues at high speed, and we reach the second check point. Same story. The Egyptian guard is half asleep, and we're waved on. We storm into the Embassy compound, put the defector in an Embassy van piled with furniture, notify the Air Attache to expect us shortly, and an aircraft is ready to take the defector to Frankfurt."

"Do you know what happened to the defector? Was he another Yuri?"

"You know, I'm not a professional interrogator, but I asked the defector the Embassy's questions and thought he was legitimate. After he flew to Frankfurt I lost track of him, but six months later I met with an agent over a drink and asked if he knew anything. He did. 'The SR guys decided he was a plant. So then they had to decide how to handle him. They decided to send him to a safe house in the U.S., but he never made it. Somehow he fell out of the DC-3 over the Atlantic....'

"I see. No questions asked."

"Right. No questions asked."

"Isn't it true that your cover changed from a tennis player to a travel agent? How could you do that without people being suspicious?"

"First, you have to be a good liar," replied Fred with a grin. "So, I'm this international tennis player in Cairo, living very well. My CIA boss, the station chief Miles Copeland, realizes my cover as a tennis player is getting thin. People wondered how I could travel the world with no money. Miles made arrangements for me to be a personal representative for *VIP Travel,* a legitimate travel agency based in Maine that was also a CIA operative."

"I see. Becoming a travel agent wasn't such a stretch. Because you were in the business you were entitled to travel at reduced rates. How did you manage to live this double life?"

"That's really a pretty tough question. I was an international tennis player, the CIA recruits me, and I'm assigned to Egypt. Then I'm a travel agent too. I just had to make up convincing stories about being a tennis player and a travel agent. Fortunately, it worked. That's just part of doing secret work. That was my job.'

"Do you remember the TV series, *I Spy*?"

"Of course. Many people say that Robert Culp's character in *I Spy* was modeled after me. I had a telephone conversation with Robert Culp years later. He never came right out and said that the show was inspired by me and my experiences, but I got the sense that it was," concluded Fred.

"When did you meet Manya?" I asked.

"Manya... Manya Jabes," Fred said pronouncing her last name lovingly.

"I was at the Sporting Club again in Cairo, playing in a tournament. This is October, 1954. Polo was also very big at The Sporting Club, and the Argentinian Polo team was visiting and playing on the Club's polo field. I was sitting in the clubhouse with nothing to do. I didn't have a match scheduled, so I decided to go out to the field and watch some polo. I'm walking behind two women, one I know, Rosette Israel. I say 'Hi' to Rosette, and she's walking with this beautiful woman. I'm introduced to her - Manya. I'm intrigued. I say, 'Manya is not a typical name. It's Russian.' 'Yes,' she replies, 'My parents were white Russian.'

"I tell her I'm Polish but I speak Russian. That gave us something in common. Then I say, 'Listen. I hope to see you again - maybe coffee or tea.' Then she floored me when she said, taking a card from her purse, 'Here's my number.'

"I caught Manya at a time when she was quite vulnerable. I learned that Manya had married very young, that her husband was very wealthy and that she had two children but they were both in school in France. She was lonely without her children and not very happy. Though her husband was very good to her, he insisted that the children go away to school. This was particularly upsetting to her. It didn't take long for Manya and me to become very close. She was interested in knowing a Slav," concludes Fred with a twinkle in his eye.

Years later Manya told me a slightly different version of how they met. We were at a senior tennis tournament in New England watching our husbands play. Manya said that all the young women in Cairo's high society and members of the Sporting Club knew of Fred Kovaleski, a tall, handsome American tennis player whom they were ready to fall in love with. Manya would have none of that. Yes, she knew he was handsome and athletic and debonair and eligible, but she was not going to show the slightest bit of interest - until they met.

Regardless of the differing recollections, both agree that the attraction was mutual and instantaneous.

Fred continued, "I contacted the CIA and told them of my plans to marry Manya Jabes and told them of her background. Well, they were not happy. Manya's parents had divorced before Manya and I met, and her father remarried a Russian physician and moved back to the Soviet Union. That was a 'no-no' as far as the CIA was concerned, as Manya's loyalties could be compromised. The CIA quickly cut me from the payroll.

There was no way that I was not going to marry my beautiful Manya.

"We wanted to get married quickly. I'm Catholic and Manya's Russian Orthodox. We went to visit a local Catholic priest, who wanted Manya to become a Catholic and attend classes to learn about the religion. I gently told the priest, 'No way,' and fortunately, I knew Albert Rizk, a Lebonese gentleman, who was the manager of the American University Club. He was very anxious to find a way for Manya and me to have a proper wedding and knew a Greek Orthodox priest whom he thought would accommodate us. A Greek Orthodox priest seemed fine to us. Arrangements were made. I asked Andre Tabourian, an Armenian, to serve as my best man.

"How did you come to know Andre?"

"He was a member of the American University Club in Beirut, and we became good friends. Later Tabourian became a member of the Lebanese House of Deputies and made a lot of money, and to my knowledge, his wealth was legitimate and not the result of kickbacks or extortion.

"The wedding was very small and took place on April 1, 1957, at the American University Club in a lovely mountain village, Brummana, overlooking Beirut. Manya was stunning, and I was the happiest man alive.

"Right after the wedding, we had a very small reception as I was very short of funds. Suddenly, during the party, I got very sick. I think because I was so nervous about being married, I was sick for five days with a fever and chills. I was not the dashing young husband I wanted to be!"

Fred was on a roll and continued his tale.

"Not long after we're married, I tell Manya that I'm a spy. She turns white and cries, 'Who have I married? A Soviet spy? No! How could I be so stupid?' I reassure her. 'No, no, I'm not a Soviet spy. I work for the CIA. I'm a spy for the United

States.' It took her a while to process this but soon her color returned to normal.

"At this point I had been in Beirut, looking for a job, and I meet this Greek-American, Peter Stevensen, at a cocktail party right after the Suez Canal crisis. He was a very gung-ho guy, a Pepsi Vice President in charge of the Middle East. I told him I had been in the travel business, but it folded because of the Suez crisis.

"He asked me, 'Do you want to be a field rep? You'd work with our bottlers.' I didn't know anything about bottlers, and he said, 'That's ok. We'll send you to Khartoum, and you can learn the business there. He offers me a job in Khartoum, Sudan, and I take it gladly. So, Manya and I, newlyweds, move to Khartoum.

"No sooner do we get to Kartoum, and my old friend from Camp Peary, now known to me as Osborn Day, learns that I'm in Sudan, and he contacts me. He's now the CIA Station Chief for Sudan. He's a wonderful guy and a good operative - very 'waspy, a Yalie,' but a wonderful guy. He tells me that his operatives have tapped the phone lines of the Soviet embassy in Sudan, but that no one can translate the conversations. He knows I'm no longer in the CIA but asks me to be a CIA contract agent.

"As a CIA officer which I was, you're the elite and privy to all top secret information. As a contract agent you're supervised and directed by a career officer and can know only what's necessary to handle the special assignment.

"I told Osborn that I know of someone who could do a better job than I. Manya. Manya speaks six languages fluently, including Russian, Arabic and French, the three languages heard on the tapes. Osborn quickly loses interest in me and asks if Manya would be willing to take the assignment. I said 'I'll ask. But you have to know that Manya is Russian and was not cleared by the CIA when I married her.' Osborn responded that he'd handle that, and he did. She was cleared, and ironically, Manya became a CIA agent. But before she was given the hundreds of tapes, our house was thoroughly inspected, bars were put on our windows, and we were given 24 hour protection."

"So, for $350 per month Manya was translating tapes, and I was learning the bottling business. One day I was on a truck delivering bottles to some outpost. But, I have to tell you, it is better to be lucky than smart anytime!"

"How so?" I ask.

"That day an airplane on its way from South Africa to Beirut ran into engine trouble and had to make an emergency landing in Khartoum. By total coincidence, flying on the plane were two top Pepsi executives, one the Vice President of the International Division and the other Vice President of International Marketing and Finance. The repairs to the plane were to take a couple of days, so the VPs decided to visit one of the local Pepsi bottlers. They meet my boss, Pete Stevenson, who mentions that he has a young American working for him, Fred Kovaleski. The VP of Marketing and Finance, Herman Schaeffer, a tennis nut, says 'Fred Kovaleski? Fred Kovaleski is here in Khartoum? I've got to meet him.'

"So when I come back from my delivery I'm called in to meet these top executives and the first thing they say is, 'What the hell are you doing in this dump?'

"It turns out that Schaeffer had gone to Penn, knew my tennis record at Penn and had followed my career. I explained, 'I needed a job and Pete offered me one. I took it.'"

"Later in the day I invited the Pepsi executives to my home, and Manya laid out a lunch for these guys you wouldn't believe. Herman still talks about it. And after meeting Manya, they were totally taken with her and again said, 'What the hell are you doing here? Jesus! We gotta get you out of Khartoum! I don't know how you two are making it here!'

"Three months later Manya and I were on our way to Capetown, South Africa."

"That's an improvement," I said. "And there's good tennis in Capetown."

"There sure is. The tennis was great even though Capetown was a 'backwater' location. It was definitely a step in the right direction. And I was doing some work for the CIA again as a contract agent. I was given individual assignments: 'Go to such and such a place, pick up a package and drop it off with so and so at such and such a restaurant' or 'Open the trunk of the 1960 Chevy parked on 'x' street, take out the package, go to 'y' restaurant and attach it to the first toilet on the left in the men's room. The work was not nearly as intense as it had been as an officer, but it was still risky.

"It's 1961 and our son, Serge, is born in Capetown. At that point, Manya said, 'Fred. This is crazy! You've got to get out of the CIA. You could be shot in the back of the head on one of your assignments or on your way home from work. It's not a good profession when you have a family.' I thought about what she had to say, agreed with her and in 1961, I retired completely from the CIA.

"But, of course, I continued with Pepsi. After we were in South Africa for two years I was asked to take a position in Adelaide, Australia for a year and a half and then to Sydney where I was made Vice President in charge of Australia, New Zealand and Indonesia.

"I thought going to Australia would be a good assignment, again with lots of tennis, but Manya cried and cried. 'What is that country? It's the end of the world. None of our family is there. We don't know anybody.' But I told her, 'Don't worry. We'll be a big cheese there.'

"We were in Sydney for ten years, and Manya grew to love it. My salary doubled, and Manya found us a magnificent home at Point Piper, a spit of land that jutted into the Sydney harbor, with a swimming pool and all the amenities - 2 Wolseley Road.

"We were leading the beautiful life. We had 'important' friends,' my job was going well, and my tennis was improving. I entered Australian National 45 tournaments - Brisbane, Melbourne, Sydney - and won most of them.

"Serge was doing well in school. Life was good! Then Manya got to know Sheila Scoter of *Vogue* magazine. They became great buddies, and *Vogue* did a special on Manya. I don't know whether Charles Revson of Revlon saw the *Vogue* article, but he was in Australia at the time. His plan was to make Revlon an international corporation with a presence in the Far East and Europe. He got in touch with me and offered me a job at double my Pepsi salary. I accepted. Revson also got to know Manya. He loved her - her class, her style. Being her husband certainly has had its benefits. I had always said that I married way above my station. And I did."

"Fred, did you stay in touch with Mrs. Hoxie during all your adventures?"

"I sure did. And one day while we were living in Australia, I got a call from Mrs. Hoxie. She said, 'Fred. I've been to Europe many times and I'm becoming bored. I'm thinking of coming to Australia.' I told Mrs. Hoxie that if she came we'd show her the time of her life. A week later I got another call from Mrs. Hoxie with the dates of when she'd be in Sydney.

"That's when I started my planning. I really wanted Mrs. Hoxie to have a good time. Years before when playing in Rome, the tournament committee had put me in the same hotel - the Flora Hotel on Via Veneto - with Adrian Quist, an Aussie Davis Cupper, and winner of Wimbledon doubles in 1938 and 1939. And he came back and won again in 1950! After we played the first day at Foro Italico, a big tennis venue, we were bussed back to the hotel. Adrian went to the bar, and I said 'This is my chance.' I followed him to the bar and sat next to him. He ordered Cinzano. I introduced myself, and we started talking. We got to be buddies. So, when we moved to Sydney I, of course, looked him up. He guided us through our move, and we actually bought a house near him. He sponsored my membership when I joined White City, *the* tennis club in Sydney where the nationals were played before huge audiences. White City had great tennis with lots of top players.

"Quist was a national hero in Australia and knew everybody who was anybody. His best man at his wedding was Sir Harold Holt, Australia's prime minister. And he was a good friend of Sir Frank Packer, publisher of Sydney's leading newspaper. I call Adrian and say, 'My old coach, Jean Hoxie, is coming to visit, and I really want to lay it on for her.' Adrian said, 'Don't worry. I'll invite all the right people.'

"Adrian certainly did his job. We had Holt, we had McMahon, the Australian Finance Minister; we had all the tennis greats including Frank Sedgman who had beaten me in the round of 16s in Wimbledon 1951.

"Mrs. Hoxie loved the party and all the attention. And she really thought her boy had made it."

"And how had she fared over the years?" I asked.

"She actually did pretty well. She established her own tennis academy in Michigan, the Hoxie Tennis Center. She had good students - Peaches Bartkowicz, a player on the Fed Cup and one of the Original Nine who established the Women's Tennis Association, and Ray Senkowski, a top player in the U.S., were among her students. Mrs. Hoxie died at the age of 75 in 1971 just before we moved back to the States. She was a wonderful lady who made my life!"

"But, you helped make her life better, too."

"Perhaps, but nothing compared to what she did for me."

"You mentioned moving back to the States. When did that happen?"

"In 1971, Charles Revson made me Vice President of Europe and the Middle East, and I was to be working out of Manhattan. Revson told Manya to fly to New York, stay in a good hotel, all at Revlon's expense, and find an apartment. Manya found us a beautiful apartment on Park Avenue, and because the real estate market had plummeted, we got a steal. In the late 80's, we moved to Washington D.C. to be near Serge, who, after being a foreign correspondent for *The Washington Post*, was returning to work at their Washington offices. We sold our Park Avenue apartment for a bundle and moved to the Ritz Carlton in D.C., where half the space consisted of residential apartments. In D.C., I joined the Edgemoor Tennis Club - strictly tennis. No amenities, no golf, the locker rooms were spartan, but Edgemoor had eight beautiful hard tru courts and excellent players.

"Washington is really where I got into senior tennis in a serious way. I entered all the national tournaments on all the surfaces and won most. I particularly enjoyed the camaraderie. I'm sure you've heard that a lot, but normally speaking, no one holds a grudge after losing a match. You go to the bar, have a beer and talk about the old days. There's no moping. And we've known these guys in our age category - many since college.

"After three years in Washington, Serge was hired by the *New York Times*, and we moved back to Manhattan - again on Park Avenue - but in a much smaller apartment. And I continue, even now, to play all the major senior tournaments. I win most of them and have to admit that being on top is a pleasure.

"I have to admit, though, that I enjoyed the wins when playing in college and on the tour much more - they were more gratifying, but as you age you learn to play a different game and get pleasure from the competition, from the friendships and from staying in shape. I'm not a gym rat, but I watch my weight and get plenty of exercise playing tennis, walking around Manhattan and occasionally working out in a gym."

"How many gold balls do you have?"

"Oh, the last time I counted I think there were 65."

"Do you have any particular tips for other seniors?"

"A lot of it depends on heredity and luck. You know I've never even had a sprained ankle, not even from jumping out of planes! And I still have my own knees and hips - no replacements, though if you need a replacement, my tennis buddies who have had them are back on the courts in no time. They swear by them."

"Are you still playing in tournaments?"

"You bet. The last one was in Poertschach, Austria this past summer. Hugh Stewart, the fellow who just called on the phone, and I are friends from our 20s. He and I played doubles there. Poertschach is a fairytale venue, and we play old friends, all in their 90s like us, from around the world in competitive matches. What can be better than that?

"Who do I play in the finals of the singles tournament? Fausto Gardini, my nemesis, the Italian Davis Cupper, who beat me in five long sets in Cairo. It broke my heart."

I didn't ask who won this time. …

What a fascinating life Fred has had - the son of Polish immigrants who became an international tennis player, an officer in the CIA, the husband of his beautiful Russian bride and fellow spy master, Manya, a successful businessman and a lover of tennis. He's still playing at 91 and perfect proof that tennis is the sport of a lifetime.

CHAPTER 2:

GEORGE and LETTY BRIA

As I turned onto their dirt driveway in Pound Ridge, N.Y., an array of giant sunflowers, waving gently in the breeze, greeted me. I parked my car in front of a well-manicured lawn dotted with flower beds and gardens. George and Letty (Arlette is her given name but George prefers "Letty" or very often "Honey") greeted me at the front door of their cottage, painted pale blue, and led me down a stone path to an old barn, dating from the 18th century, made with hand-hewn timber, gray and knarled with age.

George explained, "This is the centerpiece of our family life in the summer."

The scene was fresh and welcoming with brightly colored lawn furniture and vases of flowers attractively arranged on the barn's ground floor. Old farm implements decorated the walls, and iced tea and cookies – only one per person – were waiting for us on a coffee table.

Prior to this meeting, I had had some telephone conversations with George and had actually met him once at a local art museum where his son, John, an artist, was exhibiting some of his recent work. George is someone you don't forget. A small, slender man (he says he shrank three inches since his college days) with a deep, resonant voice, looked much younger than his 90-plus years. No white hair; the dark fringe around his bald head was barely flecked with gray. Full of enthusiasm and intellectual curiosity, he led me to his favorite painting and explained why it captured his interest.

In the barn, I had my chance to talk to George and Letty, whom I had not met previously. She, too, was darling. Petite, refined, reserved, with carefully coifed blonde hair and fashionably dressed, Letty was born in 1916, only a few months after George. They took me back to a distant, often harsh time, with a challenging, frightening childhood for Letty in Turkey and Egypt and with George, born on March 2, 1916, in Rome in the middle of World War I.

George soon moved to Florence with his family. His father, Luigi, managed a noted Anglo-Italian pharmacy, Roberts & Co., on the fashionable Via Tornabuoni. At this time, Italy was in turmoil despite having been on the Allied's winning side in World War I. She yearned for some of the territorial "spoils," namely Nice, Savoy and Istria but she got nothing. In addition, Italy had lost more than 600,000 men in the war, its resources were depleted and it feared the rise of Communism after the Russian Revolution in 1917. Black-shirted Fascist revolutionaries battled the Socialists and Communists in the streets of northern cities. Their support was essentially right-wing and gained momentum as more of the middle class and industrialists came to their side. The Florence police force, perhaps Fascist sympathizers, did little to quell the terror. George remembered the shooting, and the sounds of rifle fire. He remembered that window blinds had to be pulled back at all times so that snipers could not fire between the slats. He remembered his father having to walk every day through possible gunfire to get to work and back. He remembered his relief when his father returned each night.

His father found the situation untenable and packed off to America with his wife and George, an only child, in July 1922, just months before Benito Mussolini, a newspaper editor and political activist, and his Fascist followers won the support of King Victor Emanuel III and took over the country. It was the start of a dictatorship that eventually linked with Hitler's Germany as the Rome-Berlin Axis and was crushed in the World War II Allied victory in Italy in 1943.

"That was quite a change – a new language, strangers – did it take a while to adjust?" I asked.

"Actually, my father, Luigi, was very familiar with life in the United States. He lived here from 1895 to 1905 when his father, my grandfather, a physician, hoping for a prosperous medical career, had emigrated to the United States with his family.

George and Letty Bria

Luigi became fluent in English and was totally Americanized. Most of his schooling was in the U.S. including his admission to Columbia University where he studied pharmacology. He made friends, experienced the culture and developed a love for baseball. My grandfather, however, suffered from heart disease and returned to Italy with his family in 1905, and he died soon thereafter.

"Back in Italy, my father completed his studies, so when we came to America in 1922, he settled his family in Waterbury, Connecticut, opened his own pharmacy, became a U.S. citizen, joined the Democratic Party and eventually was elected three times to the Waterbury Board of Education. But from the very beginning he started me playing baseball.

"Every chance he had, he'd organize pick-up games among the neighborhood kids just so I could learn the game and be a player. I also took a liking to tennis and started playing when I was ten or so."

"How about your Mom? Did she adjust easily to her new life in America," I asked as Letty passed the cookies.

"I don't know. My mother, Cesarina – I always loved that name - kept to the old ways, and she made sure I stayed fluent in Italian, even insisting that I write an essay in Italian on Giuseppe Garibaldi just for her, when I was writing about George Washington for my English class."

With that background, George excelled at languages and writing throughout high school and at Amherst College. Graduating in 1938, he continued his studies at Middlebury College and earned a Masters in Italian before embarking on a 40-year career in journalism.

"Letty, tell me about some of your experiences during World War I."

"They were not happy times," she stated.

Letty, too, faced relocations and hardships because of the turmoil in Europe and the Middle East during and following World War I.

"I was born in December, 1916, in Constantinople, Turkey, at the time a very cosmopolitan city. My mother, Jeanne Beghian, was an Armenian, and my father, Jean Phillippous, was an Italian."

The powerful Ottoman Empire had acquired vast territories in Europe, Asia and Africa, including Turkey, but in the early 1900's the Ottomans began to lose their grip over their possessions. The Empire's decline was made worse by its decision to join the Central Powers, Germany and Austro-Hungary, in World War I against the Allied Forces.

"During this time the Ottomans committed heinous crimes against my mother's people, the Armenians, where hundreds of thousands were massacred or sent on death marches to the Syrian desert. Thankfully, my family was untouched by this slaughter, but we lived with fear. And, Turkey was suffering grave food shortages. We survived for two years on almost nothing.

"My family was encouraged when Mustafa Ataturk came into power. He spearheaded a movement toward independence from the Ottomans and formed a new independent Turkey based on democratic ideals. Ataturk became Turkey's first President and he began to turn Constantinople, renamed Istanbul, into a modern Turkish city.

"Initially, we were hopeful that our family business manufacturing prefabricated houses, a new idea at the time, would survive and prosper. As a child, I remember visiting my uncle's office and being fascinated by the display of miniature model homes – almost like beautiful little doll houses. But despite Ataturk's promises to westernize Turkey, he took over our business, and in 1922 my whole family, including aunts and uncles and cousins, fled to Cairo to rebuild our lives."

Letty paused to collect herself as she remembered those hard times.

I asked, "Do you want to take a break?"

"Thank you. I'm OK."

The family's start in Egypt was shaky. Within six months Letty's uncle died, and Letty, then 6, was sent off to a convent boarding school in a Cairo suburb for two years. While she was living in the convent, her mother met Andonian Hagop-Jacob, an Armenian scholar and former secretary to the American Ambassador to the Ottoman Empire, Henry Morganthau, Sr. He was the patriarch of the well-known American Morganthau family - his son Henry, Jr. was FDR's Secretary of the Treasury, and his grandson, Henry Morganthau, was New York City's District Attorney for decades. Apparently Jeanne's relationship with Andonian became quite serious, and in 1924, when Letty was 8, she was plucked out of the convent and returned to Istanbul with her family but without her father. She never saw him again and had no contact with him but for one letter. She knew little about her father's background except that he was born in Milan, Italy and that his family was in the banking business. Today, Letty wonders what happened to her father. When did he die? Did he ever re-marry?

"Do I have half siblings? I have tried to reconnect with the Philippous family but so far with no luck."

Letty paused again as she reflected on her lost family.

George said, "This is very hard for Letty."

Letty continued, "Our financial circumstances were fragile as Armenians were not always welcome in Egypt despite Ataturk's reforms. But, I was lucky in a sense. My aunts and uncles owned an apartment building where my mother and I were able to live. And to make ends meet, we took in boarders, mostly white Russians who had escaped the new Communist regime in the Soviet Union."

In 1926, now 10, Letty and her mother, who had recently obtained an official divorce from her father, left Turkey to marry Andonian who was living and working in New York as the director of an art gallery. Letty's mother quickly found work teaching French at Brooklyn Friends Academy, a Quaker school, and Letty attended Brooklyn Friends on full scholarship. She adapted well to her American surroundings, but the Depression took its toll on the family.

"Andonian lost his job at the art gallery, and new work was hard to come by. And I remember all too well making my own clothes and living on canned rations. But, I did well in school, and in 1934 I entered the freshman class on a full scholarship to Smith College, [a women's college in Northampton, Massachusetts]. My roommate was Mary Whitton, my best friend since grammar school."

And here the stories of George and Letty begin to intertwine as Mary began dating George, then at nearby Amherst. Mary and George were married after graduation in 1938, and Letty was in the wedding party.

George started as a reporter for local Connecticut newspapers, and in 1942 became a correspondent with the Associated Press in Boston. He had barely arrived when the historic Cocoanut Grove nightclub fire erupted, killing 492 people. George was sent to cover the harrowing spectacle of grief-stricken relatives identifying bodies laid out in a huge improvised morgue.

"The experience overwhelmed me, but I realized this was the career I chose. It was horrific. Meanwhile, World War II was moving on with the Allied invasion of Sicily and southern Italy, the overthrow of Mussolini and his arrest by the king, Emmanuel III, and the drive to capture Rome as

German divisions swarmed in to occupy the capital and the rest of the country to the north," remembered George as he began to gather steam in his narrative, as though he wanted me, the listener, to appreciate the immediacy, the drama, the tension. He succeeded.

Highlighting his skill in Italian, George applied to go overseas, and the AP moved him to the New York foreign desk for training.

"Huge stories were handled there," he continued, "such as, from Italy, the great battles of Cassino and the Anzio beachhead, the 'rescue' by German commandos of Mussolini from Italian captivity and transport to northern Italy to rule as a Nazi puppet."

As an AP correspondent, George had a draft exemption, and in May 1944 he sailed for Algiers "in a convoy of more than 100 merchant ships protected by destroyers and even cruisers.

"The ships were carrying bombs, lots of them," he explained. "And I listened to Morse code messages while on board and learned of the retreat of the Germans after the Normandy invasion and the capture of Rome.

"Even though I got there too late for the Allied victory in Rome, there was still plenty to do in those hectic days," George remembers. "I was there primarily because I spoke and read Italian fluently. I interviewed budding anti-Fascist politicians. I mined the Vatican newspaper, L'Osservatore Romano, for the Church's views. I established a cordial relationship with a famous Italian soldier, Marshal Pietro Badoglio. I saw him after Hitler barely escaped an assassination attempt in the famous July 1944 bombing of his headquarters. Badoglio said 'the plot by dissident members of the military meant Germany was defeated.'"

With the D-Day invasion of Normandy, media attention shifted to the drive for Berlin, and many correspondents moved to that front even though bitter mountain fighting continued in Italy.

"The AP contingent slimmed down to Noland 'Boots' Norgaard, a famed war correspondent as bureau chief, a few others in the field and me in Rome," he said. "Although still blacked out at night, the Eternal City was breathing again after the harsh German occupation. A thriving black market sprang up, with American and British cigarettes a hot item. Young kids hawked them in the streets with cries of, 'We sell America. We sell England."

Such human interest stories abounded, but George often wrote the main war story from Allied headquarters, marking the bloody progress of the multinational United Nations forces, as they were then known, up the peninsula to final victory in the Po Valley in May 1945.

"Two events stand out in my mind from those days," George said. "One was the capture and execution of Mussolini by Italian partisans. The other was the surrender of the Germans to Allied generals in a Quonset hut in Florence."

George needed no prompting as he continued. He was clearly reliving the events.

"I was in Rome when Mussolini, disguised as a German soldier, was pulled off a train by Italian partisans before he could reach possible asylum in Switzerland. He was given a summary trial, was found guilty, and was executed with his mistress, Claretta Petacci. Their bodies, along with those of a few other Fascists, were then taken to Milan and hung, upside down, a mark of utter disgrace, from the girders of a gasoline station for crowds to vilify. This scene became one of the most indelible images of World War II.

"I flew to Milan in a military plane with the Allied Forces military governor, Colonel Poletti and others, but by the time we got there the bodies had been taken down and moved to an improvised morgue. Still, another gruesome sight awaited us. The semi-naked bodies of Mussolini and Claretta lay side by side on the floor, shrunken in death. Other bodies were stacked like pieces of wood along the walls, victims of summary executions or vendettas in the unruly last days of the war.

"As a young boy on a vacation in Italy in 1926, I had seen Mussolini in his glory, haranguing a crowd from a balcony to shouts of "Duce, Duce!" Now here he lay, a miserable bullet-ridden corpse."

Months later in Rome, George interviewed the Communist partisan leader identified as Mussolini's executioner, Walter Audisio, whose *nom de guerre* was 'Colonel Valerio.'

"He told me Mussolini died a coward, babbling, 'but, but, but'" George added. "Valerio said he did not intend to shoot Claretta, but she threw herself in front of Mussolini, crying out, 'Mussolini must not die!' He then turned his gun on her too."

George further explained, "Although the details and circumstances surrounding the death have been debated over the years, the narrative of Audisio, the executioner, has largely survived. He went on to become a Communist member of Parliament and a senator.

"The Germans surrendered in Italy on May 2, 1945," continued George, "but the actual handover to the Allied command took place several days later at a ceremony in Florence. Two things stand out in my mind from that ceremony, one comical and the other awesome in its symbolism.

"The proceedings took place in a large Quonset-type building in a public park on the outskirts of Florence. I used to roll a hoop there when I was a child, and, amazingly, here I was covering this big story. Allied generals headed by American General Mark Clark were lined up at the far end of the structure. The German officers arrived in limousines. The GIs outdoors had a field day snapping pictures. General Clark had a small terrier that somehow was loose in the building and when the top German general entered, it barked angrily, ran toward the General and grabbed on to his handsome, leather riding boots. That caused some consternation and a few titters before the dog was caught.

"What happened next I shall never forget," George continued. "As the German general neared Clark and the other Allied officers, he extended his hand, but no one moved to clasp it. His hand hung in the air for a long moment. This was the end of a terrible war unleashed on the world by Adolf Hitler, and nobody in the Allied camp was in the mood for a handshake."

The surrender in Italy preceded by six days the overall surrender of Germany on V-E Day, May 8, 1945. The Japanese followed in August after the atom bombs dropped on Hiroshima and Nagasaki.

"Did you remain in Italy after the surrender?"

"Yes. With the end of the war, the focus in Italy turned to whether the monarchy could survive a huge popular mood for a republic. Political parties favoring a republic drummed on the fact that the Royals had fled to southern Italy, abandoning their people. The old king, Victor Emmanuel III, was also compromised by his early support of Mussolini, and he abdicated in favor of his son, Umberto, who was destined to rule only 40 days before the country voted to become a republic on June 2, 1946.

"Trying to cover all sides of the question, I had met the Minister of the Royal House. He had a scary name, Marquis Falcone Lucifero, meaning Lucifer in English. He got me an interview with Umberto in the Royal Palace. Umberto had led a glamorous life as crown prince before the war. He was still charming, but he spoke in banalities about the monarchy as a unifying force. Umberto's reign was brief but Lucifero lived to age 99!"

Flying in an official U.S. Army Constellation, George accompanied the new Italian prime minister, Alcide De Gasperi, a Christian Democrat, when he met with President Harry Truman.

"The Constellation was a propeller-driven, four-engine airliner, and a transatlantic flight was still a bit of an adventure in those days," explained George. "We bucked headwinds so strong that we had to turn back to the Azores for refueling. It got us a brief tour of those picturesque Portuguese islands in the Atlantic.

"De Gasperi was an unassuming man. He looked like a modest librarian compared to the pyrotechnic Mussolini in his heyday. Truman liked him, and he gave De Gasperi a much-needed loan."

While all this was happening, time was passing and George was facing passport difficulties encountered by naturalized Americans living in their native countries. They had to leave after two years or risk losing their citizenship. The AP moved George to Germany.

"I went to Frankfurt on a sleeper train from Switzerland. I'd wake up at stations in between, and all I could see was ruins," George said. "Everything, absolutely everything had been destroyed leaving only mountains of dust and ruble. Now there had been ruins in Italy, but not the mass devastation that greeted me in Germany, grim reminders of the Allied air raids and what it took to defeat the Germans.

"The postwar Germany of those days was divided into four zones: American, British, French and Soviet, the four-power rule of the victors," George related. "This quickly deteriorated since it was hard for the Russians to agree to anything the others did and vice versa.

"Berlin itself was under four-power rule, even though geographically the city was deep inside the Soviet zone. Rising tensions erupted into an historic showdown: the Soviet blockade of land and water routes to Berlin. The Allied response was The Berlin Airlift to supply the city's sectors under the control of the Americans, French and British with humanitarian aid. It was the beginning of the Cold War," lamented George.

"German civilians had nothing - no homes, no work, no food. Family members were lost or had died – all you saw was a sea of displaced persons."

The crisis lasted from June 1948 to May 1949 when the Soviets lifted the blockade and allowed goods to be transported by land and sea. By that time American and British planes had flown over 200,000 flights with 4,700 tons of food and fuel. George flew many times in the cargo planes, often under difficult conditions - in fog, in rain, in strong winds and under the assault of withering anti-aircraft fire.

"Thankfully the planes were brought down by air controllers' voices and not by anti-aircraft weapons," George added. "Photos of Berliners cheering inbound planes blossomed on front pages all over the non-Communist world," George reported. "Clearly, the Russians had lost that round."

Returning to the States in 1950 was difficult. George had been in Europe for almost six years with only one brief trip home to visit Mary and his daughter, Judy. Ultimately, the lost years were dealt with, and Mary and George were "remarried." Soon after their son John was born.

Meanwhile, after graduating from Smith as an English major, Letty, eying an editing career, landed a plum job at the Book of the Month Club where she headed the correspondence department. She received and reviewed the readers' letters of praise and criticism and responded thoughtfully. Letty was a true trailblazer as women working outside the home were rare - at least until the United States entered World War II.

"I kept myself busy with work as I had not yet found that 'special' man to share my life, my interests, my future until... until I was tricked by a friend into a blind date. Paul Brauer, a psychiatrist five years older than I, didn't charm me at first, but my mother was quite impressed with him and encouraged the relationship."

It took twelve dates before Letty was convinced that maybe her mother was right. She and Paul were married in 1941 and had two children: Janet, now an attorney living in Philadelphia with her physician husband, Steven Weinberger, and Alan, a psychiatrist in Palo Alto, California. Shortly after the wedding Paul joined the Army as a physician and was sent to the European front where he stayed until the war's end in 1945. Soon, Letty and Mary, living nearby, renewed their bonds.

The Brias and the Brauers, each with two children, socialized so frequently that their children called their parents' friends "Aunt" and "Uncle." The Brias and Brauers settled into pleasant routines of post-war America: working and raising their families. When the Brauer children were older, Letty returned to her literary pursuits, writing and editing. For almost 20 years she worked as a writer and editor of a publication for physicians, *MD Magazine,* concentrating on general cultural topics. After her retirement, she continued to write as a freelancer.

Upon his return from Europe in 1950, George spent the next twenty years at the AP's international desk in New York editing foreign correspondents' accounts and serving as Chief Correspondent to the United Nations from 1972 to 1975. He interviewed George H.W. Bush several times when Bush was the U.S. Ambassador to the UN and became very fond of him.

"He was very popular and knew how to use the diplomatic corps," he said. "Everybody liked 'George' as he wanted to be called."

Once George Bria and Mary were invited to Ambassador Bush's apartment in the Waldorf Towers, the official residence for our Ambassadors to the UN.

"Mrs. Bush was there too. They were both so welcoming. George even took me into his bedroom to show me some art works and clippings," George recalled.

George remained with The Associated Press until 1981, when he "retired" at age 65. But it really wasn't retirement. Now he had time to enjoy his passions: gardening and tennis.

His gardens were his pride and joy. So much so that he thought perhaps he should write some articles about his gardens and how he got them to flourish. So, he combined his gardening skills with his writing skills and began writing articles that were published in the *New York Times* and *Horticulture* and *Fine Gardening* magazines. Soon, his old boss, the Associated Press, noted how popular his writings were. He was asked to write a column for them.

"We can't give you much money," they cautioned.

"That's ok," and for fifteen years, George wrote his column, distributed worldwide. Some were even published in Russia's "Pravda" and "Izvestia."

"They especially liked my columns about beets," he noted. "I loved seeing my byline in remote places.

"No cold war in the garden!" he proclaimed.

"In 2004," George said, "I didn't want to write about tomatoes anymore." Despite letters and emails asking him to continue, he said, "No. That's it."

In 1998, Mary passed away. Letty delivered the eulogy for her longtime friend.

"It was beautiful," said George as he told me the story. "I cried."

Soon after, Letty, feeling sorry for George, invited him often to her apartment in Manhattan and played matchmaker, introducing him to "available women."

"But, the one I was interested in was Letty," admitted George.

But Letty was not available. Soon though, Dr. Brauer died in December 1999 after a long illness. Being a little shy, George started sending emails to Letty.

"She started answering them," he exclaimed with a hint of amazement.

Letty, sitting quietly in her comfortable lounge chair piped up and said, "We courted by email. I couldn't wait for the next one to come."

After receiving their children's blessings, Letty and George were married at her daughter's home on June 17, 2000. The ultimate compliment was a report of the wedding in the Styles section of the Sunday *New York Times.* George pulled out the article, and read his favorite part.

"I always liked her, from the first time I met her," he is quoted as saying. "She was always in the back of my mind, and when we were free, I courted her. We're just right for each other, if you want to know."

Letty added, "The account continues, 'We both felt we had very little time to lose.'"

I looked from one to the other, both smiling fondly and contentedly at each other - such a pleasure seeing these two people, well into their 90s, enjoying their lives together.

So what have they been doing since they "had very little time to lose?" Well, it is sixteen years later, and they have been very busy. Gardening, of course, but tennis especially keeps them both young and active.

George had played tennis as a child, had entered some local junior tournaments and even joined the Amherst tennis team his freshman year but hadn't had time to concentrate on the game until in his 50s while living in Pound Ridge. Joan Silbersher, a legend among Westchester County tennis players, was a founder of the Pound Ridge Tennis Club and also its pro. With her help and more time, George played tennis regularly at the club. One of his frequent games was weekend doubles with Ted Sorensen, former advisor to President John F. Kennedy. He and George had many memorable matches, but George's favorite occurred when they both reached the final of the Pound Ridge Tennis Club's Seniors Cup. The story goes that one of Ted's friends told him, that the best way to beat George was to slice.

"Slice to his forehand. Slice to his backhand. George doesn't like slices."

George recalled, "Ted sliced the hell out of me and won the first set 6-4. So I said to myself. 'What's going on here? I'll slice back!' Well, it turns out Ted didn't like slices either because I won the next two sets love and love."

A few years ago, Ted and George met at an event in New York City after not having seen each other in years. Ted had had a stroke resulting in poor vision and was not playing tennis any more.

Because of Ted's bad eyesight when George approached, he said, "Ted. George Bria. How are you?"

Ted responded, "George Bria! Are you still alive?" Oh yes, very much so. And they had a good laugh and reminisced about their "big match."

At the urging of another local pro, Jeff Aarts, who taught at the indoor Chestnut Ridge Racquet Club, George worked to improve his game. Again, he entered some tournaments and got himself a ranking as high as No. 7 in the Eastern Division of the United States Tennis Association and No. 15 in the national 85's in the early 2000s.

He smiled and told me, "I was known for my speed. I could reach those drop shots."

Drop shots! The bane of senior tennis. As you're standing at or near the baseline, your opponent slices the ball with back spin so that it barely clears the net and drops dead on the other side. These shots are tough for anyone to run down but particularly for the older players.

Letty had always played some tennis over the years, "but I could take it or leave it. I'm not a competitor," she said. "But George got me into it. We'd get up early in the morning to be on a Chestnut Ridge court at 6:30 a.m. to practice our games before anyone else got there."

"She has a wonderful forehand," added George with pride.

Her game was getting so good that George entered her into a women's 80 and over tournament in Albany, New York, first in 2000 and again in 2001. And she won both times!

"Can you believe it?" offered Letty.

But that's not the best story. In 2004, both Letty and George entered an 85 and over tournament in LaJolla, California. Shortly after, an international seniors 85 and over tournament was being held at the Philadelphia Cricket Club in Germantown, Pennsylvania, and who would be playing in the women's division but Dodo Cheney! Dodo Cheney is a legend: the most durable female player in tennis history. In her youth, she was the first American woman to win the Australian Championships in 1938. She racked up many other titles in doubles, and later, as a senior won more than 300 "gold balls," the seniors' trophy for winning a national tournament. Dodo's usual partner, Dorothy Brundage, was unable to play that year in Philadelphia, but she had heard of Letty's successes in Albany and La Jolla. Wanting the strongest substitute she could find, Dodo asked Letty to be her partner. Letty was terrified. Dodo does not like to lose.

Actually, Dodo never loses. Nevertheless George convinced Letty to take up the challenge.

George and Letty arrived in Philadelphia, and immediately Dodo wanted to get in some practice, but actually she was more interested in checking out Letty's game before playing their matches. After they completed their warm up and Dodo was getting ready to leave, she said to Letty, coldly, 'Practice your serve.' Letty, hearing this obvious criticism became even more anxious about the impending partnership, but George tried to allay her fears.

"The secret weapon is the spinning drop shot. Use that, and you'll be a winner," George counseled.

Letty and Dodo made their way to the final. The first set was very tight, with their opponents prevailing. Letty mustered her courage, remembering George's advice about drop shots. She and Dodo eeked out the second set. Going into the third and final set, Letty gave herself a pep talk and saw George's proud, smiling face. Dodo played her usual excellent game, and Letty got in some good serves and drop shots. Cheney and Bria won! Letty became an international champion at 88, and she has a cherished gold ball to prove it.

"I was overwhelmed," admitted Letty.

Dodo and Letty were also entered in the singles division of the tournament and, of course, they faced each other, Dodo winning 6-4, 6-1. Letty was thrilled to have won as many games as she did.

"The tournaments are fun because you're playing against people your own age, so the skill level is not so disparate as it would be if playing against younger players," said George in summation. "And… you don't mind adding years to your age! You look forward to being the rookie in the next age bracket."

Letty added, "The thrill of winning an international tournament at my age just lifted my spirits for years and made me feel so much younger!"

Letty, in addition to playing tennis twice a week and gardening, participates in an exercise group that has been going strong for fifty years.

"Originally there were twenty of us in the group. Now it's down to five, but we meet twice a week with a personal trainer. We stretch, though not too strenuously, and do aerobic exercises for an hour."

I hadn't visited with George and Letty in a while and wanted to get caught up. In April, 2015 I drove to Manhattan to meet them at their apartment on the Upper East Side in a very upscale neighborhood. I was greeted by the doorman who asked my name.

"Ah, yes. They're expecting you."

I went to the elevator as directed, got off on the twelfth floor and knocked on their door. George greeted me with a warm smile. He brought me into their living room with its wall to wall window looking north toward the East and Harlem Rivers. The stunning scene was reflected in the floor to ceiling mirror on the opposite wall. The apartment was Letty's home during her marriage to Paul which she kept. It is now their permanent residence. George gave his Pound Ridge home to his children two years ago. Actually, that year was eventful. George, at the age of 97, decided he should not be driving a car any more.

"I hadn't caused an accident but feared that with a loss of dexterity, it wasn't out of the question. Actually I was tired of doing all the driving. Without a driver's license, living in Pound Ridge would have been impossible. You need a car there."

So, with the loss of a car and the home in Pound Ridge, Manhattan became their home where they live comfortably all year long, even during the harsh winter of 2013/2014.

George said, "There were times when I didn't step out of the apartment for a week or more. But, I could sit here in the living room and see all that was going on. The view from our window - snow falling, wind blowing, passersby bundled up in heavy coats and warm hats, cars struggling on the FDR to keep from sliding into a nearby car - while we were warm and comfortable. We had nothing to complain about."

At the age of 97, George also decided that his tennis days were over. He was having difficulty with his balance. Tennis, his love, was no longer much fun, and he decided, no more. It had been a long and wonderful affiliation, but now he enjoys it vicariously by watching all the tennis on the Tennis Channel, NBC and ESPN.

Letty, unfortunately, in the prior fall while getting off the train at 125th Street as she often did when traveling from Pound Ridge to New York, fell. Her last memory was looking for an elevator. The next thing she knew she was in a hospital. To fill in the gaps, a good Samaritan, Gary Cunningham, a Brit, saw Letty fall and called for an ambulance. Gary, in New York to visit his son, a student at the Field School, accompanied Letty in the ambulance to Lenox Hill Hospital. Letty's daughter Janet, on her way to an event at Smith, called Letty's cell phone to check in. To her surprise, the phone was answered by an unfamiliar man's voice. Gary told her what had happened. Startled by the details, Janet called George, then in Pound Ridge, who rushed to the hospital. Letty was conscious but a brain scan revealed a small bleed. George was distressed, of course, but Letty responded well to the treatment and within a few days passed a crucial test. The hospital staff had become very fond of the Brias, and when the results came in, a cheer went up throughout the floor. Letty recovered completely, though it took some time.

In May, 2013, both George and Letty attended their college 75th reunions at Amherst and Smith. George, the class secretary since 2002, was the only returning alumnus from his Class of 1938. He was given a distinguished service award, and a photo on their living room wall shows George accepting the award with all the returning alums clapping and smiling in awe. And Letty attended her 75th reunion at Smith. It was Memorial Day weekend, and the weather didn't cooperate with rain and even some snow. But Letty enjoyed being with her classmates, and only offered a mild complaint about the weather.

"Do you have some tips for super seniors on how to improve their games?" I asked.

George began enthusiastically. "I call my secrets for youthfulness, 'The five C's: commonality, chance, courage, challenge and cashews.'"

Clearly, George had given this subject some thought.

"Letty and I are blessed to have so many common interests: literature, gardening, tennis, friends, family, lifestyle. We read the papers together, we discuss current issues together, and, of course, we enjoyed our tennis together. Actually, we still do, but we watch it and marvel at the professionals' skills together.

"You have to take chances; you have to be willing to be venturesome. Letty's tennis victories late in life are the best example of that. And I was behind her all the way, encouraging her to take chances. The gold ball was her prize - and mine too!

"You have to be courageous. Now I had back problems - spinal stenosis - and in 2005 when I was 89 I had a titanium rod implanted. Titanium! That's what my tennis racquet is made out of. Letty had her fall. We've both had medical issues over the years, but we bit the bullet, took the risk of surgery and are better for it.

"Being willing to challenge yourself is similar to courage, I know, but I'm talking about accepting the challenge of getting yourself ready to play competitively. Even though the age categories have fewer entries as you get older, you still have to get 'tournament tough' by eating right, practicing and working out. Prepare yourself for the challenge, and you'll feel so young and healthy.

"Last, cashews. You know cashews are very good for you. I was a chocoholic but kicked the habit rather recently," George confided.

Letty interrupted, "Actually, that was twenty years ago!"

"I guess you're right. Seems like yesterday. But, diet is important. Eat lots of vegetables and fruits. We always have a plate of crudite to munch on, and, of course, cashews too."

Referring to the *New York Times* Styles section article, Letty's daughter Janet was quoted as saying, "I've been telling the story of my mother's new romance not just because it involves my mother, but because of the hope that it offers to others. It's very life-affirming for everyone to hear about what can happen, even when you're 83 or 84."

Or even when you're 100! That's the story of George and Letty: life-affirming and proof that you can be young and stay young despite your age. Tennis helps that happen.

CHAPTER 3:

GARDNAR MULLOY

Gardnar Mulloy, fourteen years a top ten singles player, No. 1 in the United States in 1952; doubles champion at Wimbledon with Budge Patty; World War II Navy Commander of LST 32; founder and master of senior tennis with 129 gold balls with an unforgettable personality - irreverent, charming, flirtatious, outspoken, quick-witted, patriotic, loyal and lifetime lover of tennis.

Perhaps you have never heard of him? You don't know what you've been missing. Actually, I was quite surprised that, when mentioning his name to devoted tennis players of today, most returned my query with a blank stare. They had never heard of Gardnar Mulloy.

When I was planning a visit to Florida to interview Donna Floyd Fales I mentioned that I'd love to meet Mr. Mulloy, but had no idea how I could arrange it. Donna, an old friend of Gardnar's and his former mixed doubles partner, said, 'Let me see if I can take care of that. I'll call his wife, Jacki.'

Not long after that conversation Donna called back and said that I'd be welcome to visit but that Gardnar had good days and not-so-good days and that I'd have to take my chances. Fair enough. I hoped for the best.

Gardnar lived in a hard-to-find section of Miami, remote from the city center. The day before I was to meet with Gardnar, Donna took me on a 'dry run.' And it's a good thing she did. On the day of my visit, I gave myself plenty of time, knowing that I'm "directionally challenged," a phrase Donna coined having been my "directory assistance" when I drove from the Miami airport to her home. Again, I had to call Donna twice on her cell phone as I was driving to Gardnar's home to get straightened out. But, I found his home, a modest one-story stucco, around the corner from "Gardnar Mulloy Way." I went to the door and knocked – and waited – and knocked again. The door was unlocked so I opened it quietly and heard voices. I closed the door and knocked again, this time a bit harder.

Jacki, a petite blonde, greeted me at the door and led me to the family room where I saw Gardnar sitting on the sofa watching the Broncos and Patriots NFL playoff game on TV with his rescue dog, Choo Loo, a ball of black and white fluff, sleeping contentedly under Gar's right arm.

I was stunned to see this still handsome, vibrant 102-year old man with a ruddy complexion, hardly a line on his face, and his sense of humor very much in tact.

"Who are you rooting for," I asked after introductions and taking out my legal pad and pen.

"Well, I worked in Denver for two years. Did you know that?"

"Yes, I read that in one of your books. So you must be rooting for the Broncos."

Gardnar smiled and was totally non-committal.

"I'm pulling for the Broncos," I offered. But still there was no response. I didn't want to interrupt his game watching, so we both watched and talked during commercial breaks.

"You grew up in Miami, didn't you?"

"Yes."

Gardnar Mulloy
at his Miami home in 2016

Jacki added in her lovely British accent, "And he built this house that we're living in when he came back from the war. His father's place is just behind us, and his Dad gave him a piece of his property and Gar did the rest."

"It hasn't been touched since," added Gardnar. "Lived here all my life."

"What was it like living here as a kid?" I asked.

"My best friend was Eddie Hodsdon. We were 'Huck Finns' fishing and doing lots of things and getting into trouble too. My Dad would give me long lectures as part of my punishment. He taught me a lot."

"Didn't you and Eddie have a business selling 'pop' to your friends?"

"We bought the 'pop' wholesale and sold it retail. It was a good business."

"Now, wasn't it your Dad who got you into tennis?"

"Yes. He built a court behind his house, and I had to take care of it. I didn't like that."

"But, he did get you started in the game, right?"

"Yes, but I liked lots of sports. But he told me tennis is the only sport you can play all your life, son."

"And you proved him right."

"I did."

After graduating from high school, Gardnar was given a football scholarship to attend the University of Miami. Though he played football his freshman year he missed his tennis and, not being shy, went to the Dean of the University, D.F. Ashe, and suggested the University start a tennis team.

"Do you remember going to the Dean at Miami suggesting that it start a tennis team?"

"Oh sure. And the Dean told me that Miami was a new university and there was no money in the budget for tennis."

"Did he say anything else?"

"He said that if I wanted to do the recruiting and coaching we could have a team."

"And that's what you did."

"Right. I even got Pancho Segura to play."

"Pancho Segura ended up winning three intercollegiate championships in a row for Miami."

"He did. But nobody knew whether he had ever gone to high school. If he did, he didn't tell anybody."

When Gardnar was inducted into the University of Miami's Sports Hall of Fame, Segura was one of the speakers and said, "Had it not been for Gar Mulloy, I would be somewhere in South America climbing for coconuts and chasing alligators for a living." Perhaps that comment was a hint about his prior schooling. In any event, Pancho (called "Segoo") went on to be a top international player in the 40's and 50's, was a crowd favorite and earned about $50,000 a year, a good sum of money then.

"But whether he went to high school or not, he did well at Miami and became a great teacher of tennis."

"Yes, except for me, he was the best," said Gardnar with a smile.

Gardnar graduated from the University of Miami in 1936 and from its law school in 1938.

"Your father had always wanted to be an attorney and pushed you to take up the profession."

"I went, but I wasn't much interested in law. I graduated at the bottom of the class," admitted Gardnar.

While at Miami, Gardnar met a beautiful blonde co-ed, Madeleine Cheney, elected as the first Miss University of Miami. They dated regularly and Gardnar always referred to her as "the love of my life." They were married on August 29, 1938 shortly after Gardnar's graduation from law school. That same year Gardnar was ranked in the top ten in the U.S., mostly from playing intercollegiate matches. His first U.S. Championship title came in 1939 when he and his father, Robin Mulloy, won their first of three Father/Son national tournaments.

Gardnar continued to play the circuit, mostly locally, including a tournament in Cuba, not far from Miami. In 1940, Gardnar and Wayne Sabin lost in the finals of the National Doubles Championships played at the Longwood Cricket Club outside of Boston. This was the year Gardnar started to get into the record books. Again, in 1941 Gardnar was the finalist with Henry Prussoff in the National Doubles, but the war in Europe closed down all the European tournaments and was having an impact on tennis in the States as well.

On December 8, 1941, the day after the bombing of Pearl Harbor, Gardnar enlisted in the Navy, even though he was married and 28 at the time. He wanted to serve his country, and serve he did. The story of his naval career is compelling.

"Gardnar, I'd like to talk a little about your war experience during World War II, but could I also refer to your books for more detail?"

"Yes. I'd like that."

Jacki, too, agreed, so with their permission, I introduce you to Lt. Commander Gardnar Putnam Mulloy.

Gardnar became a "ninety-day wonder" spending days of intense course work, drillings with heavy guns and trying to complete the impossibly long homework assignments. The schedule was grueling. "At the end of the course we took an all-day exam, but I doubt if they expected any of us to pass it," commented Gardnar. But he did and graduated with an officer's commission as an ensign and was immediately posted to the Naval Air Station at Jacksonville, Florida where he was given the assignment of teaching tennis to pilot trainees. He thought it was a waste of time, in part, because the pilots weren't interested, nor was he, and he asked the Commandant to go to sea.

Soon Gardnar was assigned to Little Creek, Virginia, "the amphibious stronghold for the Atlantic Fleet." According to Gardnar, "amphibious combat was involved in charging onto a beach and getting killed." He was nervous but "also tingling with excitement" because he knew he was finally going to be useful. After extensive training in amphibious warfare, Gardnar was promoted to Lieutenant, j.g., then Lieutenant and ultimately was named Commanding Officer of Landing Ship Tank, U.S.S. LST 32, with 13 officers and 154 men under his command. From the time he first saw his ship, as the '32' was being launched with the traditional bottle of champagne, he knew '32' was his ship and he would take care of her and her crew.

Beach landings and sea training began immediately after the launching. Finally, '32' and the crew were ready, and at the same time, there were rumors that they were going overseas. Before that occurred, however, Gardnar undertook "midnight requisitioning" to be sure that '32' was well stocked for the journeys ahead. He, with selected crew members, scurried around to find canned goods, electric light bulbs, spare engine parts, maps, charts, miles of rope, but equally important, hundreds of steaks, pork chops and vegetables stacked in '32's frozen compartments, all "borrowed" from other ships and shore facilities.

But that wasn't all. Gardnar requisitioned two 35 mm. projectors and Hollywood feature films, along with the required training films. Each night while crossing the Atlantic, a training film was shown as was "standard operating procedure." But the training films were quickly followed by the featured Hollywood films. Gardnar knew he had the best outfitted ship in the U.S. Fleet, and needless to say, morale was high on '32.'

Early in 1943, LST '32' sailed out into the Atlantic loaded with all kinds of equipment – tanks, jeeps, trucks, and strapped to the main deck was a 50-ton small-size landing craft, an L.C.T., complete with crew. LST '32' and the other LSTs in the flotilla were guarded by a number of destroyers, heavily armed to protect them against German U-boats eager to deploy their torpedoes. If a ship dropped out of formation, the convoy proceeded, and the lagging ship would be on its own in German-infested waters.

Gardnar noticed that '32' was slowing down; the engineering officer radioed that the starboard engine had failed. Soon the crew lost sight of the convoy. Gardnar feared the U-boats would come up fast. They were a sitting duck – an easy target. Anxiety was high. Then, the engineering officer radioed again. Thankfully, the engine was operational. Gardnar exclaimed, "We nearly ran it out of its bearing catching up with the convoy."

Heading for Northern Africa and passing through Gibraltar, Gardnar and his crew experienced their first air raid. German planes attacked in force and "all hell broke loose," explained Gardnar. "They dropped flares until the convoy looked to me like a huge neon sign. The bombs followed."

The convoy ships were firing in all directions.

"It looked like a gigantic fireworks display – very beautiful but very deadly. I was scared stiff," admitted Gardnar.

In his book *As It Was,* he described how his mouth was full of cotton; he couldn't utter a word. Then he saw a ship and tanker blow up with flames, and smoke obliterated the air. Gardnar was nauseous. But then, he regained his composure and gave the order to start shooting. After a night of hell, '32' and the crew survived without any damage. The next morning a plane wing from a German medium bomber was found on their deck. He was proud of his men and his ship.

At this point, the convoy broke up all along the coast of Africa with ships going to their individual destinations. LST '32' was ordered to go to Bizerta, Tunisia where, on its way, it encountered more withering air fire, but Gardnar had had his baptism of fire. This time he was unperturbed.

Gardnar's first amphibious assault was also the first major amphibious assault of the war – Sicily. They sailed to Sicily's Gela Beach where the first wave of men and materiel were dispatched, and the ship returned to its rendezvous point. Waiting for orders to return for follow-up loads, a radio message, "Prepare for an air attack" was received. A wave of U.S. carrier-based fighters flew over. The radio message was misleading. The fighters were American, but one of the merchant ships, a civilian ship, started firing and other ships, including naval ships, followed suit. Gardnar did not give an order to fire. In fact, he was horrified that the American ships were firing on their own aircraft especially as the pilots were waving their wings to indicate they were friendly. Extensive basic airplane identification training followed this unfortunate incident.

The next invasion was several weeks later at bloody Salerno. After several delays because of bad weather, the first wave of troops and supplies went in. Shortly after, the Nazis brought up 75 mm cannons mounted in trucks and tanks to fire on '32' and the other LSTs. Gardnar saw an LST making the beachhead with her bow doors open when a 75 mm shell exploded right in her tank deck. "She sank in ten minutes, losing practically all the soldiers and crew," observed Gardnar.

Nevertheless, the assault continued with the LSTs returning with supplies and replacements until the beachhead was established. A great many ships and men were lost in the effort. The horrors of war were clearly evident.

Meanwhile the Allied Forces were pushing north toward the village of Cassino in Italy, where they were met by strong German forces. Neither side was able to make any headway, with the loss of men on both sides reaching staggering numbers. A landing at Anzio was planned. Gardnar's initial beachings were quite easy, but the follow-up was rugged because the troops were pinned down.

The return loads were either American casualties or prisoners. Doctors worked feverously to take care of the stretcher cases lined up by the hundreds on '32's tank deck. The injuries were horrendous; men were screaming with pain; blood was everywhere. The stench and suffering were unbearable. Many died en route.

Gardnar and his men noticed that the German prisoners were either very young or quite old – an indication that the Germans were desperate for manpower. Gardnar and his crew became hopeful that the end of the war was in sight. Nevertheless, Gardnar interviewed some of the captured German officers and was astonished that they believed they were actually winning the war and that their capture was merely an isolated incident.

Gardnar knew that beach landings were hell, but he came nearer to dying of fright one night when he went on patrol with the torpedo boats. The skipper of one of the boats was a friend and since Gardnar had a couple days off, he asked to make a night run with him. The excursion started calmly – a still night and a smooth Mediterranean. Suddenly, as they neared Genoa, their radar picked up a battle squadron of large enemy ships. One of the boats made a wide circle, putting up a dense smoke screen, while the remainder of the boats roared in as close as they dared to the enemy.

"Everything seemed to happen in split seconds," said Gardnar. They fired two torpedoes at what looked like two cruisers. Searchlights winked on and off. As the torpedo boats got out fast, the enemy opened fire with their big guns. In no time the sea was turbulent; waves were crashing against them, tossing the boat feverishly.

Then it was over.

After some weeks of routine activity, Gardnar was ordered to take part in the invasion of the Isle of Elba. The operation was expected to be easy as only 2,000 German troops were thought to be on Elba. Gardnar and his '32' went in with a small task force but ran into tremendous resistance on the beach head. They were pinned down by crossfire, and he lost several men. Nothing was more hurtful to Gardnar than losing part of his beloved crew, but he had to carry on. Eventually carrier planes were called to strafe the beach, and the beach was secured. After the carnage had ended, Gardnar learned that their forces captured or killed about 20,000 Germans, far more than the original estimate of the number of Germans occupying Elba.

Some weeks later, when in Bizerta, North Africa, Gardnar was ordered to take a cargo to Anzio. Never was there a better cargo - 75 nurses of the 21st Evacuation Nursing Corps. The cargo was loaded with great speed, care and efficiency. Out to sea again, '32' was the happiest ship in the U.S. Navy with the men and women enjoying each others' company, and, for a while, forgetting about the savagery of war. When '32' reached Anzio, the crew reluctantly parted with the cargo. It was a sad occasion, especially when they knew the nurses were heading into a battle zone. But, what was almost unbearable was learning later that despite the red crosses that the nurses wore, they were strafed and most were killed.

The next port of call was Palermo for a "refit," in order to sail back to Naples to become involved in large-scale practice assaults on the beaches and islands around the town. At last they were preparing for "the big one" – the invasion of Southern France. Gardnar was ordered to take a force of Commandos and a British Radar Unit to the Isle of Port Cross, just off the French Coast near Toulon. At midnight before D-Day, they steamed in close to the island's shore, disembarked the 600 commandos into their rubber boats and watched them stealthily paddling their way on to the beach. They had six hours to subdue and capture the island. Then it would be dawn and '32' would be on the other side of the island to land radar equipment.

At dawn, they started to slip through the channel, guided by three British minesweepers clearing a way to the port. Suddenly, a cruiser standing out to sea started sending blinker messages that the island had not been secured. LST '32' fell back but returned twelve hours later when the island was in Allied hands after a long, tough battle ending with an American carrier force attacking and bombing the island into submission. The radar gear was unloaded, and the commandos came down to the beach to welcome Gardnar and his crew who were obviously grateful that the commandos got through the ordeal successfully.

Next, Gardnar was ordered to Palermo where railway tracks were screwed down on the tank deck, then ordered to Italy to pick up a load of freight trucks and finally to take them to North Africa. At this point the war was finally winding down with Allied victories, and Gardnar was relieved of his command – a pleasant shock – and ordered to report back to Little Creek. His new orders were to report for duty in the Pacific as a Group

Commander of LSTs and a promotion to Lt. Commander. A few days later, Gardnar boarded a destroyer escort bound for home.

"Gardnar, did you ever get to the Pacific to take command over a group of LSTs?"

"No. The war ended, but those damn LSTs won the war."

Then he added, "Churchill made that comment after the war."

Gardnar returned home to Miami to his wife, Madeleine, his two daughters, Janice and Diana, and his Dad, soon building the house where he lives today. And he went back to tennis despite having lost three years of playing at his prime.

"How did you come back as an older player and actually play your best tennis?" I asked.

Gar replied, without hesitation, "I don't drink – never did. I don't smoke – never did. I eat healthy food and exercise – always have."

After a brief timeout for the football game I continued, but mistakenly said, "You were a fine singles player but best known for your doubles wins with Tony Trabert."

Gardnar, before I could get it out of my mouth, corrected me, "Billy Talbert!"

"Right, right. That's who I meant, Billy Talbert. Sorry. I get Trabert and Talbert confused sometimes."

I heard a "Hurmfff."

"How many times did you and Talbert win the U.S. title?" I asked. "I think it was a total of six times: 1942, 1945, 1946 and 1948. Then again in 1950 and 1953."

"Yes. We were a great team. One of the best."

Actually, they won four Grand Slam tournament titles, five national championships and several Davis Cup matches.

"One of those victories was after you had joined the Navy." I observed.

"1942, before we shipped out. I got leave to play."

Gardnay Mulloy in his prime

"Gardnar, now I'm going to jump ahead to 1952. Do you remember that year?"

"Probably, but you tell me what happened then."

"Well, you got to the singles finals of the U.S. National Championships when you lost to the Australian Frank Sedgman."

"Yes. Frank was a lot younger than me."

"But despite that loss, you were ranked No. 1 in the U.S. that year."

"Yes. One year I was ranked the No. 1 tennis player in the U.S."

In fact, Gardnar excelled in singles reaching the top 10 in the U.S. for fourteen years in addition to being No. 1 in 1952. He has 46 career titles and has wins against such tennis stars as Lew Hoad, Dick Savitt, Bill Talbert, Tony Trabert, Sidney Wood, Pancho Segura, Pancho Gonzales and Ken Rosewall.

"Now how about the Davis Cup? You played on seven Davis Cup teams, right?"

"Yes. Many times. I was honored to represent my country."

"As a matter of fact, you were on seven Davis Cup teams, and three of those times – in 1946, 1948 and 1949 – you helped your team win the Cup. And twice, you were not only a player on the team but also the team's captain."

"That's right. I always loved playing Davis Cup. I liked serving my country in World War II and I liked playing for my country in tennis."

I paused a minute to appreciate what Gardnar had just said.

"Here's another statistic you may not remember. In 1957 at the age of 43, you played on the American team. You were the oldest U.S. Davis Cupper ever."

"Probably so. And I kept playing. I think I still have the record."

"1957 was a good year for you, wasn't it?"

"That was the year I won Wimbledon."

Gardnar's greatest triumph was winning the Wimbledon doubles title at the age of 43 with Budge Patty in 1957. And he has a wonderful story to go along with the victory. I reminded him of it by taking him back to an event in 1951.

"Gardnar, in 1951 you and Dick Savitt, the top American player that year, were playing an exhibition match at Lady Crossfield's Garden Party, right?"

"Yes. I remember that well. She was some sort of royalty."

"After the match, tea was served promptly at 4."

"Yes. And I sat next to Princess Elizabeth."

"Right. She hadn't been crowned Queen yet. She was still a princess."

"Yes."

"And you had a conversation with the princess."

"Of course, we talked about a lot of things, but I really wanted to know why she never came to any of our matches."

"The Wimbledon matches?"

"Right."

I added, "Before she had a chance to answer, Lady Crossfield interrupted in her clipped British accent and said that as the royal princess she had many official duties to fulfill and Wimbledon wasn't on the list."

"That's what she said, but I suggested the princess didn't come because she couldn't get a ticket and I'd be happy to get her one."

Gardnar was never without a clever quip.

"Now, six years later, in 1957, you and Budge Patty had the match of your lifetime."

"Yes."

Taking out Gardnar's book, *The Will to Win*, I referred to page 9 and read, 'I cannot remember whether or not I actually heard the umpire say the words, 'Game, set and match. There seemed to be a second of suspended time between the fact and the realization. Dimly I was aware of cheering crowds. … Then it hit me. With Budge Patty I had at last won a title at Wimbledon and I was forty-three years old. … The screaming and cheering of the crowd finally got through to me and I looked around at a white dazzle of waving hands, paper hats and handkerchiefs. Some spectators were even jumping up and down in the stands.'

I stopped reading, and Gardnar said, "Yes. That's how I felt. Then the Referee came down from his stand."

"And he told you what?"

"That the Queen was going to present the trophies," added Gardnar with a smile.

"You and Patty had gone into the tournament unseeded, and you beat the favorites, the top seeds, Australians Lew Hoad and Neale Fraser, in the Championship match."

"You got that right."

"When you received your trophy from the Queen did you have a chance to say anything to her?"

"Yes. I asked if she remembered me. And she said 'of course I do!'"

Then with a sparkle in his eye and a winning smile, Gardnar added, "How could she forget me?"

I was so amused I actually laughed out loud and thought this 102-year-old gentleman is still full of spunk.

"Did she say anything else?"

"She said she was late to the matches that day because I had forgotten to get her a ticket."

Again, laughing, I said "What a great story! And the Queen not only has a good memory, but she also has a good sense of humor."

"That she does. It's a moment I'll never forget. And I'll never forget the win. After many years of trying to win I finally made it at 43."

"Your Dad was right when he said that tennis is the only sport you can play all your life."

"He was."

"Gardnar, I want to change the subject," I said.

"OK."

"You are one of the few top men players who continued to play in the so-called 'senior events.'"

"I did to stay healthy."

In 1958 at 45, Gardnar qualified to play senior tennis in the U.S. He entered all four national championships on clay, grass, hard courts and indoors on wood. He won them all. But there was another senior tournament organized, exclusively for veterans known as the Gordon Cup.

"You played in the Gordon Cup matches, didn't you?"

"Yes. The Gordon Cup was for veterans, and I was a veteran. Of course I played – and I always won," Gardnar said with a smile.

"Well, you had just won Wimbledon recently so that's not surprising," I added.

Gardnar's smile remained with a wistful look in his eyes.

As Gardnar's Davis Cup career wound down and his days entering Grand Slam tournaments ended, he gladly started playing the Veteran tournaments, though small at the start and not as competitive as what he was used to. But soon, a few stars – Frank Sedgman and Bitsy Grant among them – gave needed support to the veterans. Before long, the veteran tournaments morphed into Senior Tennis tournaments, and a vast number of older players with their wooden racquets became attracted to the thrill of senior tennis competition.

I asked, "Gardnar, you played senior tennis competitively into your eighties."

"That's right."

"What was it about senior tennis that kept you in the game?"

"Just that… keeping in the game. You improve your lifestyle as you age. You stay young."

"In the U.S., the trophy given to the winners of senior events is a gold ball. How many gold balls have you won?"

"At last count – 129."

"That's got to be a record."

"It is," agreed Gardnar proudly.

"Gardnar, do you remember when you were playing in a senior tournament in the 1990's held at the Army-Navy Club in Washington?"

"Sure. That's when I met President Clinton. He was watching my match from behind the fence."

"Right. And you noticed the President, so you stopped playing and went over to meet him."

"Yes. And the umpire said he'd default me if I didn't keep playing."

"But you went anyway because the chance to meet the President of the United States was too important to miss."

"That's right. I was a fan of his. I introduced myself and he said he knew who I was."

"So while you were a fan of his, he was a fan of yours and had followed you career for years."

"That's what he told me."

"When you went back to the court to play, did the umpire default you?"

"No. He had second thoughts."

"What else is special about senior tennis?"

"Whatever the age, there are matches, friendly or otherwise."

"You don't have to enter national or regional tournaments to enjoy senior tennis."

"No. Just play with your friends or make new friends. Join a team; join a league; play in club tournaments. My motto is 'have racquet, will travel.'"

"So wherever you are you have a racquet handy."

"Of course. Great for making new friends."

"Gardnar, you said this in your book: "If you don't quit tennis before you are 50, you are gloriously hooked for the rest of your life. Tennis is made for the age that comes after you realize you're not the champion you strived to be, or are a former athlete of a sport you can no longer play....It doesn't matter, as there's a place for you to enjoy the game. Senior tennis is the best stimulant because you don't have the pressure of the championship. The A, B and C players enjoy the game at their level and the beginner is pleased with any improvement. All you couch potatoes and lounge lizards better get off your butts and smell the flowers before it is too late. Grab a racquet and enjoy the fun."

"From your teaching days and from your lifetime of playing tennis you know that to be true, don't you."

"Oh yes. I've seen it. I know I'm right."

I was totally taken with Gardnar Mulloy and said "You are amazing! I hope folks take your advice to grab a racquet and enjoy the fun!"

Before I left, Gardnar asked me, "Are you married?"

"Yes."

"How many husbands have you had?"

"One."

He paused a moment, then said, "Hmmm, only one. Do you have children?"

"Yes. Two daughters."

"How old are they?"

"Let me think. Deb is 51 and Amy is 48, almost 49."

Without a pause, Gardnar announced, "You're an *old* bag!"

Again, I laughed out loud, and said, "And I'm an old bag still playing tennis!"

"Good." Then Gardnar continued, "A couple wives died on me. But now I have Jacki. Jacki is a savior."

I could tell she is. Her life is devoted to keeping Gardnar happy and comfortable. As Jacki was leading me out of the family room, Gardnar yelled, "Come back soon when you can't stay so long!"

I laughed again, told him I would and thanked him for all the fun I had had meeting him.

He smiled and got back to watching the Broncos/Patriots game.

I stopped at the piano in the living room to look at all the photographs of Gardnar and family members. Jacki took the opportunity to tell me how she and Gardnar first met – on the telephone.

"Really? How's that?"

"I'm British, you know, and lived near Wimbledon. My friend was dating 'Tappy' Larsen."

"Art Larsen? The one everybody called 'Tappy' because during matches he tapped everything in sight?"

"Yes. Tappy was very superstitious. Anyway, my friend was having a party for him and asked me to come to be a dinner partner to Gardnar Mulloy. I told her I didn't think I could make it as I had a prior engagement but would try. I didn't go, and the next day I got a call from Gardnar saying he was sorry that I missed a good party and maybe we'd meet another time.

"Some six years later, I watched him play a match at Wimbledon. When the match was over I introduced myself as the woman who didn't show up for the party, and he remembered. We kept in touch for years after that. Then in the late '90's, early 2000, after his second wife had passed away, we started seeing one another. I came to his 90th birthday party, I helped him write his book *As It Was*, and we were married in 2008."

"That's a good story. I'll have to add that to Gardnar's story."

"And did you know he received the French Legion of Honor medal?"

"No."

Jacki continued, "I read in the *Miami Herald* that the French consulate was looking for a likely contender, and I thought Gar would be perfect. They sent me an application, I filled it out and sent it back, and shortly, I was notified that he was their choice. Gar received it just last July – actually on July 15, 2015 – and he is the oldest recipient since Napoleon created the honor in the 1800's."

I was sad to leave Gardnar and Jacki Mulloy and their beloved Choo-Loo. I had worried that the visit would be a disaster, but, on the contrary, was pleased how well it went. Gardnar was still charming and totally "with it" at 102, and the time with him was a joy. I feel so fortunate to have had the opportunity to visit with him, a true tennis legend, who has accomplished even more as a Navy Lt. Commander during World War II, as a tennis coach and mentor, as a loving son, father and husband and as someone all of us seniors should cherish. Just eight days before his 103rd birthday, Gardnar passed away on November 14, 2016, but he left an amazing legacy.

"Senior tennis offers rich rewards that will improve your lifestyle, as it has for many of us. So go for it; you can't miss," said Gardnar in one of his books. Sage advice from one who knew.

CHAPTER 4:

TONY FRANCO

"What makes senior tennis so unusual is that you look forward to growing older," announced Tony Franco.

Seems hard to believe, doesn't it? But that's the truth. Senior tennis players can't wait to reach the next level: the 45s, the 50s, the 55s, etc. because then they're the rookies in the field and most likely a bit faster and stronger than their older – though only by at most four years – opponents.

Born on July 16, 1925, in Philadelphia, Pennsylvania, Tony, at six months, moved with his family to Peru, his father's birthplace, for four years. Peru was under the dictatorial rule of Augusto Leguia, who silenced his opponents and ignored the civil liberties recently granted in a new constitution. Tony's father Antonio was named a Peruvian consul and was transferred to New Orleans, Louisiana where the family lived briefly.

Tony has one recollection of living in New Orleans. One day when coming home from nursery school, Tony, frustrated, asked his mother, "How come nobody can understand me? Are they deaf?"

No. They weren't deaf, but he was speaking Spanish and his new friends only spoke English.

Shortly after arriving in New Orleans, the Leguia government fell after a successful coup, and Antonio realized his job and his family's lives were at risk. They returned to Philadelphia, where Tony's mother's family had lived for generations.

Tony was always a "sports nut" and knew the names of all the professional sports stars, their batting averages, their running statistics, their yards gained, their touchdowns or their win/loss records. One day, when in the seventh grade and weighing not much more than 70 pounds, he knew the JV football team was having try-outs. He thought he'd try out, but upon opening the door to the gym and seeing the size of the boys trying out, he had second thoughts.

One yelled to him, "You coming to try out?"

Tony responded wisely, "You think I'm crazy?" and left.

Tony decided he would have to pick a sport that didn't require muscle and brawn. Tennis seemed a good choice. He started following the well-known, small but successful tennis players, Bobby Riggs and Bitsy Grant. If they could do it, so could he. He began hitting tennis balls against the garage wall and occasionally talked his friends into playing on a nearby court.

In 1938 when Tony was 13, his father was transferred and the family moved to Puerto Rico. Tony continued using the garage wall as a backboard but played no games and took no lessons. Tennis was not very popular in Puerto Rico. But in 1940 and 1941 American military families began moving to the naval base in Puerto Rico as World War II raged in Europe, and the U.S. beefed up its preparedness. A community of American expatriates grew, the naval base beaches and tennis courts became popular with the servicemen and their families, and the

Tony Franco

"teen center" with its juke box, coke machines, snacks and dance floor was a favorite among the teenagers. Civilian friends of the military families were welcome, and Tony became a "permanent fixture," mostly at the two cement tennis courts.

"One day," he said, "I played eighteen sets. I was on that hard court from 9 a.m. to 6 p.m."

Tony was befriended by another tennis enthusiast, Admiral John Howard Hoover, commander of the Caribbean Sea Frontier, who would later have an outstanding World War II record. Admiral Hoover was taken with Tony and occasionally asked him to play doubles with him on the Naval Base court. Tony was only too eager to oblige and was especially impressed when games were arranged, and he was picked up in a chauffeured Navy vehicle.

In September, 1942 when he was 17, Tony entered the University of Pennsylvania as a freshman, and decided that, being only 5'3" and weighing 90 pounds, tennis would definitely have to be his game. The crew coach at Penn, Rusty Callow, however, tried to recruit him as a coxswain for his rowing team.

Tony said, "I want to win a letter for being good, not for being small."

Coach Callow responded, "So what can you do?"

Tony answered, "I can play tennis."

Tony made the varsity team playing at third doubles. But, his tennis career was cut short a year later when he turned 18 in July, 1943 and enlisted in the Navy.

Tony was sent to Sampson Naval Base in Sampson, New York for boot camp. After completing the initial training in May or June, 1943, Tony applied to submarine school in New London, Connecticut. The small and highly selective submarine school, a popular assignment, was overwhelmed with volunteers and classes were full. While waiting for openings, the other volunteers were assigned to work details on the base, mostly digging ditches. The Master at Arms, Chief Spritz, a real tyrant, wanted "his boys" to toughen up. He had them digging ditches every afternoon. One day Tony discovered some nearby tennis courts at the Officers Club and thought perhaps he could get a job maintaining them. Even though the courts were hard and required very little upkeep, Tony went to inquire. Yes, he could work on the courts and do other odd jobs as needed. Chief Spritz was not happy when he learned that Tony had gone behind his back to finagle another job. During inspections, the Chief targeted Tony and "called him out" for minor infractions. When the submarine school sent out its acceptances and rejections, Tony was found to be "temperamentally unfit" for such an assignment, most likely upon the Chief's suggestion. He was summarily sent off to Pier 92 in New York City and shipped to Liverpool and Plymouth in England, then to Normandy and Omaha Beach in August, 1944. The Normandy invasion preceded his time there as D-Day was June 6, 1944, but there was still much work to do. Tony served on an LCT – a landing craft tank.

"When not carrying big Sherman tanks, we carried personnel, cargo and other vehicles, which was what we were doing mostly," Tony said. "We would rendezvous with liberty ships, privately owned merchant ships that anchored miles off shore. We would go out to them from the harbors, load up and take the load to North Africa, Salerno, Enzio or Omaha Beach."

In December, 1944, at Christmastime, Tony was hospitalized in Plymouth for, of all things, ingrown toe nails. He had been running to and fro on the LCT, often stubbing his toes, and they became so inflamed that he had to cut off the top of his boots to relieve the pain. The hospital was filled with wounded soldiers, survivors of Normandy and other battles and Tony was too embarrassed to let visitors know what his affliction was. He was particularly embarrassed when carolers came to cheer up the troops by singing Christmas carols.

He hid his chart and thought, "Oh my gosh. These carolers have been through the Blitz and made all kinds of sacrifices, and they think I'm a war hero.'"

After his discharge from the hospital, Tony returned to the LCT. The day before V-E Day in May, 1945, the ship docked for two days at Quai d'Ivry in Paris, and the captain gave the crew 24 hours to leave the ship and celebrate. Paris was alive with cheers, tears of gratitude, flowing beer and wine. Strangers approached Tony and his shipmates with smiles of joy, thanking them for their service and sacrifices. France was finally liberated. Tony spoke enough French after having had two years of it in high school, and combined with his fluency in Spanish, he was able to communicate and understand the good wishes.

In July of 1945, Tony had orders to go to the Pacific for the invasion of Japan. He was in Puerto Rico on leave when the war ended. His orders were changed: remain at the Puerto Rico Naval Base for an assignment to its hydrographic office. Earning overseas pay and an extra stipend for food when he was living at home and eating meals for free was, indeed, a bonus. But the best bonus was that he got to work on his tennis game again.

Tony was honorably discharged from the Navy in August, 1946, and one month later he was back at the University of Pennsylvania and playing at No. 1 in singles and doubles for the next three years. During his years in the service, Tony grew and put on weight, transforming the 90 pound weakling into a 165 pound, 5'11" player. Penn, in the Ivy League, faced top players such as Dick Savitt, Cornell's No. 1 player, who later won Wimbledon in 1951. But his toughest match was in the spring of 1949 when Penn played the College of William & Mary. William & Mary's team was so good that the top player on the Canadian Davis Cup team, Brendon Macken, played No. 5 for the team. Tony, playing at No. 1, faced Fred Kovaleski, playing No. 1 for William & Mary.

The score? "It's censored," Tony told me.

Tony graduated from Penn in 1949 and returned to Puerto Rico, where he was hired by IBM, his first and only employer, to manage the IBM office in San Juan. Even though his roots were in Puerto Rico, as was his family's, this assignment was not what Tony had in mind. As a young bachelor, he would have preferred more exciting venues either in Rio, Havana or Mexico City. Nevertheless, in his spare time, he concentrated on tennis. In 1950, the Hilton Hotel chain opened the Caribe Hilton, with a new tennis facility in San Juan. Welby Van Horn, well-known in tennis circles as the founder of successful junior development programs, arrived a year later to be its head tennis pro. Puerto Rican tennis began to blossom. In addition, the San Juan Country Club became popular with good tennis players. Tony joined the club and played with, among others, Charles Pasarell, a fine Puerto Rican tennis player and father of Charles Pasarell, Jr., known as "Charlito" who would later win the national junior championship and become one of the top American players in the 1960's and 1970's.

His father commented once to Tony, "If my parents spent as much money on me as I do on Charlito, I too would have been a champion!"

After Charlito retired from the tour, he and his partner, Ray Moore, founded the Indian Wells tennis tournament in California, the largest combined ATP and WTA tour event. They later sold it to Larry Ellison, co-founder and CEO of the software company, Oracle, Inc., who has made it into one of the most popular and profitable tennis tournaments in the world.

As comfortable as life was in Puerto Rico, and thinking that living at home was not an ideal situation, Tony, now 25, asked for that transfer to Rio, Mexico City or Havana. Instead, IBM wanted Tony to open a new office in Tegucigalpa, Honduras. Again, not what Tony had in mind, but he accepted the offer and ended up staying in Tegucigalpa for twelve years, from 1951 to 1963.

At a party in February of 1953 Tony met a young American woman, Edith Unsworth, who was visiting her sister, Marie, then married to a successful Honduran businessman. Edith was a popular new face with long, shining, jet black hair accenting her ivory skin, and Tony approached her. He learned that she was from Jackson Heights, New York, very near the West Side Tennis Club in Forest Hills, then the site of the USLTA (U.S. Lawn Tennis Association) National Championships. Tony was anxious to know whether Edith played tennis.

'Surely she was a player,' he thought.

But Edith did not play. Nevertheless, Tony was undeterred and said, "Well, I can teach you."

For the rest of her vacation, they spent several hours on the tennis court. Edith thought she was getting quite good. What she didn't realize was that Tony hit all the balls right to her and at the perfect pace for a beginner so that when she went out on her own, it was a disaster. Edith did not become a tennis player. But, over the years, she has become Tony's devoted fan and knows more about the game of tennis than most.

When Edith left Honduras at the end of February, she and Tony kept in touch. In the meantime, Tony managed to get in some good tennis and kept up his good work at IBM. When Edith visited Honduras in 1955, she and Tony spent much more time together. Tony, carefree with money to spare, flew to New York City a few times, and on New Year's Eve 1955, while enjoying dinner at their favorite restaurant, El Chico Restaurant, Tony asked Edith to marry him.

Edith and Tony were married in the Lady Chapel of St. Patrick's Cathedral in New York on June 16, 1956. Soon they moved to a lovely apartment overlooking the city of Tegucigalpa. With an altitude of 3,000 feet above sea level, the air was clear and dry. Daily temperatures were in the 80's but not at all tropical.

"Damn it. Another beautiful day," was a common comment from visiting businessmen.

Much to Edith's delight, labor was cheap, and it was common for middle class families to hire household help.

"We had a full-time maid and laundress," admitted Edith. "They were very helpful, especially since our social life was busy."

Tony even described it as "exhausting." Their party-loving friends, Hondurans and American expatriates, entertained the newlyweds frequently in their homes.

Tony added, "Life was good, but with three or so parties every week, it could be a breeding ground for alcoholism."

In 1963, Tony finally got the assignment he had been longing for and was transferred to Mexico City which then was a beautiful city with no crime, no drug cartels, no pollution and a good exchange rate. The city, originally established by the Aztecs in the early 14th century, is nestled in the large Valley of Mexico, situated in the high plateaus of south central Mexico surrounded by mountains and volcanoes. The Francos settled in happily, first in an apartment on the Reforma, and next, an apartment in Polanco with breathtaking views overlooking Mexico City. The days were clear but chilly at 7,500 feet.

"Every morning the sun peeked out from behind the volcano Popocatepetl," said Edith. "Mountains and green forests spread out before us, and the homes nearby, all in pastel colors with terra cotta roofs and high stone walls, were covered by bougainvillea of all colors."

Tony joined the Reforma Club and went from an unknown winner of the C tournament to the finalist in the A tourney.

Then, unexpectedly, in November 1969, IBM asked Tony to return to the United States temporarily for training in press relations and internal communications. After the training, he was to return and take a new position at IBM's Latin American Headquarters in Mexico City. He and Edith had become very accustomed to the comfortable lifestyle and climate of Mexico and were reluctant to leave, but Tony was told the new assignment in the States would last only a couple of years. They decided to accept the offer.

In early 1970, the Francos bought a home in Briarcliff, New York, a modest split level where they still live today. Edith had the greatest adjustment with two toddlers and no full time maid, no nurse maid, no laundress, no gardener. But life in Westchester County was very pleasant with good schools and related school activities, lots of friends, and most important, lots of tennis. The Francos were becoming very "Americanized." Tony joined Westchester County's town tennis league where the competition was of a very high caliber. And, he had recently turned 45, which meant he could enter the wonderful world of senior tennis.

The Francos were not sent back to Mexico City. Instead, Tony was assigned to the IBM offices at the UN Plaza in New

York City, and in 1974 he was moved to IBM's Headquarters in Armonk, New York, were he stayed until his retirement in 1989.

Tony's first Eastern 45-and-over event was top heavy with Bobby Riggs, Bill Tully and other heavyweights, but by the end of the year he managed to have a No. 10 ranking. By the time he got into the 50s, he was ranked first in the East.

In 1986, Tony, 61, played Bobby Riggs, 67, famous for his challenge and loss to Billie Jean King in the 'Battle of the Sexes' match but also for being ranked No. 1 in the world and winning both Wimbledon and Forest Hills in 1939. The 1986 match was played on clay at the Little Rock Country Club, Little Rock, Arkansas, where Chris Evert's uncle, Jerry Evert, was the club pro.

"I just didn't want to look too bad or embarrass myself," Tony remembered.

Franco and Riggs met in the round of 16, and the local TV reporter who was covering the matches, when announcing Riggs' opponent, said, "Tony who?"

As the match unfolded, Edith, sitting on a hill overlooking the court near a young couple mesmerized by the play, overheard them exclaim, "This is going to be an upset!"

Edith kept saying to herself, "Oh no. Riggs will find that higher gear and pull it out."

But he didn't, and Tony won the match 6-3, 6-3.

Afterward, the same local commentator interviewed Riggs, who was quite generous in defeat. Riggs said "I ran into a buzz saw!"

When Tony returned to Westchester after his triumph, he was greeted by his weekly tennis buddies, Curt Beusman, Larry Kreiger, Len Floren and Bob McFadzen, with whom he played for years every Sunday morning at 10 a.m. at the Saw Mill Club. These gentlemen, always eager to poke fun and knowing that

Riggs was a big gambler, suggested that Riggs must have bet against himself and threw the match.

"Not likely!" Tony replied, "He couldn't have found anyone to bet on me."

From then on Tony's new name among his friends was "Buzz Saw" and to commemorate his big victory they presented him with a T-shirt emblazoned with "BUZZ SAW" written across the back.

In June of 2007, Tony was playing at the Oglebay Senior Open in Wheeling, West Virginia. At dinner after the first day's match, he had some chest pain that didn't go away by the next morning.

"Just a little heart burn is all it is," suggested Tony.

He went to the courts ready to play the next round but still didn't feel himself. He reluctantly told the tournament director he'd have to default. The tournament director's son, a physician, was a volunteer at the tournament. He immediately called for an ambulance to take Tony to the nearest emergency room at a hospital in Wheeling where Tony was diagnosed with a myocardial infarction, i.e., a heart attack. From there he was taken by ambulance to the University of Pittsburgh Medical Center, where he had two stents inserted.

It turns out Tony had high cholesterol. "I didn't pay enough attention to Edith's advice to stay away from the salt," he said.

How long did this episode keep Tony off the courts? About two weeks. Actually, when he got home to Briarcliff, he saw his cardiologist who advised Tony not to play competitive tennis. Not being particularly happy with the advice, he contacted another cardiologist at New York Presbyterian who said, "Go ahead and play." That advice Tony followed.

Tony and Fred Kovaleski, his rival from college days, never met again on the tennis court until 2000, a mere half century later, in the finals of a 75-and-over national seniors' tournament on grass courts at the Orange Lawn Tennis Club. The score was very one-sided, as were the next four times they played each other in national finals. Kovaleski always prevailed.

"Fred was the top guy that all of us were trying to beat," said Tony, "but I never even won a set."

Tony and Fred met a second time two years later at Orange in the finals of the National Grass. Again, Tony lost. In 2005, Tony turned 80 and entered the 80-and-over category. Who does he meet in the finals of the grass at Orange? His nemesis Fred Kovaleski. Kovaleski wins again, and he wins a second time that year on clay in Arlington, Virginia.

Not long after that loss, Tony's grandson, Tony, suggested, "Maybe you should try playing Mrs. Kovaleski."

Tony and Fred didn't face each other again until 2010, at Tony's favorite venue, the Longwood Cricket Club, outside Boston, in the final of the national grass court 85-and-over tournament. That year, Tony was the youngster and had youth on his side. It was a hot, humid day. Tony won the first set 6-4. At 4-5 in the second set, Fred was serving. At deuce Tony won the point, giving him a match point on Fred's serve. He lost it, and Fred went on to hold serve for 5-5. At that point, Fred walked to the net, extended his hand and retired.

Even though the USTA record shows a win for Tony, he doesn't feel he deserved it. Tony to this day believes that his friend of 61 years tried to let him win that match point rather than default.

But in 2013, Tony had his first real win over Fred at the National Grass Court final at Longwood. The score was 6-3, 7-5. Finally, a victory. A stunning fact about senior tennis players is that they never give up. They remember the scores of their matches. They remember who, when and where they played. They continue the fight with new strategies and finesse. But, despite the dogged competition, the players are loyal friends and play together as doubles partners which Tony and Fred did in 2013 in the annual Atlantic Coast Cup held at the West Side Tennis Club in Forest Hills.

The Atlantic Coast Cup, the annual intersectional event of team tennis covering all the states from Maine to Virginia, is a prestigious event for seniors in the 45s, 55s, 65s and 75s. Tony has captained the Eastern Division in all age categories over the past forty years. Now over 85, he's hoping to start an 85 and over category for the team competition, but it hasn't happened yet. In the meantime he continues to play in the 75s.

The two-day event takes place every summer with the teams alternating as host. The competition is intense, but after the first day's play, the host team presents a cocktail party and banquet where all the team members and their spouses/partners mingle, stories are told and the fierce rivals on the courts are transformed into fun-loving, spirited, loyal friends. The captain of each team introduces his team members and often jokes about the success or failure of the day's matches, and the audience adds its own flourish to his comments. But the serious play returns the next day, and the team that wins is awarded the Atlantic Coast Cup, engraved each year with the winning team's name.

In all, Tony has won 44 gold balls, the ultimate trophy in USTA senior tennis, winning 20 in singles and 24 in doubles on all surfaces - grass, clay and hard, indoor and outdoor. That number is remarkable because Tony didn't win his first gold ball until he was in the 75s.

"Nothing like getting a good partner," he mused. "I won 23 of the 24 gold balls with my good friend, a Californian, Graydon Nichols, and we won the world championship four times playing together in the 80 and over."

Tony's international wins in singles occurred in Perth, Australia and Antalya, Turkey, the scene of his biggest win in 2006, when he became the No. 1 player in the world in the 80 and over category by beating Jean del Homme of France in a three-set final.

In 2015 and 2016, Tony and Graydon Nichols accomplished the ultimate. Tony won four singles tournaments on all four surfaces and they won four doubles tournaments on all surfaces in the 90-and-over category. That's two Grand Slams in two years. Quite a feat.

Alas, there is no World Cup in the 85s. The International Tennis Federation sets the rules for senior international play requiring at least eight countries to participate in each category. Unfortunately, to date only Great Britain, South Africa, Canada and the U.S. have teams ready and willing to compete.

Tony also has another outlet. He competes internationally as a member of the International Tennis Club of the United States of America, one of 41 such clubs around the world binding the international tennis community together in friendship and competition. Tony has played for the IC in Australia, New Zealand and many times in matches between the United States and the Canadian and Mexican ICs, always annual events.

What keeps Tony young?

"It's hard to explain," Tony said. "One feels a certain euphoria which carries over into daily living when playing well competitively. You're healthy physically and mentally. You have a positive attitude about life in general, with little thought of mortality and aging. Tennis seniors think they're young. It's that simple - a matter of mind."

"Luck, too" he said, pointing out his heart attack, two arthroscopic procedures at 65, a total right knee replacement at 71 and a total left knee replacement at 87. Some people, looking at the glass half empty, wouldn't think of a heart attack as good luck, but, of course, Tony focused on the quick recovery. And he looked at the knee surgeries as totally elective to maintain his quality of life.

"I didn't have to have them done," he said.

He could have gone on with his life, but what would life be without tennis? The marvels of modern medicine.

"Many senior players have had similar surgeries such as Gene Scott, a top ten player in the 1960's, member of the U.S. Davis Cup team, founder of and writer for *Tennis Week* and member of the I.C., until his untimely death in 2006," Tony said.

"He had two new hips and remained the best in the world. King Van Nostrand, another with many, many world and national championships, had both knees replaced in his 60's, and he continues to dominate.

"Being pain free again renews your spirit and spurs you on to work hard, train more and compete. The advances of today's orthopedic medicine empower us."

Tony's weight is the same today as it was when he graduated from Penn. But it probably wouldn't be if he didn't have some prompting from Edith. She keeps him off too much salt and red meat. But, he's not a fanatic about his diet, except that he never snacks. Good common sense and moderation.

When he was younger, Tony admitted to smoking cigarettes, but when the Surgeon General's Report came out in 1964 warning of the dangers of smoking, he quit.

Tony recalled, "When I played as a young man in the 45's, the players always fled to the bar for drinks and cigars. Not now. Beer and wine in moderation satisfies thirst but absolutely no smoking."

Stretching exercises every morning - 12 leg lifts, arm arcs, 40 sit ups - are a part of his routine. While I interviewed Tony, he got down on the floor to demonstrate. As he started to get up, he grimaced and grabbed his left leg, and I thought, 'Oh no.' But, he said, "It's only a Charlie horse" and rubbed the leg a few seconds. Presto, it was gone.

Another daily routine is doing the *New York Times* crossword puzzles. The Sunday puzzle he does in under 40 minutes. He did admit that once in a while he has to get an assist from Google! So how many 91 year olds even know how to find Google?

"The Friday and Saturday puzzles are tough," he said.

"Since I had my second knee replacement, I couldn't play my last year in the 85's, but I'm ready for the 90s. I'm a youngster again and with a brand new body part!"

Tony quotes Roger Pharr of *Tennis Magazine* as saying it all: "Sometimes I win, sometimes I lose, but I meet a great bunch of guys who love the game just as much as I do."

The camaraderie among the players who have played with and against each other for over 40 years is unique. The wives and significant others participate, too, and are a part of the many years of close friendships.

Tony's good friend Larry Kreiger, the creator of the "Buzz Saw" nickname, often says, "Senior tennis players don't age. They get older, but they don't age."

When asked if he plays golf at all, Tony deadpanned, "I'm not old enough yet."

CHAPTER 5:

DAVID DINKINS

I first met Mayor David Dinkins when he was honored for his contributions to the world of tennis at an event hosted by the United States International Club at Cipriani's in New York City. The meeting was brief, and he would never have remembered it, but at the time I was struck by his calm and dignified demeanor. With a compelling smile he humbly thanked me for my good wishes.

Years later, in early November 2014, my husband and I were guests of a good friend who was on the dias at the Al Smith Dinner in New York City. I knew of the annual Al Smith Dinner, of course, as a New Yorker and as one who has enjoyed reports of the event's speakers, especially during the Presidential Election campaigns. During the cocktail hour before dinner, the guests either ogled all the celebrities or talked among their friends. Out of the corner of my eye I saw Mayor Dinkins talking with some gentlemen. He was quite nearby, and I caught his eye. He smiled. That was enough of a sign for me to go to him and introduce myself, which I did. I knew he was a tennis player and avid fan and had been responsible for helping the U.S. Open tennis championships stay in New York. I asked how his tennis was these days, and he said, "Well, I stopped playing last year."

"That's too bad," I responded.

"Well, I'm 88 now, and I figured it was time. But I'm still a big fan."

"Oh, I know, I see you on TV sitting in the President's Box all the time."

The Mayor smiled, almost shyly, his eyes sparkling.

I told Mayor Dinkins that I was in the midst of "a project." I didn't say, 'a book' because that would jinx the whole undertaking. Anyway, I continued that my project consisted of interviewing men and women playing senior tennis who were still thriving on it.

I asked, "Could I interview you?" You never know if you don't ask.

And the Mayor said, "Yes," found a napkin, took a pen out of his coat pocket and wrote down his name, his phone number and his email address.

I was stunned.

Then he added, "My secretary's name is Lynda. Give her a call. She knows everything."

Well, of course, the next day I called and spoke to Lynda, who said she'd get back to me.

"The Mayor is very busy."

"Oh, I'm sure."

Lynda did get back to me, and we set up a meeting for Friday, December 4th at 1:30. I was delighted.

Friday, December 4th was breezy but bright and sunny for an early December day. It was a perfect day to drive into the city, but I had to give myself plenty of time. I didn't want to be late! I found the impressive building housing the Columbia University School of International and Public Affairs where Dinkins has an office as a Professor of Public Affairs. Street side parking was difficult, not unusual for New York City, but after a couple drive-bys, I found a spot on Morningside Drive only a

David Dinkins

few blocks away. I parked, ran to the school's entrance, got on the elevator and headed for the Mayor's office, tucked in the back of a long corridor of office cubicles. The door was open, and I went in to be greeted by Lynda. She was welcoming, but said that the Mayor was on the phone.

"He'll be with you shortly."

While waiting, I studied all the plaques and momentos placed carefully on glass-enclosed bookshelves. The door to the Mayor's office was open, so I could hear when the last call on hold was finished. Lynda led me in.

The Mayor, smartly dressed in a blue blazer, blue shirt, red polka dot bow tie and matching pocket handkerchief, was wrapping up his work, and closing the file before him. The office was homey, not at all pretentious and was filled with framed photographs of his family, his most revered friends and international heroes, Nelson Mandela and Paul Robeson, and his many, many tennis friends. And that's what the mayor wanted to talk about - his family and his tennis friends. He introduced me to his family through the photographs - his wife, whose moniker is "my bride" or "honey;" his son, David, known as "Davey;" his daughter, Donna, "Daddy's Little Angel;" Donna's daughter, Kailila, his "Little Cupcake;" and Jamal, "Daddy's Little Tiger."

Dinkins was a spunky little kid - industrious too - growing up mostly in Trenton, New Jersey with his dad, William Harvey Dinkins, Jr., but "Pop" to him, and briefly with his mother and grandmother in Harlem after his parents separated.

"My parents never told me why they separated, and I could never understand it. But I lived in Harlem with my mother, Sarah Lucy, known as Sally, and her mother, Nora Bacon, who were both domestics working for $1 a day. We moved from apartment to apartment - just before the rent was due - but I never felt poor. I never went hungry, and I always had clean clothes, many hand-me-downs from the wealthy families my mother and grandmother worked for. And I always made friends wherever I lived."

"Mayor Dinkins, I read your book, *A Mayor's Life: Governing New York's Gorgeous Mosaic,* which I thoroughly enjoyed, so some of my questions will refer to incidents that you recount in your book, is that okay?"

"Yes, of course."

"Tell me about when you were living in Harlem with your mother and grandmother and you and some of you friends decided to make an extra special 'skate-scooter.'"

"My buddies and I, when we were six or so, rigged up some 'skate-scooters,' soap boxes nailed to 2 x 4s with metal roller skates as wheels. But, to make the skate-scooter really good-looking, we needed to find some reflectors. Now the only place to find reflectors was mostly on car license plates. So a bunch of us found the perfect reflector and started to free it from the car when a black police officer spotted us and knew immediately what was going on. We all took off, but because I was the smallest, he caught me. He could have taken me to the station house, but instead he did something worse. He took me home to my mother and grandmother who gave me a good shellacking I'll never forget. I haven't stolen a reflector since" he said, smiling.

"I was pretty smart too. I'd watch the vendors who sold fruit and vegetables from their pushcarts and noticed that they didn't have shopping bags to give to their customers. So I bought shopping bags from a wholesaler, three for a nickel, and sold them for two cents apiece. When I finally made a dime, I went to the five and dime store and bought my mother a present. That was a proud moment for me."

When Dinkins was still in grammar school he returned to Trenton to live with Pop, probably because the schools were better in Trenton and his father was doing well financially.

"Tell me about your Dad."

"Pop was a very smart man who started out with a one-chair barber shop on the first floor of our house in Trenton which became a four-chair shop by the time I returned. And he had become a real estate broker and insurance agent. He taught me a lot too. And he gave me responsibilities. My first job when going back to live with him was shining his barbershop customers' shoes. I had another job too – taking checks to Pop's creditors. Back then you didn't mail payments, you delivered them in person. He'd go to his strongbox and hand me money he had saved to pay for electricity, heat, phone and of course for church. Then there was a special category for savings. He taught me never to forget savings. He also taught me the difference between "gross" and "net" – always remembering that expenses had to be deducted. That lesson helped me later when I was negotiating the agreement to keep the U.S. Open in New York."

Remember Spanky and his gang, the *Little Rascals*? Back in Trenton, Dinkins with his tight group of friends reminded me of the "rascals" and their hilarious escapades. I reminded the Mayor. He smiled.

"We didn't have all the nicknames, but I do remember one, Junky Joe, otherwise known as Hilmar Hensen," said Dinkins. "Junky Joe was a name that fit him much better than his given name, though I don't think he let anybody know of it when he became a teacher and school principal. He, another buddy, Les Yaling who later became a Tuskegee Airman and successful dentist, and I were down at the canal to cool off one hot summer day. I imagine the whole gang was there, but I don't really remember. Anyway, Pop had built us a makeshift diving board, and we'd do our dive bombing jumps into the canal accompanied by hoots and yelps of laughter. The only problem was, we didn't know how to swim. After one jump, I went down, surfaced and went down a second time. Junky Joe and Les jumped in and saved my life."

Fred Shenck, later President Jimmy Carter's deputy Undersecretary of Commerce, Leon Higginbotham, later Chief Judge of the U.S. Court of Appeals for the Third Circuit, and Les's brother Hartley Yaling, who became an obstetrician-gynecologist, completed the gang. Little did anyone know that these innocents would have such stunning careers.

The Mayor continued, "Saturdays were special. The gang scoured the nearby neighborhood of more affluent folks, looking for empty soda bottles to turn in. Once the bottles were returned and we had nickels in hand, we headed for Pryor's Doughnuts, where we could get a baker's dozen of day-old doughnuts for a nickel. But, even better, Pryor's was right across the street from the Strand Theater. From 1 pm on, we watched four hours of movies, cartoons, serials and news, eating our doughnuts and whatever else we could finance at the snack bar. We watched from the balcony though. Blacks were not allowed downstairs."

"Did that bother you? Having to sit in the balcony?"

"I never paid much attention to the slight. My buddies and I were having too much fun watching the movies," said the Mayor.

"We used to buy cigarettes for a penny a piece even though none of us smoked," he continued. "One time we gathered enough money to buy a whole pack! Junky Joe took the pack home. That was a mistake. He got caught, and his dad knew who the other culprits were. We all got in trouble."

The gang wasn't very good at playing pick-up baseball, the Mayor told me.

"But we loved our football," he said. "We had an old, beaten up football. The bladder was completely dried out, so we stuffed it with leaves and continued our pursuit of athletic greatness."

When the boys were older, Junky Joe formed a band called *Jim Jam Jivin' Jamboree.*

"They were actually pretty good," Dinkins said. "Junky Joe played the drums and Leon, the future Judge, played the sax, all 6 foot, 4 inches of him, and the girls went wild. I couldn't play anything, but had the job of carrying the instruments for their gigs so I would get into the dances for free."

"As you got older did you find jobs other than carrying Junky Joe's equipment?"

"Sure. I worked as a waiter at a fancy country club. At another time I got a job trucking freight at the Pennsylvania Railroad Station transporting goods from the loading dock to the platforms. And I also worked part-time at the U.S. Post Office. I was never without a job.

When Dinkins turned 17 in July of 1944, the war was raging, and Dinkins wanted to be a part of the effort.

"Everyone was going into the service, and I wanted to be one of them," he said. "But I didn't want to go into any branch of the service. I wanted to be a Marine! I liked the way the Marines looked in their dress blues with the red stripe down the pant leg. And I liked the way they fought. I learned about the Marines through the newsreels at the movies. Even though I was only 17 and weighed about 125 pounds, I was determined.

"The only way for me to get into the branch I preferred was to enlist *before* I turned 18, otherwise I probably would be drafted into the Army when I reached my 18th birthday," he said. "I was determined to enlist even though my chances were slim. The Armed Forces only started to accept black candidates after President Roosevelt issued an Executive Order permitting the integration of black men into the services."

But even then, there were restrictions. Undaunted, the Mayor had to find a Marine recruitment station. Young candidates were supposed to go to a station in their hometown or city, but Trenton didn't have a Marine recruitment station.

"So I went to Newark and was turned away cold," Dinkins said. "'We have our quota of Negro Marines,' I was told and was ushered out the door. I pushed on and traveled to Jersey City. Same thing - our quota is filled. Then I went on to Camden and their quota was filled. But I wasn't going to give up. I took a bus to New York City. I figured that New York City is so big, perhaps their quota was higher and there was still room. I walked in, and the first question was 'Where do you live?' I told them 'Trenton' and they said, 'You have to go to a recruitment office in the state where you reside.' But I had done that, I told them. 'But,' they said, 'There are no exceptions.'

"Even that didn't stop me," he continued. "I took a train to Philadelphia. Same result. 'You have to live in Pennsylvania to sign up for the Marines here.' Of course I was discouraged. I went home to concoct another strategy. I went back to Philadelphia and told them I wanted to be a Marine. I told them how I had tried every recruitment office around, and I think the officer felt sorry for me so he let me fill out papers and take the physical exam. I couldn't believe it! But during the exam they said I had high blood pressure. I told them, 'I don't have high blood pressure. My pressure's fine, but they showed me the results. I found a doctor near the recruitment office who agreed to take my blood pressure: normal! Now what? I went back home to reconnoiter and saw my family doctor in Trenton who had been an Army surgeon. Normal! So, I returned to Philadelphia. They took my blood pressure in my left arm - too high. 'Try my right arm,' I begged. Too high. 'Try with me standing up.' Too high. There had to be some way the blood pressure would register normal, I thought. 'How about lying down?' Still too high. I think because I had been such an annoyance, the officer prepared a letter for my draft board and gave me a copy. In substance it said, 'This man passes the physical and selects the Marine Corps. Put him in the Marine Corps.'"

The Mayor learned later that he may have had "white coat syndrome," or "white coat hypertension," a benign condition occurring when patients, being anxious about seeing a physician, exhibit high blood pressure (hypertension) in the office which returns to normal once they leave.

Finally! David N. Dinkins, all 5 feet, 7 inches and 130 pounds of him, was going to be a Marine. But he had to wait until he was 18 to sign up. All through his senior year, he only thought about becoming a Marine and remembered little of what went on in school. On his 18th birthday, July 10, 1945, Dinkins signed up. Two weeks later, he was on his way to Montford Point, Camp Legeune, North Carolina where the black Marine recruits were trained.

On his way from Trenton to Montford Point, Dinkins had his first taste of Jim Crow behavior in the deep South when buying a bus ticket to Camp Lejuene. The ticket taker said, "Round back, boy."

Dinkins and another recruit travelled together, but on the last leg of the trip, his buddy missed the train. The good news was that his buddy finally made it to Montford; the bad news was that he was carrying Dinkins' orders.

"So what happened next?" I asked.

"'You don't have your orders?' asked a big black sergeant who greeted me at Montford," Dinkins said. "I replied 'no' and the sergeant took one look at me, decided I was an incompetent and summarily decked me.

"That was my introduction to the United States Marine Corps!" declared Dinkins.

"The services were segregated then. The black recruits received their basic training at Montford Point, not Parris Island, South Carolina where all the white recruits were trained."

But, once in the Marine Corps, Dinkins didn't question the distinction. He did the drills, the long runs over rough terrain in the blazing summer heat that caused men to drop. He did whatever the sergeants ordered him and his fellow Marines to do. And even though the war ended shortly after the future Mayor became a proud Marine, he wasn't discharged until August 21, 1946. In the meantime, the drills and long runs continued relentlessly.

"The Marine Corps wanted us disciplined, tough and fit when we left the Corps," Dinkins said.

It was not until August, 2012 that the Marine Corps properly recognized the contribution of the black Marines who trained at Montford. The nation's highest civilian honor, the Congressional Gold Medal, was awarded to all the men - 20,000 - who served there between 1942 and 1949.

"I was 85 when I proudly accepted that medal," said Dinkins.

The GI Bill, officially called the Servicemen's Readjustment Act of 1944, established hospitals for servicemen and veterans, low interest mortgages and stipends covering tuition and expenses to colleges or trade schools. From 1944 to 1949, nearly nine million veterans benefitted. Dinkins was one of them. With the help of the GI Bill, he attended and graduated, cum laude, with a Bachelor of Science degree in Math from Howard University in Washington, DC. He then received a fellowship to continue studying math at Rutgers University in New Jersey, again on the GI bill. While in his first year of graduate school, Dinkins began to wonder whether a career in math was really what he wanted. He remembered one extremely difficult exam consisting of one problem which took him four hours to answer. After handing in his paper, he asked a bright young woman in his class whether she had trouble answering the problem.

"No," she replied. "It took me about 20 minutes."

That's when Dinkins decided he was in the wrong field. When he told Pop he was quitting graduate school, Pop wasn't happy. "You're dropping out? You can't do that," he cautioned.

But Dinkins did, and soon followed in his father's footsteps by going into the insurance business.

Prior to graduate school, when Dinkins was a senior at Howard, he was strolling down Howard's Seniors Walk, a pathway for the exclusive use of seniors. He saw in front of him a young woman with beautiful legs and decided he needed to catch up with her. Indeed, she was very attractive, but was only a freshman and wasn't supposed to be using the Senior Walk. But that mattered little to Dinkins. Joyce Burrows would become his soul mate, the love of his life. They were married on August 30, 1953, shortly after Joyce graduated from Howard.

While the newlyweds waited for an apartment to become available in upper Manhattan, they lived with Joyce's parents.

"I married well," explains Dinkins. "Joyce's mother, Elaine, I loved, and her father was a successful self-made man and my mentor. Daniel L. Burrows was his name, but he confided to me, 'the "L" didn't mean a damn thing.'"

Mr. Burrows had been active in Harlem Democratic politics and was a New York State Assemblyman for several years. He encouraged Dinkins to go to law school and enter politics. Dinkins took his advice, and, again with the help of the GI bill, he attended Brooklyn Law School, graduating in 1956.

"And I passed the bar on my first try," he added proudly.

Soon Dinkins had an associate's position in a prominent black law firm, Dyett, Alexander & Phipps, earning $25 per week. Mr. Phipps left the firm when he was elected to the New York State Assembly and Dinkins replaced him as a partner in the firm. Dinkins realized the importance of expanding their practice and getting new clients. The best way to accomplish that, he thought, was by word of mouth. And there was no better way to network and get known in the community than to become involved in Harlem's Democratic Party. Soon he was a member of the George Washington Carver Democratic Club, and Dinkins was on his way to a career in politics.

His political career officially began as an Assemblyman in the New York State Assembly in 1966. He and three other prominent black politicians, Percy Sutton, Basil Paterson (father of former New York Governor David Paterson) and future U.S. Congressman Charlie Rangel worked collaboratively on many projects and became known as "The Gang of Four."

Dinkins was well-liked and highly respected in Harlem's black community. He moved from the Assembly to being President of Manhattan's Board of Elections from 1972 to 1973 and then City Clerk from 1975 to 1985. He ran for Manhattan Borough President three times, finally winning the seat on the third try in 1985. Referring to his struggles to win the Borough Presidency, he often recalls the famous comment made by Vitas Gerulaitis, a top U.S. tennis player, when finally beating Jimmy

Connors after suffering 16 losses in a row against his rival. "Let that be a lesson to you all. Nobody beats Vitas Gerulaitis 17 times in a row!"

Dinkins' next goal was the prize: to be the Mayor of New York City. He put together an excellent campaign staff led by Bill Lynch, former Chief of Staff of the powerful union AFSCME (American Federation of State, County and Municipal Employees) and Norman Steisel, former Deputy Budget Director in Mayor Ed Koch's second term. Dinkins was especially fond of Steisel. Like him, Steisel *loved* tennis.

"How he plays the game tells me a lot about his character," remarked Dinkins. "He played the game as it should be played, with integrity and grit but always a gentleman."

Dinkins knew that his fight to become Mayor was not going to be easy. First, he had to defeat the incumbent, Ed Koch, in the Democratic primary. Second, if successful in the primary, he had to defeat Rudy Guiliani, the Republican candidate, in the general election. The odds were against him. Both races were arduous but Dinkins knew, "That's politics," he said.

Beating most of the pundits' projections, Dinkins won in the Democratic primary with 51% of the vote. With that margin, Dinkins happily avoided a run off and had money to spare for the general election. Again, in the general election, the odds favored Guiliani, who had Roger Ailes and David Garth, two successful strategists, on his team. Again, the campaign was difficult, but surprising many, on November 7, 1989, Dinkins defeated Guiliani to become the first and only (so far) African-American Mayor of New York City.

His fondest memory as Mayor was Nelson Mandela's visit in June, 1990. Dinkins wanted to introduce Mandela to New York City with an inspiring event at Yankee Stadium, as the stadium was often used for special events such as the visit of a Pope or a large rock concert, but George Steinbrenner, the owner of the N.Y. Yankees and the stadium's tenant, refused to cooperate. Coincidentally, Billy Joel had booked the stadium for his sell-out concert, "Billy Joel at Yankee Stadium" and had heard about Dinkins' plea to have a gala reception for visiting Nelson Mandela. Joel graciously donated one of his three nights so that thousands of New Yorkers could meet, hear and be inspired by Mandela. The stadium was filled to capacity. When Dinkins introduced Mandela, he gave him a Yankees hat and jacket. Mandela immediately put them on and wore them proudly, waving and smiling broadly to the crowd. The next day his photo wearing the Yankees jacket and hat was front page news. Soon after, Mayor Dinkins received a telephone call.

"Mr. Steinbrenner is on the line," announced his secretary. Steinbrenner, after seeing the photo, agreed to pay all the city's expenses for the event.

But even more thrilling for the Mayor was the time that Mandela spent with him and his family at Gracie Mansion. He described Mandela as being gracious, compelling, kind, and good-humored. The Mayor holds dear the photograph of Mandela with the Dinkins family, holding his granddaughter, Kailila, in his arms.

Perhaps the biggest achievement by Dinkins as Mayor was when he successfully negotiated to keep the U.S. Open in New York. Dinkins loved tennis and followed it closely, but more important, he knew that the U.S. Open brought significant revenue to New York City. When upgrades were needed to the USTA National Tennis Center in Flushing Meadows, needing additional city parkland, Dinkins took action to allow the tournament to continue to be upgraded against threats that the tournament could leave New York City.

In 1968, tennis became an "open" sport permitting professional and amateur players to enter tournaments, as was done in golf. Until then, tennis players who played at the West

Side Tennis Club in Forest Hills, the most important tennis tournament held in the U.S., had to be amateurs. Amateurs were not allowed to accept prize money. As a result, some of the better players turned "pro" and started their own tournament tour, but their "tour" suffered from little financial backing and scattered organization. Their purses were small. Struggling to make a living, many good players quit; others didn't even consider a career in tennis unless it was to teach.

When the Open era began, finally, dramatic changes occurred. Amateur and professional players entered the open tournaments, and tennis was elevated to a popular spectator sport. The tennis stadium at the West Side Tennis Club could not accommodate the growing crowds. The United States Tennis Association ultimately decided in 1978 to move the Open to the Singer Bowl built for the 1964 World's Fair. Renovations were made, and the stadium was renamed the Louis Armstrong Stadium in honor of the world-famous musician Louis Armstrong, who lived nearby.

By the late 1980's, the U.S. Open had become so successful that the USTA needed to upgrade its facility to keep up with the growth of the event and needed to use more parkland in Flushing Meadow to create a new stadium, now known as Arthur Ashe Stadium. As leverage, the USTA threatened that if they were not allowed to expand its footprint in Flushing Meadow, it might be forced to find another tournament location outside of New York City. Dinkins knew that if the USTA planned to leave New York City, the loss of the U.S. Open would not only be a loss to loyal sports fans but also more importantly, a significant loss in economic impact to New York City.

"People come from all over the world to attend the U.S. Open," argued Dinkins. "They're not just local fans who hop in the car or take the subway with the family for a day at Yankee

Stadium. The U.S. Open fans bring their families from Europe, Australia, Serbia, Croatia, wherever and stay for a week in our hotels, dine in our restaurants, buy presents to take home. They're an enormous boost to our economy!"

In spite of these arguments in favor of keeping the Open in New York, Dinkins faced opposition. They believed the project was too costly, one that New York City could ill afford with all its other needs.

However, during negotiations which were handled primarily by Carl Weisbrod on behalf of the city, it became clear that the city and the USTA essentially agreed on one critical matter: the New York metropolitan market was too important to lose. Negotiations with the USTA, the ATP (Association of Tennis Professionals), the WTA (Women's Tennis Association), the FAA, (Federal Aviation Administration), the City Council and other agencies began and went on for more than two years.

First, the USTA complained that there was not enough land for the project, that the land was on a landfill, that the unions would be difficult, that the expense would be prohibitive and that the infrastructure getting people to and from the location was in terrible shape.

Local residents were opposed to the idea. Located in the Borough of Queens, its President, Claire Shulman, fortunately became a strong supporter and advocate of Dinkins' plan. She helped appease the objections of Community Board #8, the representative board for the residents in that area. Community Board #8 objected to the loss of the popular park built on the former World's Fair site used by Latinos, Asians-Americans, African Americans, the poor, and low and middle income residents. One much loved part of the park was a pitch-and-putt golf course. Community Board #8 argued that all those amenities would be lost to a constituency that's often ignored by the politicians. President Shulman convinced her community of the merits of the new tennis facility and found a way to move the pitch-and-putt to another location.

"Much credit too must go to Claire's attorney, Nick Garufiss," added Dinkins.

Another hurdle was what to do about the air traffic. The proposed center was right in the middle of flight paths into and out of LaGuardia Airport. Ivan Lendl, a leading player, said, 'We're outa here if planes fly over our heads.' The ATP and the WTA threatened to create their own Open and move it elsewhere.

Dinkins negotiated with the FAA to find a solution. Finally, the FAA agreed to divert air traffic for the two weeks of the U.S. Open. The USTA wanted an agreement in writing to that effect. The FAA refused. Ultimately, Dinkins agreed that the city would pay a fine, with a cap of $325,000, payable to the USTA if the FAA failed to keep all - every flight - air traffic away from the site. To this day the city has not paid a dime. The FAA kept its word.

Also dicey was the structure of the lease. What would the term of the lease be? Would the city own the stadium and the outside courts or would the USTA? Would the city lease the land to USTA? If so, would the rent be based on *gross* receipts or *net*? Would the tennis center be available for use by the city and the public during the 50 weeks a year when not being used for the U.S. Open?

Dinkins knew the problems the city had collecting rent from Yankee Stadium and Shea Stadium based on net proceeds. When the lease is based on net proceeds, the tenant deducts what one might consider unwarranted costs from the gross to lower the net receipts, leaving the city with less than it had anticipated. Dinkins remembered the lesson learned from his father as a young boy: the difference between *net* and *gross*. He and his team negotiated a commitment that the U.S. Open would remain at Flushing Meadows for twenty-five years, with rent starting at $400,000 with incremental increases, plus 1% of gross revenues and options to extend the lease to a total of ninety-nine years. The 1% gross revenues included profits from sales of food, clothing, sports paraphernalia, restaurant business and television rights.

Pursuant to the lease agreement, the city retained ownership of the land; the USTA paid for the construction and renovation of all the facilities; the city was responsible for improvements to the Grand Central Parkway, entrances and exits, which were sorely needed - with or without the tennis center.

Dinkins argued that the $150 million spent by the city will "keep the world's greatest tennis tournament in the world's greatest city." Others were less enthusiastic, but Dinkins proved to be right - very right!

Baseball stadiums are generally used 81 days a year. When the Yankees or the Mets make it to the playoffs and the World Series, a few extra days are added. Football stadiums are used even less: one day a week for 9 to 11 weeks a year. To protect against the complex remaining idle, the lease provided that the facility could be used by the public and the city when not hosting the U.S. Open.

The New York City Council was responsible for approving the project, and in 1993, with the election campaign between Dinkins and Guiliani in full swing, pressure on council members to vote against the project was fierce. Ultimately, shortly before the general election in November, the Council voted to approve the project. The timing was tight and Dinkins hoped that if Guiliani won, he would not carry through on his threat to squelch the deal. Guiliani did win the election and brought the issue before the City Council attempting to rescind the lease, but the City Council voted against his proposal.

The new and improved USTA National Tennis Center has generated more annual income to New York City than the Yankees, the Mets, the Knicks and the Rangers combined. Colleges and schools conduct tournaments at the tennis center; tennis instruction is given at the tennis center; courts, fitness facilities and a hospitality center are available to the public for a fee paid to New York City.

Later, Mayor Bloomberg, while in office, gave Dinkins the ultimate compliment when he commented that the USTA National Tennis Center, "is the only good athletic sports stadium deal not just in New York but in the country."

Revenues increase every year. In 1991 revenue totaled $145 million. By 2015, the revenue had grown to more than $750 million according to one study. In addition, 13,000 seasonal workers are employed at the tennis center and in the community during the Open. The U.S. Open has become the best attended sporting event in the world and is broadcast to 188 countries worldwide.

"I love the tournament. I love the sport. I love New York City," exclaimed Dinkins.

Dinkins made it happen. I'm not sure that Dinkins gets enough credit for this accomplishment, but he doesn't seek the glory. He's happy having the plaza in front of the East Gate entrance named "The David Dinkins Circle." And he is happy to have daily tickets in the President's Box each year. After his tenure as mayor, Dinkins served as a member of the USTA's Board of Directors, where he was instrumental in having the facility named the USTA Billie Jean King National Tennis Center, after the phenomenal tennis player, advocate and his good friend.

Mayor Dinkins was a late bloomer as far as tennis is concerned, but once he took up the sport, there was no stopping him. As a young boy, he had played some ping pong and when in high school and college "had messed around with tennis a bit but I had no instruction and no idea how to play the game"

In 1974, during the tennis boom of the '70's, Bill Hayling, the brother of one of Dinkins' best friends from childhood, put a racquet in Dinkins' hand. By this time Dinkins was 47 years old, but he had kept himself in pretty good shape over the years and was ready. After that, he played every day, whenever, wherever.

Dinkins joined a black country club in Scotch Plains, New Jersey, at the height of the tennis craze and became a part of the wave of new players in the sport. Since then, many people have given up on tennis because it takes time and effort to get good. But not Dinkins.

Mayor Dinkins came to know Arthur Ashe, one of America's finest tennis players, benefactor of tennis, civil rights activist and gentleman, as both were well-known figures - one in politics, one in tennis - each with similar interests even though a generation apart in age. And they even share the same birthday - July 10th.

"I became very close to Arthur and his wife Jeanne," said Dinkins "And I was with them when they first met. I think it was the United Negro College Fund that was having a tennis benefit at Madison Square Garden. Part of the festivities was a 'celebrity' tennis match between Ron Gault, a former U.S. Justice Department attorney, advisor to Mayor Koch and good friend of mine, and me against Andrew Young, the civil rights activist, Congressman, former Ambassador to the United Nations and Mayor of Atlanta, and Gordon Parks, the famed photographer. I don't remember who won, but Jeanne, a photographer, was at the event as a guest of Gordon Parks. They were introduced, and the rest is history."

The Ashes and the Dinkins spent many happy times together. Dinkins cannot say enough about Arthur Ashe and the influence he made on tennis and the world, not only as a marvelous tennis player and gentleman but also as an activist against apartheid and discrimination against blacks.

"I spoke at Arthur's funeral, and I said, 'Arthur was a credit to his race - the human race,'" he said.

When Dinkins was struggling to learn the game, Ashe said, "If you want to see what a tennis player should look like, go see Charlie Pasarell."

Dinkins did one better. He went to Pasarell's coach, Welby Van Horn, a highly respected tennis coach and former professional player. Van Horn started his coaching career in 1951 when he became the head pro at San Juan Puerto Rico's new Caribe Hilton tennis facility. There, he coached Charlie Pasarell's father, also an excellent player and then his son, "Charlito," who became the top-ranked American player in 1967 and a good friend of Ashe. In the 1970's, Van Horn had a summer tennis camp at the Choate School in Wallingford, Connecticut and Dinkins attended in 1974 and 1975. He described Van Horn as a "funny fellow."

"Van Horn always cautioned his students that there's no easy way to learn tennis. Too many players were 'cats' and not enough 'dogs.' The 'cats' were players who ran around the court just trying to get the ball back. The 'dogs' were serve-and-vollyers who served well, ran to the net and put the ball away."

Dinkins gives Van Horn credit for creating his game, though he wished he had a better backhand.

While Dinkins was perfecting his game at the Van Horn tennis camp, Ashe, in the summer of 1975, was playing at Wimbledon. As the No. 6 seed, he made it to the final where he faced Jimmy Connors, the No. 1 seed and heavy favorite. Ashe then startled the tennis world, winning 6-1, 6-1, 5-7, 6-4 to become the first black man to win the Wimbledon men's singles title.

In 1969, Arthur Ashe, Charlie Pasarell and lover-of-tennis and benefactor Sheridan Snyder co-founded the National Junior Tennis League, which has the mission to bring tennis, fitness and life's lessons to inner-city, underprivileged boys and girls as well as handicapped and wounded warriors. Dinkins became a member of its Board of Directors.

Over the years, NJTL has established youth tennis centers nationwide and has been instrumental not only in bringing promising new players to tennis academies but also by encouraging them to hone their academic skills to go on to colleges and universities. Children are given scholarships or grants for tennis instruction; they're given extra help to make them better students in the classroom, learning the importance of good study habits and achieving academic success. Through the USTA Foundation, working together with NJTL, children are able to earn scholarships to college.

"Can you tell me of a couple success stories?" I asked.

"Marc Clemente, originally from the Philippines, for one. He is a product of NJTL, having started as a 10-year-old at the Central Park clinics. He graduated from Columbia University, played some professional tennis touring in Southeast Asia, started a successful coaching career, part of which was at NJTL, and now he is in sports marketing having worked with the Tennis Channel, CBS and the Today Show, before going to The Singapore American School as Director of Marketing and of Tennis.

"Another fine product of NJTL is Katrina Adams, the current president of the USTA," the first African-American and former professional tennis player to lead the USTA.

Katrina grew up in Chicago and in 1975 joined a tennis clinic when she was 6. But, the next year she joined the NJTL program in Chicago and has remained involved ever since. She went on to play at Northwestern, winning the NCAA doubles title and then joined the pro tour, having a world ranking as high as No. 67 in singles and No. 8 in doubles. For the past ten years, she has been the executive director of the Harlem Junior Tennis and Education Program, one of NJTL's facilities. She has also been a commentator on Tennis Channel since 2003 and now leads the USTA.

"I'm very proud of NJTL achievements. And I'm hopeful too that these young people will stay in the game until they're as old as I am," concluded Dinkins, beaming with a smile.

Can you imagine playing doubles with the likes of Roger Federer, Rod Laver, John McEnroe, Monica Seles, Serena Williams, Ilona Kloss and Billie Jean King? Each week until Dinkins stopped playing at age 88, the Mayor's secretary sent out email blasts to 64 of his best tennis-playing friends, finding out who's available for the matches that week. They're on the list and play whenever they can.

"My son Davey is also on the list," said Dinkins proudly. "He's 60 now and has become a pretty good player!"

"Ilona Kloss was on my list. One day I picked her up and, to my surprise, Billie Jean was with her. Billie Jean was recuperating from an injury so didn't play, but she wanted to watch our match. When we arrived at our usual court at Roosevelt Island where I always played with Billie Jean, the crowd went wild. She inspires not just the little girls but boys too and not just in tennis. In all areas of our daily lives, she inspires."

Soon after Seles, then the world No. 1, was stabbed and injured on court during a tournament in Hamburg, Germany in 1993, Dinkins met her in Monte Carlo. She was playing in a Pro Am there and Dinkins was immediately impressed by her as she struggled to recover mentally and physically from the attack.

"I'd always been a fan of hers. Then after the stabbing happened, we became fast friends," the Mayor explained.

She didn't return to professional tennis for more than two years, but Monica played in Arthur Ashe Kids' Day, a program held at the Tennis Center and sponsored by NJTL with support from the USTA. Her partner? The Mayor. Their opponents? Mike Wallace of CBS "60 Minutes" fame and Martina Navratilova.

The Mayor said, "We were at match point, Mike was at net, and by some fluke he stuck his racquet out at just the right moment and hit a short volley that we couldn't get. But that loss didn't dampen the friendship between Monica and me. We're still very close.

"Plain and simple, it's a fun sport! Of course the most fun is winning," said the Mayor. "But millions simply become better people through tennis."

"How's that?" I asked.

"For one, you do yourself a favor and keep in shape. I was always a singles player, but later started playing doubles. When you reach your 80's, doubles is better for you," he added with a smile. "I stopped playing when I turned 88. But, I still love the game, love the people I've met and the thrill of watching top tennis.

"You meet great people who become life-long friends. Psychologically, you feel youthful and energetic. You think young. You learn to play by the rules because if you don't, you get called on it. Players who cheat - word gets around and they're not invited back. As I mentioned when playing with my Deputy Budget Director Norman Steisel, you learn about one's character when playing tennis.

"I remember watching Ashe play Jimmy Connors one night, I think, at Madison Square Garden. At a crucial point a linesman called one of Connors' shots out. Ashe corrected him saying, 'No, that ball was good' giving the point to Connors.

Ashe was such a fine ambassador of tennis and an example of what integrity is."

He continued, "You tend to be more positive and optimistic, at least that's been my experience. But, the best part is bringing this game to children. They become better kids and can be involved in the sport forever."

Right on, Mayor Dinkins!

CHAPTER 6:

HENRY TIBERIO

Henry Tiberio seemingly always has a pleasant and composed expression. He has bright blue eyes and not one wrinkle with skin almost as smooth as a baby's. Henry is 93 years "young."

"Henry is much loved in the New England tennis community and for good reason having won every senior division in New England and has for many years taken on the national tournaments as well," said Bob McKinley, the host captain at the Atlantic Coast Cup senior tennis competition held at the Essex Country Club, Manchester, New Hampshire in July, 2014.

But that's not all. For many years and up to the present, he has been giving back to tennis as a teacher and mentor as a USPTA (United States Professional Tennis Association) teaching professional. He works part time now and concentrates on older players giving them advice, techniques and strategies that he has learned over the years.

"I teach players in their 60s, 70s and 80s. I relate to them even though I'm 93 because I'm still competing," said Henry. "They appreciate that and know I'm a player and know what I'm talking about."

Growing up, Henry said he was not much of a player.

"I started playing tennis with my brother when we were 11 and 12," he said. "We'd walk to a public court in town before school, play, and then walk a mile and a half to school. That's why I have good, strong legs even today."

After high school, Henry went to Duke University in Durham, North Carolina on the V-12 program.

"You know that's when the Government put you through college," he said. "I signed up for the Navy and when I graduated I was sent to Washington, D.C. I never saw combat, but I was the "keeper" of secret mail for the captains and admirals. I couldn't even go to the bathroom unless I took the mail with me. At the end of the day, I'd turn it all over to the brass."

When Henry left the service, he moved to Massachusetts and worked for thirty-six years for the state of Massachusetts in children and family care.

"We'd try to get children out of foster care and back to their families," he said. "Or if that didn't work out, we'd arrange for adoptions. It was good, fulfilling work."

While at Duke, Henry played on the tennis team "but only when a teammate didn't show up." However, he really started to take the game seriously when he reached the age of 50. That's when he learned about the pleasures of senior tennis.

"What is it about senior tennis that is so special for you?" I asked.

"Tennis is truly a game for life. It keeps you moving and thinking. You have to think, you know, about what shot your opponent is going to hit next. Moving and thinking. That's what the game is all about. And if you're moving and thinking, you're engaged and living a longer and happier life.

"One day, a friend who knew I liked to play tennis told me about this beautiful place to play in Beverly, Massachusetts. I'd never even heard of Beverly, Massachusetts. Anyway I took

Henry Tiberio

a look and it was beautiful. Originally the club was started by the United Shoe Machine Corporation for its employees. They had over 6,000 employees at the time and they manufactured 85 percent of the shoes in America," said Henry proudly.

You get Henry on a topic - any topic - and he takes the ball and runs. His enthusiasm for life comes through in the stories he tells.

"The club, known as The Beverly Golf and Tennis Club, is still going strong today and is the host of many great New England tournaments," he said. "So, I joined the club. It had 12 great clay courts. Then one day, I was playing singles and reached down at the back of the court to pick up a ball. The back of the court was separated from the next tier of courts by a screen but there was a two-foot space at the bottom, so I could see through. I look up and see a beautiful pair of legs. I didn't see the rest of the body, but those legs were beautiful. So after we finished playing I found a spot where I could get a better look. And that was my Frances. She is the most supportive, beautiful woman who has been my wife ever since."

"Does Frances play?" I asked.

"Oh yes, and she's quite good, but she doesn't play in the seniors tournaments like I do, but we still play mixed together," he said. "I think mixed doubles is going to be the game of the future in the seniors. This couple in New England, a husband and wife - I can't think of their name right now, but I will.... ah, Ken Miller and his wife. Anyway, they started this series of tournaments called 'The Slams' which are played every year in New England. It's a circuit. The grass tournament is played at a club in Point Judith, Rhode Island; the hard court tournament is played in New Haven and the clay is played here at the Beverly Golf and Tennis Club. This year 90 players entered the clay court tournament. They had flights in the 55s, 60s, 65s, 70s and 75s. No 80s, 85s or 90s. It's a wonderful tournament, and I think the Millers should be inducted into the New England Hall of Fame for what they've accomplished."

Taking a short breath, Henry continued.

"You know we have wonderful tournaments in New England," he said. "Of course we have the Atlantic Coast Cup which we host every fourth year. But we have the Friendship Cup with Canada. It's an annual event. We alternate venues. One year we play the tournament here in New England, the next year we play in Canada. It's always good tennis, and what better way to make friends from another country who love tennis as much as you do?"

He is proud too of the part New England has played in the history of American tennis.

"This Club – The Essex Club was for many, many years the host of a national women's tournament on grass - a warm up tournament for Forest Hills," said Henry. "We had all the greats playing here - Doris Hart, Maureen Connolly and many others. It did a lot for New England tennis."

Wanting to get back to the subject of senior tennis, I asked Henry to tell me more about what he gets out of senior tennis and why he loves it.

"Well, I keep playing because I want the younger people to look at older folks and see that we are vital," he said. "We're healthy. They don't have to be polite and sympathetic because we're up in years. They can see that we're fine and enjoy a good quality of life. I'll have people say, 'Gee, Henry, how can you play such good tennis now when you weren't much of a player in the past?' and I say, tennis is a lifetime sport and you can get better as you age. No doubt about it. And then entering these senior tournaments gives me such a positive attitude. I had the thrill of my life this summer. I played in the national 90-and-over grass tournament at Longwood this past summer. I made it to the final when I played Fred Kovaleski. I've played Kovaleski many times. I never even won a set from him. But, this year he wasn't moving to the right very well and I took note. We split sets and then our third set was a tie-break set. We had five match points between us, four for me, one for Fred. I feel it's a strong self-preservation instinct that gets me the ads. Then I wait, hopefully, for an opening for an easy match point. I finally won 10-7 in the third. That was the best win of my life!"

Clearly that win made Henry feel 20 years younger! But he offers some advice too.

"Don't be macho and play down to a younger age category," he said. "Just admit your age and play in your own age group."

CHAPTER 7:

KATRINA ADAMS

When I met Katrina Adams, the President of the United States Tennis Association, in her USTA offices in White Plains, New York, she greeted me with a big smile, dressed stylishly in black boots, black tights and an oversized black sweater. We settled down on a comfortable sofa and began Katrina's story.

She grew up on the west side of Chicago with two older brothers and her parents, both of whom were teachers. The Martin Luther King, Jr. Boys Club had summer activities for children nine to 18, and in June of 1974, when Katrina was seven, the summer activity was tennis. Katrina's parents were teaching in summer school so Katrina tagged along with her big brothers to the Boys Club. Even though she was much too young for the tennis programs, Katrina bugged the instructors for two weeks before they let her participate. By the end of the summer, she was named the Most Valuable Player.

Katrina turned eight in August of 1974, and she entered her first tournament, the ATA (American Tennis Association) Nationals in New Orleans no less. She and her parents made the long drive to the ten-and-under tournament, and it paid off. Katrina got all the way to the final before losing.

"I wanted that *big* trophy," said Adams, remembering her disappointment when losing that first final. "I only liked *big* trophies back then."

I can just imagine the spunk of this little eight-year-old girl and how it developed and grew over the years.

From there her tennis career took off. She played on the USTA junior circuit, and at the Whitney Young Magnet High School where she was the top singles player in 1983 and 1984.

"I went to the 18 national indoors in Kansas City where all the college coaches were recruiting. But, I was only 16, young for a rising senior, and none of the coaches talked to me. I thought I'd like to go to UCLA, USC or University of Florida, but no one seemed interested. That was a huge disappointment, but the Northwestern coach knew of me from my high school career in Chicago. I went to Northwestern's recruitment weekend and loved the school. I met the girls on the team and loved them too. It seemed a good fit for me. I corresponded with the coaches and in April I signed the letter of intent.

"At Northwestern, I won the NCAA doubles with Diane Donnelly and was a two-time All-American. My junior year, when I was 19, I left Northwestern, and in January, 1988 I turned pro. I regret never getting my degree, but one of these days I'll pursue it when the time is right, but for now, I'm pretty content being where I am.

"I retired from the tour in 1999 after getting as high as No. 67 in the world in singles and No. 8 in the world in doubles with Zina Garrison. I played with Zina my first three years on tour, and I had my best years with her as my doubles partner. She was my best friend and a mentor early in my career. I was an aggressive player and she was passive, so we had perfect chemistry as a team that allowed us to be successful. I played with several other partners, including Lori McNeil, Debbie Graham, Larissa Savchenko, Mariaan deSwardt, Chanda Rubin

Katrina Adams competing for
Northwestern

and others, but Manon Bollegraf from Holland was my other longtime partner, and we were also quite successful as a team."

"After you retired in 1999 did you go into broadcasting?" I asked.

"No. For four years I was a USTA National Coach working in Atlanta, Georgia with our nation's top juniors as a regional coach. The top juniors in my region were Carly Gullickson, Jamea Jackson, Brian Baker, Robby Ginepri and many others, some with national rankings.

"After coaching, I wanted to pursue my dream. I had majored in Communications at Northwestern and wanted to be a tennis commentator/analyst on TV. In 2003, I contacted ESPN, but they didn't have any room for me. So then I contacted the Tennis Channel. The Williams sisters were No. 1 and No. 2, dominating the women's tennis world at the time, and I thought the Tennis Channel needed me more than I needed them. They needed diversity."

"That was pretty gutsy of you," I said.

"I suppose, but apparently I impressed them with my confidence and approach. I contacted Larry Meyers of the Tennis Channel and went to his office unannounced, actually without an appointment. He was interested and wanted me to meet with the Talent Director, but at the time he was on a conference call. I sat outside his office for an hour. Finally, he came out of his office, and asked, 'Can you come back later?' I said 'Sure.' Then he said, 'Call first,' so I did. He asked if I had a reel/tape of me doing work on TV, and I told him 'No.' 'Well, see if you can get a tape done before your next visit.'

"Fortunately, I had a friend in Atlanta, Sam Crenshaw, who was with a news station. I visited him on the set, and he said, 'Ok. Let's go.' I had never been on a TV set before, but Sam had some old footage of a tennis match which he played, and I did the commentary. I was even using a teleprompter which I had never done before. And, unknown to me, the entire production staff was on the set - about 30 people, including producers and directors - whom I never saw as they were in an adjoining room separated by a non-see-through window. When the session ended, Sam spoke into the microphone and asked, 'How was that?' and the production crew responded, 'Perfect.'

"I sent the tape to the Tennis Channel in October, and in April a producer called. He asked, 'What are you doing on April 10th?' I didn't really have any plans for April 10th, so he said, 'Good. You're going to be on air in Lowell, Massachusetts for the Fed Cup, when we go live for the first time. Venus, Serena and Alexandra Stevenson will be playing.' And that's how I started in television."

"As I said before, pretty gutsy. Good for you! So aside from the TV work, what else were you doing?"

"In October 2005 I became the Executive Director of the Harlem Junior Tennis and Education Program, and I'm still there, supporting our mission and raising funds and awareness for our youth to use tennis as the vehicle to earn a college scholarship while maintaining a focus on education and wellness."

"Were you involved in the Arthur Ashe Kids Day at the USTA Billie Jean King National Tennis Center?"

"Very. That's a great day for the kids and an opportunity for youth to pick up a racquet for the first time and then experience an amazing show in Ashe Stadium watching tennis, TV and movie superstars on the court and stage - the Williams sisters, Nadal, Federer, Djokovic, Andy Murray, Rihanna, Justin Bieber, Alec Baldwin, Will Farrell. The kids love it!

"And Mayor Dinkins is always there. He has always been involved with the NJTL Awards Luncheon which is held on Arthur Ashe Kids Day, an opportunity for the youth to participate. Dinkins is a huge supporter of the National Junior Tennis and Learning Network and supports my program HJTEP (Harlem Junior Tennis and Education Program) and NYJTL (New York Junior Tennis and Learning) locally here in New York City."

"He's very fond of you," I added.

"I know. He calls me his daughter. And I really got to know him better when I became a member of the USTA Board of Directors in 2005. He has done a lot for tennis, especially in New York. He has been my No. 1 fan, and I adore his passion for youth, for our sport and for his determination to make a difference for all of us. I refer to him as 'my other father.'"

"Certainly, tennis has opened doors for you, hasn't it?" I asked.

"For sure, it has. I've had a remarkable path. Being a professional player in any sport is one thing, but in tennis the sport is global. And because of that I am honored to have endless relationships around the world. Also being a TV commentator keeps me present in the sport and allows me to develop relationships with all the current players. Tennis has given me so much, and now as President of the USTA I have a chance to give back to the sport that I love."

"Do you have specific goals that you are hoping to achieve as President," I asked.

"I have three initiatives. First, is to grow Hispanic participation in tennis. The Hispanic population is growing in the U.S., but it has the smallest participation in tennis - only 1% of all tennis players are Hispanic. We need to get the right message across - that tennis is a life-long sport. We're starting to make some headway.

"Second, we have more and more high school kids playing on high school teams. There are 350,000 high school players, but once the season is over, the vast majority of them don't play until the next year. We're trying to engage them in a fun, team environment. They may just be recreational players, but we want to keep them involved once the season is over. I named a task force to investigate and to come up with ideas. One idea that we have used for a few years now, is to have 'Play Days' where the students come together for a day of fun playing tennis without any pressure. There's no ranking, no recruiting, just an opportunity to have fun playing the game. And they can engage in multiple Play Days throughout the year.

"The third initiative is to rebuild the focus on sportsmanship in our game. It has gone awry with too much bullying and cheating. Again, I named a task force which has done some careful research and created an oath with the intent that all players at the national and sectional levels must sign. And not just the players, but the parents and coaches must also sign."

"What about college tennis? Is that bringing more young Americans to the pro tour?"

"Definitely, collegiate tennis is growing our sport, but I'd like to see more Americans in the system. You know, the U.S. is the land of opportunity for college athletes so the foreign players seek out the American universities and colleges. But right now four of the top five international junior players are American: Taylor Fritz, Tommy Paul, Michael Mmoh and Riley Opelka."

"The USTA is also focusing on its player development program, right?"

"Yes. We have the Player Development headquarters in Boca Raton, Florida. We have lodging for the kids, but it's not like Bolletierri's [referring to Nick Bolletierri's teaching complex] where the players stay for a whole semester and get schooling as well as tennis instruction. We have one to two week programs of intense instruction given by our 'national coaches,' all former professional players. The programs are very popular, and we're looking forward to some positive results. We are building a new state of the art facility in Orlando, the Home of American Tennis, which will house our Community Tennis Department as well as Player Development. The USTA National Campus will provide opportunities for players of all levels and from all across the country to visit and experience the new norm in American Tennis."

"Including senior players?"

"Yes. Including senior players."

I asked, "Do you have any initiatives to support senior tennis?"

"Well, super seniors are leaving the game because of illness or injuries or they're taking up golf and pickle ball. We're concerned and are encouraging our teaching pros to utilize bigger balls and perhaps smaller courts that we use for the kids under ten. We ask that when new courts are put in to provide blended lines making the court smaller so that boys and girls under ten - and the older players too - can enjoy the game more."

"Katrina, do you participate in any of the senior tennis events?"

"No. I have no desire to compete in senior tennis tournaments. I played at the highest level, and since I left the tour, I just want to play for fun. Many of my colleagues play in sanctioned senior tennis events, and I applaud them, but that's not my interest. However, I'll always play because I love the sport.

"That's really what's important. You continue and will continue to play regardless of whether you enter big tournaments."

"Katrina, you're still in your forties which doesn't seem too senior to me, but what is it that you love about playing tennis in your 'senior' years?"

"First, it allows me to do something I love - to play the game. I love the feel of the ball. I love that it keeps me nimble. I love that it keeps me mentally strong. In tennis you have to focus. Tennis keeps me healthy and fit. It's actually a fun way to achieve self-preservation. And, I build lasting relationships through playing tennis. It's wonderful exercise and I love spending an hour on the court with a friend. And I meet new friends through tennis. There's no sport like tennis that can do all of these things for you."

"Do you have any tips for senior tennis players?"

"Stay in tennis. Don't hang up your racquets because you aren't as nimble as you used to be. Play on the smaller courts with lower compression balls. You can still get a great workout and be competitive and enjoy the sport. If you want to improve when not on the court you can watch the Tennis Channel. There are one-minute drills shown throughout the day, 24/7, that are very useful. The internet also has videos on You Tube or tennis.com, so it's very easy to fine-tune your game visually. I also recommend concentrating on flexibility as this will cut down on injuries. And, just take a good walk to stay in shape. The thinking now is that running doesn't seem to be as important as a good walk."

"Who in tennis do you feel is most responsible for your many tennis achievements?"

"There are several people. First, my parents. Without their love and support, I couldn't have stayed in the sport long enough to reach the pinnacle as a professional player."

Katrina Adams as President of the USTA in 2015

"Who thought that that long drive to New Orleans when you were eight would lead to such a career?"

"Right. It's pretty incredible. But then the many coaches that believed in me as a junior, collegiate and professional player - that obviously has been instrumental. And other supporters, family members and friends have supported me in my achievements.

"However, do you see this album that was created as a gift to me commemorating the "Original Nine?" asked Katrina as she pointed to a handsome book on her coffee table.

Picking it up I saw on the outside cover a photograph of the "Original Nine," the nine women tennis players who in 1970 defied the USLTA who did not support their effort to demand prize money equal to that awarded to the men. Risking their careers, the nine players - Americans Billie Jean King, Rosemary Casals, Nancy Richey, Peaches Bartkowicz, Kristy Pigeon, Valerie Ziegenfuss, Julie Heldman and Australians Kerry Melville Reid and Judy Tegart Dalton - signed contracts for $1 to set up the Virginia Slims tour of eight professional tournaments spearheaded by *World Tennis* magazine publisher Gladys Heldman and her good friend, Joe Cullman, the CEO of Philip Morris. The USLTA suspended the Original Nine, but by the end of 1970 the Virginia Slims Circuit had 40 members. Later, in 1973, the Virginia Slims Circuit absorbed the Women's

Grand Prix circuit, and the WTA (Women's Tennis Association) was formed.

"I know I am what I am today because of these nine women," said Katrina. "Because of their strength, determination, stubbornness and vision, I was able to have a successful professional career as a tennis player. Playing the sport at the professional level I can imagine what they went through, and I wanted to honor them at the 2015 U.S. Open as a thank you to let them know that they are not forgotten. Those in attendance were greatly appreciative and we had a great time. Those who couldn't attend were with us in spirit."

What will Katrina's future be? We don't know, but I have no doubt that she will continue to inspire young tennis players, improve the game as it is played, think globally to encourage more international competition, encourage older players to continue playing and give back to the game she loves as she is doing now - graciously and very competently.

CHAPTER 8:

DONNA FLOYD
FALES

The morning after my arrival to spend a weekend with Donna Floyd Fales and her husband Gordon in Coral Gables, Florida, I followed her in her 2002 red Camry to the Royal Palm Tennis Club in Miami where she was playing a match against a 65-year-old gentleman, John Trainor.

The temperature outside was 52, the wind was blowing fiercely, but that was immaterial to Donna. At 75, she still has fast feet, classic strokes, strong, well-placed serves, uncanny court sense while conforming to the old-school style of holding two balls in her left hand.

After a strong warm-up and a toss to serve, John won the first game. Donna's service game started with a running backhand shot down the line which fell inches out.

"She's off the court and aims for the lines. It's very dispiriting," John quipped to me.

Donna missed a few shots and lost her serve. Soon, she was down 2-5, before she started to connect with low, well-placed forehands and backhands.

"She's got those classic strokes that go low over the net," John again commented to me from the court. "Only world-class players can do that."

Donna stayed steady and evened the set at 5-5. Suddenly, John pulled up short, took a few slow steps and complained that his calf muscle was acting up.

"Not to worry," Donna said. "We can stop."

"No, let's keep going."

The match continued, but again paused at 5-6, 30-all with Donna serving, when John said, "I need a minute."

Donna offered again to stop, but they continued. Donna then held serve for 6-6.

At this point John decided he better stop. I wouldn't suggest that he sensed a shift in momentum. Donna does not like to lose, and I doubted she would lose this time.

While walking back to our cars, the players compared ages, and John was quite surprised that Donna, who beats him regularly, is ten years older than he is.

Donna confided later that she has a hard time finding players who will give her a good game, but she mentioned one, Ozgur Altan, the Turkish counsel general in Miami, who has improved his game enormously since they started playing. And how old is he? 43.

Donna was born on October 14, 1940 in Atlanta, where she lived until 1952, when the family moved to Virginia. She took to tennis naturally as her parents were both players, particularly her Dad. He not only played but also organized tournaments, clinics and other tennis activities in his spare time.

"In 1955, I won the Virginia State Women's Championship and my father won the Men's Championship," said Donna. "I was only a sophomore at Wakefield High School in Arlington and ended up being the youngest women's champion at that time in the tournament's history. And my father won the men's

Donna Floyd Fales

championship. That was a happy time for the Fales family."

Also in 1955, Donna entered and won the fifteen-and-under national championship.

"All the players in the tournament were the top juniors in the country – Nancy Richey, Sally Moore and Albertina "Tina' Rodi. I beat them all in that order winning in the final against Rodi," said Donna. "In 1958, I played Beverly Baker at the Pennsylvania Grass Court Women's Championships at the Merion Cricket Club near Philadelphia in an early round. Beverly, one of the marquee entrants, was the No. 2 woman in the U.S. and No. 3 in the world that year. I prepared for the match by analyzing her game which was unusual because she was ambidextrous and particularly good at reaching wide balls on both sides. I decided to hit right at her. I won the first set 9-7, lost the second 1-6 but came on strong in the third, winning the final set 6-3.

"Bill Clothier, a top USTA official and the tournament director, came up to me after the match and said, 'Young lady. You've cost me a lot of money.'"

Donna was bewildered by the comment. Certainly, he wasn't taking bets, but Donna soon learned that the top players in the tournament were given free housing and free "meals on the porch," from noon to 2 pm, a coveted honor allowing them to watch all the matches in progress. They were permitted to select their dishes from a menu and given a travel stipend. The "perks" seem quaint now, but before the Open era when players were not given prize money, they were very welcome. Sadly, Donna lost in the next round, but for a 17-year-old she was making her mark.

The next big tournament for Donna, also held at the Merion Cricket Club, was the Middle States Championships. This one she won, and her trophy was presented to her by Grace Kelly, a Philadelphia native, actress and soon to be the Princess of Monaco. No wonder this young dynamo pursued the sport.

From high school, Donna attended the College of William & Mary College in Williamsburg, Virginia, and won the U.S. Intercollegiate singles title in 1959. Donna's win was "pre Title IX" and few universities or colleges had women's teams, however, William & Mary always had a strong tennis tradition.

Donna, in the Class of 1962, majored in History. William & Mary, very proud of Donna's record in tennis, sponsored her trip to Great Britain in 1961 to play the grass circuit there, including Wimbledon. Donna was given a part-time job by the college to help defray some of the cost. Then, in 1962, the college permitted her to graduate six months early in order to travel to Africa and Europe to play in tournaments and exhibitions.

The year before, Donna's good friend and top tennis player, Donald Dell, had contacted the USIA (United States Information Agency) for permission to travel independently to enter tournaments in Africa and Europe with his tennis-playing friend Allen Fox. The USIA gave them permission as long as they arranged their own itinerary. Donna heard about this adventure and convinced the college that she should have a similar experience. The college agreed. More important, would her parents agree?

"My father said, 'You're traveling by yourself?'" said Donna. "'Yes,' I replied, and reassured him that I was doing everything through the USIA, and that I would be in touch with the USIA and the embassies by mail. Then, once I get to Europe I'll be playing in all the majors there.

"'Do you understand what you may encounter as a single woman in Africa and Europe?' he asked, and I reassured him that I would be careful and that there would be other tennis players with me. My father relented, and my first stop was Cairo, where I won the women's singles and mixed doubles with Fred Stolle, an Aussie who took me under his wing. Fred and I remain good friends, and now he lives not far from me in Florida.

"The next tournament was in Alexandria, where I again won the women's singles and Fred and I won the mixed. This was all very exciting. From Egypt I went to Khartoum, Sudan, where Bill Hussey, an official in the State Department, had arranged an exhibition, then clinics in Nairobi, Kenya and Kampala, Uganda. I was most impressed by Sudan, a newly independent republic freed from British rule. The British living there were quite elegant; men in tropical white suits and hats and women, stylishly dressed, waving fans in the heat."

From there, Donna traveled to Salisbury, Rhodesia, now Zimbabwe, where she met a tobacco auctioneer who had once played tennis against her father. Donna's attempts to enter Iran were unsuccessful. Single women were not permitted to travel alone in Iran nor play against men. Instead, she travelled to Johannesburg, South Africa, where she played in the South African national tennis tournament.

"I can't remember how I did in Johannesburg – must not have done well," she admitted.

As I listened to Donna describe her journey, I found it incredulous. This is 1962. It's the Cold War. She's travelling by herself in strange countries, not knowing anyone, except the auctioneer in Zimbabwe. What was she thinking?

From Africa, Donna went to Europe, where she met up with many tennis players from England, France, Italy and Australia. The "Aussies" – Fred Stolle, Roy Emerson, Neale and John Fraser, Warren Woodcock – were there too and all looked after her. Donna entered tournaments in Naples, where she beat Judy Tegart; in Rome losing to Margaret Court; in Paris beating Christine Truman. Then she was on to Wimbledon, but had a difficult first-round opponent, Nancy Richey, who won 11-9, 10-8.

"After Wimbledon, as a part of an exchange between the United States and Russia, Donald Dell, Frank Froehling, Billie Jean King and I entered the Russian national championships played in Moscow," she said. "Moscow was cold and bleak. The Soviet architecture was grim - stacks of cement blocks forming unattractive government buildings. Our hotel management did not allow us to be alone. There was always someone in the hallways to follow us when we left. We didn't know if our rooms were bugged, so we were very careful about what was said. And we did not provoke. We were to abide by their rules.

"We were constantly on guard. I remember Billie Jean and I went to a puppet show unaccompanied. When we got out of the theatre, we didn't know how to get back to the hotel. I couldn't believe I would put us in such a situation. I'm always very careful about directions and knowing where I'm going. Anyway, we gave the cab driver the name of the hotel, and he got us there, but we wondered whether he, too, was a plant watching us."

In the spring of 1961, not long before Donna went on her extended journey, she met Gordon Fales, a handsome young Officer Candidate in the Coast Guard OCS (Officer Candidate School) located not far from William & Mary. They dated quite seriously, until she left the following February for Europe and Africa. During her trip, Gordon was not forgotten. Donna wrote letters to him at least three times a week, and he wrote her as frequently. Through the letters, Donna realized that she wanted to marry Gordon, and the feeling was mutual. When she returned to the D.C. area, she decided to stay put for a while, primarily to get to know Gordon better and to, hopefully, plan for a wedding. She got a position with a Congressman, Kenneth Roberts of Alabama, and worked for him but only for two months.

Gordon and Donna were married on December 8, 1962 and the couple moved to Manhattan, where Gordon was working for American Airlines, and Donna continued to play on the tour. She was among the Top 10 players in the U.S. from 1960 to 1963 and in 1965 and 1966. One of Donna's best wins took place at the women's Eastern Grass Court Tennis Championships in South Orange, New Jersey when she defeated Rosie Casals in the final. Allison Danzig, the famous sports reporter with the *New York Times*, described the match in its August 1, 1966 edition:

"Donna Floyd Fales... won the championship today with an attack of such power and cleverness as to break down the resistance of Rosemary Casals...A standing-room crowd of 3,500... saw the little 17-year-old Miss Casals, the conqueror of Mrs. Billie Jean King... hammered and harried into submission, 5-7, 6-3, 6-0... Unperturbed over the loss of the first set that she had seemed to have in hand, the blond Mrs. Fales lifted her game to greater heights in the second set. Few women players the world over could have matched her performance in her command of every variety of stroke and the faultlessness of her court craft as she ran her little opponent almost to the point of exhaustion and won nine games in succession from 3-all.... Every virtue of the first-class tennis player was exemplified by Mrs. Fales today. Her flat forehand and her service had depth and power. Her low, skimming undercut backhand had length and reliability. The finality of her volley and

overhead, her command of both the lob and the drop shot and the mobility and inflexibility of her defense combined with her court generalship and anticipation were too much for even as tough a fighter as Miss Casals."

In addition, Donna played on and captained the U.S. Wightman Cup team in 1963 and 1964 and captained the U.S. Federation Cup team for four years. Twice in that span the U.S. was victorious in Berlin and Athens. She made it to the quarterfinals in three of the Grand Slam tournaments: the French, Wimbledon and the U.S. Championships. Her career was blossoming, but in 1966 Donna cut it short at the young age of 27 to start to raise a family.

"Open tennis was about to begin, but until then all of us players were amateurs financing our own expenses. Only the independently wealthy could continue. I was married and pregnant with my first child and had to stop the tour. But players reaching the age of 27 or 28 can only get better as they get older. Look at Betty Stove from the Netherlands, and Judy Tegart of Australia. They continued into the Open Era and were my age. Their games got better and better. They matured physically and mentally."

Donna took a "leave of absence" from tennis as a player to raise her two sons and a daughter, but she continued to be very involved in the tennis world as a coach of the women's tennis team at the University of Miami from 1977 to 1980 and as a volunteer with the USTA serving as the chairman of or a member of countless committees from 1963 to 2004. She was a board member of the International Tennis Hall of Fame and the U.S.I.C., (International Club of the United States) and ran the prestigious Orange Bowl junior championships from 1991 to 1997.

"Running the Orange Bowl was an enormous job," Donna said. "The Orange Bowl is known throughout the world as *the* tournament for juniors to show their mettle before transitioning into pro tennis. The event takes place for two weeks in Miami, and I had the help of Jim McDonald, an experienced coach and director of tennis events in the Miami area. We set up the policies and procedures, arranged housing and meals for 600 juniors, set up the draws -- an exhausting undertaking that took long hours and many days to complete -- and ran the tournament itself, hiring staff, umpires, linesmen, everything it takes to run a major tournament. But, it was always very satisfying."

Another enormous tennis-related job Donna took on was serving as Board President of the NJTL (National Junior Tennis League) from 1975 to 1989.

The NJTL was started in 1969 by Arthur Ashe, Charlie Pasarell and tennis benefactor Sheridan Snyder to bring tennis, fitness and education to underprivileged boys and girls in urban areas.

"The idea was to get kids on the courts and off the streets," said Donna. "We used the courts in public parks and provided brightly colored 'NJTL' T-shirts for the kids to wear. When we tried to get USTA funding, I'll never forget this. The meeting was held in Arizona, and the USTA wouldn't embrace the program because the dress code was not all whites. Can you imagine? Fortunately, in the 1970's the USTA changed its posture, and NJTL was merged into USTA programs. Then, in 1974, I was asked to start a chapter in the greater Miami area which I did. That program evolved into the Greater Miami Tennis Foundation, which by 2005 with funding from generous patrons, grew with 35 parks in use and over 35,000 kids on the courts during our summer programs."

To say Donna gave back to tennis is an understatement. Her organizational skills, ability to work with others, creative thinking, good humor and her unconditionally generous spirit have brought many young people into the game of tennis and have, I am sure, improved their lives tremendously.

While visiting, one morning Donna was up at 6 am to bike a mile or so to meet her friends, three or four women in their 60's, for a three-mile walk, followed by the bike ride home. "But Donna, it's dark when you're out there biking and walking," I said.

Donna smiled but didn't respond. Then, the next day she was playing tennis with John.

"That was a Saturday so we had a leisurely schedule," she said. "We didn't get started until 9."

On weekdays, Donna is up at 6, gets in her walk or sets up a tennis game for 7 and is back home in time for breakfast and a shower before 9.

"On Sundays, I generally go to church and then play a friendly game of golf in the afternoon."

"But, you also find time to play competitive senior tennis, right?" I asked.

"I really didn't get into sanctioned tournaments again until I turned 65 in 2005. Before then I played some local mixed doubles matches with my good friend Eddie Rubinoff, a former University of Miami champion and top U.S. player in my day back in the '60's. But in 2005, I was ready for the challenge and became a 'senior player.' I'm finding super senior tennis very much to my liking. We have all lived our lives and don't have to prove ourselves. We are who we are. We're more relaxed and the competition is excellent, but we can enjoy it even more than we did when younger.

"To get started in 2005, I entered two tournaments in the U.S. – the grass and the clay – and saved some time to play in the ITF [International Tennis Federation] World Championships.

I couldn't justify taking any more time away from work and family."

The International Tennis Federation sponsors competition among nations that for senior tennis is the equivalent of the Davis Cup and Fed Cup, with top tennis players from around the world chosen to represent their countries. The play is divided into two categories: senior tennis for players 35 to 55 and super senior tennis for players 60 to 90. Each age category is given a cup named after a well-known player: for instance, the Gardnar Mulloy Cup for the men's 80 and over category and the Althea Gibson Cup for the women's 70 and over category. The competition is the most prestigious team event on the ITF senior's circuit. The championships actually include two tournaments, one as a member of a national team, the other as individuals.

"In 2005, the 'Worlds' were played in Antalya, Turkey, at a beautiful resort, Ali Bey, on the Mediterranean with 60 red-clay courts," Donna said. "Ali Bey is a common destination for Germans, Russians and Turks with the sea, 24-hour food service, live entertainment, shops, tennis and water sports. The two tournaments, the world team and the individual championship, were held back to back, one week for each, and the gala dinner for all participants is the most lavish in the world held outdoors around a large pool, always under a full moon, it seems. The food is spectacular, and an orchestra, dancing and fireworks top it all.

"This is where I played my most satisfying matches. Being a newcomer to this group, I was not seeded but was placed in the draw because the committee acknowledged some wins I had had that year in the States. We had a draw of 64 in the singles. In the second round, I beat Seagran Furan of Germany 7-6, 7-6 after being down 1-5 in the second set. Then I beat Inger Delamare from France 6–4, 6-4. In the semis I met Janine Lieffrig of South Africa who, by the way, had a win over Francoise Durr at the French Open in the '60's. I won the first set 6-4. In the second set, I was up 5-1, then 5-4, 40-15, on my serve and lost it. Lieffrig took the second set 7-6. In the third, I was down 1-4, 40-15. Then somehow I started winning points and came back to win with a drop shot on match point.

"In the finals against Rosie Darmon of Mexico, I lost the first set 7-6. We split sets, and I was down 1-4 in the third. The day was brutally hot; the match went on for three hours, but I managed to pull out the third set at 6-4 to win the match and the championship.

"To start my super senior tennis career that way was thrilling. The next day I saw Rosie, and she said, 'I can't walk today. That match took everything out of me.'"

Donna certainly knows how to win the hard way.

"What is it that keeps you playing senior tennis?" I asked.

"Winning the hard way is one satisfaction," she said. "Sure, it would be fun to win matches 6-1 and 6-2 but that wouldn't be very competitive. I love the competition and I like to keep myself in shape so that I can win the tough matches. Conditioning is key."

As Donna described her matches, I was impressed how she remembered the details so clearly. After interviewing other players, I realized that most of them also remember the details.

"I also played in the women's doubles tournament too," Donna continued. "I was teamed up with the French player Inger Delemare, who didn't speak English. I decided that the best way to communicate was to draw out the strategy, so on the court I drew 'x's' and '0's to indicate her position and mine. I drew arrows to show shifts in positions, and we made it to the finals!"

"In 2010, I played again in Antalya for The Althea Gibson Cup, for women 70 and over. We won the team competition, and I won the singles.

"The 2013 year wasn't a good year for me. I lost four finals: a team match against Great Britain; the individual singles to Michelle Bichon of France whom I had just beaten in team play; mixed doubles with Fred Drilling against two Austrians Peter Pokorny and Sophie Garaguly and doubles with Cathy Anderson against Heide Orth of Germany and Frances Maclenna of Great Britain. But the venue, Portschach, Austria, a lakeside summer resort with views of the Alps overlooking the lake, was spectacular.

"But I came back in 2015 and won the team event in Croatia in the Queen's Cup for Super Seniors, 75 and over. The ITF Worlds were played in Umag, Croatia, another beautiful summer resort on the Adriatic Sea which is in view while you are playing your matches."

Donna said her new favorite event was the Friendship Cup sponsored by Mary Wilson, played in Poertschach, Austria for seniors 75 and over, the United States against Europe with 10 players on each team.

"Then there is much more camaraderie in senior tennis than in open tennis," said Donna as she gave more reasons why she plays super senior tennis. "If you have a match against a German woman, for instance, and she beats you, you have a drink together after the match. It's still very competitive though. But you're more relaxed. You've lived your life and you know who you are. There's no need to try to prove yourself. Being active, strategizing, running – it's all a part of this great game. Winning at it is a bonus. There's a euphoria and an appreciation of each day.

"I also think I'm playing better in the seniors. I'm developing new shots. I always had a good drop shot, but now

I'm working on short forehands. I hit cross court to the service line at an acute angle taking my opponent off the court. It's pretty effective. A lot of my friends play bridge, so I decided that when I turned 70 I'd take it up again. Well, I did try it, but it's not for me. It's too sedentary. The little ladies like to play in the middle of the day, and I've got other things to do."

"What are your tips for senior tennis players?" I asked.

"They're simple: keep moving; prevent injuries with good conditioning; learn to drop shot and lob – they're lethal weapons. And remember, it is the last player standing who wins the gold ball."

CHAPTER 9:

BETTY EISENSTEIN

On a clear, hot, early August day in Washington, D.C., I followed Betty Eisenstein's explicit directions from Bethesda to her home. Turning on to her winding street, quiet and lined with handsome, tall shade trees, I found her home, a lovely brick town house. I rang the doorbell and soon heard someone scampering down the stairs. The door opened, and I was greeted by Betty, a diminutive, smiling, frisky, bright, 91-year-old dynamo. She was as glad to see me as I was to see her, and she wasted no time taking me up a flight of stairs to meet her husband Julian who was seated at his desk reading a book.

Betty began to reminisce about her early days with Julian. While she was studying for a doctorate in European History at Radcliffe after having graduated from Vassar in 1945, some of her friends were encouraging her to meet a young gentleman, Julian Eisenstein. Coincidentally, Julian and Betty had a chance encounter at a dance where Julian, handsome in his tux, was with mutual friends.

"We were introduced, started dating immediately, and over the course of a few months we were engaged. When I told my mother, she was in a state. 'Elizabeth,' she said, 'You've always been such a sensible young woman, how can you be so irresponsible?' I reassured her that Julian was a fine young man, but she wasn't so sure. She wanted to see for herself and invited him to visit the family home in Harrison, New York.

"Julian, an only child, who came from a very small town in Missouri, was slightly overwhelmed by the number of family friends and guests who were with us that weekend. He was, likewise, surprised by the size of our home. 'This is the biggest house I've ever seen in my life!' he exclaimed as we approached.

"Thankfully, the visit went well. My family was never impressed with people with money; they were, however, impressed with people with brains! And when they learned Julian was graduated from Harvard, summa cum laude, and was now working on his PhD in Physics and that he was a fine athlete, demonstrated when he joined the tennis games, they decided my sudden engagement wasn't so rash after all."

"Tell me about your family, Betty," I said.

"I grew up in another world," she said. "I was born in a brownstone mansion on Fifth Avenue, between 68th and 69 Street near the Frick Museum, on November 11, 1923. My grandfather, Adolph Lewisohn, a German Jew, came to the United States from Hamburg, Germany when he was 18 years old and made a fortune in copper mining out West. He married and built the Fifth Avenue brownstone, but sadly, not long after, his wife died. But, within a few months his son, my father, married, and Grandfather asked the new couple to come live with him. They did so, and three of their four daughters, I being the third, were born in that house. My mother never felt at home there. 'It was like living in a hotel,' she'd say, and she spent every weekend at the house my father had built in Westchester. Both my parents enjoyed tennis, Mother especially, and they managed to build two tennis courts! One court was clay, the

Betty Eisenstein in her study wearing some of her international trophies

other was a hard court. During the winters, we made the hard court into an ice rink!"

In her non-stop fashion, Betty continued.

"I grew up with tennis. My father always said, 'Golf takes you away from family, but tennis brings you together.' So from the time I could hold a racquet I played. I grew up with two older sisters, and I always tried to keep up with them. My nickname was 'Me Too.' I wanted to do everything they did, and I think that's how I got so competitive. Sink or swim I was going to keep up.

"My family also invited their friends to play, so there was always lots of activity on the courts. By the time I was 10 or so, my game had gotten so good that I was asked to join the adults in their games. That was a milestone for me."

"Did you play tennis in college?" I asked.

"I went to Vassar as a freshman, just three months before Pearl Harbor. We had a women's tennis team, and I was on it, but we never played. The school was focused on military drills for would-be WACs [Women's Army Corps] and WAVES [the Navy's 'Women Accepted for Voluntary Emergency Service']. But, I did play when I was home during vacations.

"I graduated in 1945 and entered Radcliffe/Harvard that Fall to pursue a PhD in European History. I played some tennis at Harvard but no competition. Julian completed work on his PhD in May, 1948 while I was still deciding on a dissertation topic. He planned to start work as a physics instructor at the University of Wisconsin in Madison in the fall. In the meantime, we were married on May 30, 1948 on the lawn of my family home in Harrison. The day was a bit overcast but no rain fell. Chairs were placed on the lawn, musicians played, and dinner and dancing followed the wedding, a Reformed Jewish ceremony.

"Our honeymoon was also from another world - a grand three month tour in Italy, Switzerland, France, England, Scotland and Ireland. When I was younger, my parents had taken my two older sisters with them on trips to Europe but had left my younger sister and me behind as we were too young. A trip was planned for 1939 when we could all go, but my father decided it was too ominous to venture abroad. The honeymoon trip more than compensated for the trips I missed."

Upon their return, the young couple moved to Madison, Wisconsin where Julian had a position as an instructor in the Physics Department at the University of Wisconsin.

"I was in for a shock," Betty admitted. "First, I had to learn to be a housewife. I didn't know how to cook. I had never even been in a kitchen before! Then, our babies came. Our first, a baby boy, only lived 24 hours after birth, which was a difficult time for us. Then our first daughter, Margaret, was born in 1951. I was quite overwhelmed with all the new responsibilities. Plus, I hated the winters! My nose froze every time I stepped out of our apartment. And, of course, there was no tennis. But, Julian had a post doctorate at Oxford, and we spent a year in England during that time, which was delightful. I became pregnant with our oldest son, Johnny, who was born in New York City when we returned to the States in 1952.

"Soon after, Julian accepted a position at Penn State, and we moved to State College, Pennsylvania. There, our third child and second son, Ted, was born in 1954, and again I had my hands full. But by this time, I had received my PhD in history from Harvard, and I was anxious to start teaching. But, Penn State wasn't interested in hiring me. I was miserable and felt very isolated.

"But, in 1956, Julian joined a team of physicists working at the National Bureau of Standards, and we moved to Washington, D.C. We rented for one year and then moved to our present home, where we've lived happily since 1957."

"Are we getting to play any tennis yet?" I asked.

"Still no tennis in my life as I was busy with the children and trying to get a part-time position as a college professor of history. I contacted Georgetown, George Washington, Howard, American, whatever college was in the area, and I didn't get a response from any of them. They just weren't interested in hiring a woman. But, I had a friend who knew of a young adjunct professor of history at American, Dorry Goodman. She was pregnant and needed to take a leave of absence. So, I was able to take her spot. The position was part time, and I made $300 a term. The course was an entry level *Introduction to European History*, but eventually I taught upper level courses and was on the tenure track."

"Now, some tennis?"

"As a matter of fact, yes," Betty said with a grin. "Our children were all going to the National Cathedral Schools, and we joined the affiliated St. Albans Tennis Club. Allie Ritzenberg, the club pro, suggested that I give senior tennis a try. I had never heard of senior tennis. He gave me a schedule of senior events and urged me to get involved.

"So, here I am, almost 50, and I enter my first tournament since I played in a juniors tournament once years ago. My first round in the 50s put me against the top seed whose name was totally unfamiliar to me - Dodo Cheney. She was extremely gracious as we shook hands on the court. She was dressed elegantly in her tennis dress, pearls and a sort of bonnet, looking a bit grandmotherly. But her appearance and demeanor gave no hint of her formidable 'take no enemies' game. I was on and off the court in half an hour, losing 6-0, 6-0.

"Little did I know she was already a legend in senior tennis. Dodo played into her 90s and continued to 'play down' as she always did to a younger age category.

Dodo won well over 300 gold balls and was inducted into the International Hall of Fame in 2004 along with Steffi Graf and Stefan Edberg. Sadly, she passed away at age 98 in 2014.

"Years ago *The New Yorker* had a piece about Gardnar Mulloy who was then in his late 80s asserting that he had won well over 100 national championships, a feat that no other tennis player had accomplished. I wrote an indignant letter to the magazine noting that women were also tennis players and that Mulloy's record was eclipsed by Dodo's."

Betty is a feisty feminist.

Her appetite was whetted, despite her stunning defeat to Cheney, as she entered the National Clay Court Championships in Houston. Again, Betty lost in the first round, but this time in a third-set tiebreaker against the No. 2 seed.

"Walking back to the Clubhouse with my head down, I ran into a lovely lady, Marga Lee Mahony, from Bedford, New York. She asked why I looked so forlorn. I told her I'd lost and was going home. She said I ought to stay and play in the consolation round. 'I don't want to get a booby prize,' was my reply, and she explained that if I played in the consolation round and won, I would win 5th place in the tournament."

All national tournaments use a double elimination system which gives losers in the first, second and third rounds a second chance by entering what is called 'the back draw' or consolation round."

"I stayed on, won the consolation and placed fifth in the tournament, which meant I could be seeded in the next tournament I entered and no longer had to face the very top players in the first round.

I asked, "Did you have more encounters with Dodo Cheney as you continued to play senior tournaments?"

"Oh yes. We faced each other several times. As I got better, and Dodo grew older, our encounters were closer - and actually became less friendly. She was not only a fierce competitor but also had no qualms about resorting to unsportsmanlike behavior. I recall her coming off the court on one occasion, saying happily *'that* woman gave me bad calls, but I gave her worse ones.'

"Later, Dodo began playing mother/daughter matches with her daughter, Christie Putnam, who had a few words with Dodo about her court behavior, and her demeanor was much improved.

"I was also Dodo's doubles partner in several tournaments which was a wonderful experience. She had changed her ways and admitted that her daughter 'scolded' her. She had stopped trying to unnerve her opponents, but she always put on a good show for the spectators. Though she's seven years older than I am, had knee trouble and didn't move easily, her shot making was always remarkable; her love of the game and unfailing enthusiasm were infectious."

"Betty, you mentioned getting better as you get older. So the old adage you can't teach old dogs new tricks doesn't apply to senior tennis?"

"Well, for me it didn't and for many others it's also not true. I became a better competitor, more court savvy and learned how to strategize and counter-punch. Preparing for tournament play involves lots of practice games which keeps me fit and 'tournament tough.' You can say that when I played my first match against Dodo at Forest Hills I was far from tournament tough. I hadn't played competitively, and that makes the difference.

"What makes USTA senior tennis tournaments unique is its age categories: the 60s, the 65s, the 70s all the way up to the 90s. As you age in a particular age division, it gets harder to hold your own. But concerns about aging are counterbalanced by the thought that in a year or so you'll be 'the new girl on the block' and can count on confronting older players instead of struggling to hold your own against younger ones. Senior tennis players are the only people I know who look forward to turning 70 or 75 or 80! That's a psychological boost to your well-being.

"Speaking of birthdays, when I was turning 74 my husband wanted to plan a party for me, but I said to him 'I'd rather celebrate by having you come with me to Naples, Florida, where my Middle Atlantic sectional team is playing in an intersectional tournament. He did come and often recalls how he sat down to lunch with 300 women and loved it.

"In a sense senior tennis is the survival of the fittest. The older I get, I notice more players dropping out. The draws in the higher age divisions get smaller, but for those of us who are healthy enough to continue, it's a gift. And as my game improved so did my equanimity. I became less unnerved by minor injuries, difficult opponents and unexpected contingencies. The equanimity carried over to the rest of my life as well. That's another plus for senior tennis."

"Betty, how many gold balls have you won?"

"Right now I have 44 gold balls and 34 silver. I'm not that fond of the silver," Betty said as her voice trailed off.

At this point in our discussion, Betty asked, "Would you like to see them?"

"Of course."

Betty led me down a narrow, winding staircase into her basement. She handled the stairs without a pause; I struggled a bit. The basement had been transformed into a cozy family room with two white upholstered, deeply cushioned sofas and matching chairs, a TV and assorted pictures and paintings on the walls, but the main feature was Betty's trophy collection.

"Thankfully, senior tennis trophies are gold balls or pretty china or framed proclamations. I don't know what I'd do with big gold trophies with a woman tennis player on top. Can I show you some lovely china trophies I won when playing the Houston Racquet Club's national seniors tournament?"

"Sure."

We maneuver the narrow, winding staircase again, and Betty led me to her bright, white breakfast nook with large windows overlooking her backyard and her neighbor's flowering Crepe Myrtle tree. Another plus for women's senior tennis: their trophies make home decorating easier.

"I have some more international trophies upstairs in my study. Would you like to see them?"

"Yes. That's what I'm here for."

Betty took me on another journey up one flight of stairs, then another.

"Betty, I see how you stay so fit and agile!" I said.

"Yes. that's probably so. I do go up and down a lot. But I have to be careful about my weight."

"How much do you weigh?" I ask the question women don't like to hear.

"Ninety-two pounds. And I'm trying to put some weight on. I'm too light."

We enter Betty's cluttered study, stacks of papers organized in random piles on a large mahogany table, a smaller table for her computer, printer and assorted office equipment, and on a hook on the far wall are her medals.

"Oh, I haven't touched these in years!" said Betty.

We take them down from the hook, untangle their ribbons and lay them out neatly on a table.

"Put them on, and I'll take a picture," I suggest.

As Betty draped each medal over her neck she described the tournaments, mostly international, but a couple she couldn't even remember.

"It's been a long time since I've even looked at these.

"This study is where I'm working on another book, my memoir."

"Another book?"

"Yes. My best-known work is *The Printing Press as an Agent of Change*. It's about the influence of the Gutenberg Press and how it revolutionized Western Europe. I call it the 'Unacknowledged Revolution' because nobody wrote about its impact on the media and the public's access to printed information. I've written other books too. Remember a professor has 'to publish or perish.' But the book about the Gutenberg Press and its aftermath sparked a lot of attention. It's even been translated into seven languages. Today, people are talking about the similarity between the pre- and post-Gutenberg world and the pre- and post-Silicon Valley world."

Betty walked me to a windowsill stacked with books - her books - books she has authored. I only now realized the extent of Betty's many scholarly accomplishments. When I got home, I did some research on her works and her many distinguished awards including fellowships from the National Endowment for the Humanities and the Rockefeller Foundation; the American Historical Association's Award for Scholarly Distinction. And she received an honorary degree of Doctor of Humane Letters from the University of Michigan.

Betty was too modest to mention these awards, but what is most remarkable is that at the age of 91 she isn't phased by advancing years and is writing her memoir.

After looking at the books on her windowsill, which we had neatly rearranged for the photo, Betty went to her computer, the biggest I-Mac on the market, sat down and started opening windows, giving one precedence over the others, and skillfully navigating her way around.

"You're pretty good at that," I commented.

"Oh, but I have a young man to help me," she said.

But, I'm thinking, 'Still, at her age? She's pretty amazing.' I asked, "Did you continue teaching after your work at American University?"

"Yes. In 1974, the University of Michigan was interested in honoring women and asked if I would come as a full professor. The offer was very tempting, and actually, it came at a good time for me. I had to get my mind off the tragic death of my young son, Johnny, only 21 when he died. I found that flights leaving Dulles Airport could get me to Ann Arbor in exactly three hours, door to door. I could leave at 9 a.m. on a Monday morning and arrive at the University in time for an afternoon class, and on Thursday afternoons, I could leave at 3:30 p.m. and be in my home by 6:30. I accepted the position and taught there from 1975 to 1988, when I retired at 65. Teaching advanced courses at Michigan was an uplifting experience, and I took advantage of the sabbaticals that were offered. I spent a year at Stanford at the Center for Advanced Study in Behavioral Sciences. Julian came also. We had a wonderful year, and I played tennis every day.

"And we've enjoyed tennis as a family too," she continued. "As I told you before, my father always said, 'Tennis brings the family together.' My family is scattered from Oregon and Washington State to Missouri, but every summer Julian and I collect them all - children, grandchildren and great grandchildren - and we go to our home in East Hampton, Long Island where we play tennis, swim and enjoy being together. And though there's no tennis involved at Thanksgiving time, we always have the family come to us in Washington, D.C. to celebrate the holiday."

"Betty, when you were showing me your medals, you told me about some of the international tennis events you entered. Tell me more."

"International competition brings together men and women who have been chosen to serve on national teams," she answered. "They represent countries from all over the world: Spain, Austria, Turkey, Brazil, Germany and others. I've played in Barcelona, several times in Austria and at the Club AliBey on the Turkish Riviera near Antalya, Turkey. The organizers hold lavish, colorful opening ceremonies. Delightful dances are performed by Turkish school girls, and we all march together under our country's flag. You'd think we were in the Olympics!

"What a gorgeous venue it was - dining pavilions, smaller restaurants on the beach and 55 red clay courts. The first week of competition is devoted to team play, and we all cheer on our teammates. The second week is individual competition. At one event I didn't have a doubles partner so my German friends urged me to join forces with an Hungarian woman. Her first name was Ersabet, the Hungarian equivalent of my name, Elizabeth. Having the same name established a kinship between us. She didn't speak English, French or German, and I don't speak Hungarian but we played together well enough to reach the finals before getting knocked out by a seasoned American team.

"I mentioned my German friends," she continued. "Playing in these international events puts you together with the same groups of women who are more or less your age. I became friendly with several German women who probably would have been my enemies in the days of the Nazis. Fortunately, tennis brings people together.

"My most remarkable win against the Germans came when competing for the Althea Gibson Cup in Palm Beach, Florida. My doubles partner was a lovely lady, Kay Wakely. She had never been in Cup play before and was nervous, but we did well enough to get us to the finals where we played a German team. It was a scorching hot day, and the young man umpiring was obviously anxious to get out of the sun and was not entertained by having to watch our slow moving game. Kay and I had won the first set and were having trouble finishing the second. The score was repetitive: deuce/ad for us, deuce/ad for them with no end in sight. Finally, we had match point with Kay serving. By this time her nerves were consuming her. Serving into the ad court, she hit the wildest serve I've ever seen. It was so far out that it completely missed the service box and hit the foot of the other German player who was standing in the back court on the deuce side. Before we realized what had happened the umpire called the game: 'Game, set, match USA.' We were dumbfounded, but the rule was explained that if a ball hits a player before bouncing, it is the other team's point. The Germans accepted the loss graciously.

"Once I was in Athens attending a conference," she continued. "The organizer, an elegant Greek lady, belonged to a tennis club located in the Athens park, and she arranged a match for me. When I arrived I was introduced to a short, heavyset Greek man sitting on the club patio with his friends. I could tell he was disappointed that I had gray hair and did not resemble the gorgeous long limbed blond California type he had in mind. His brusque, contemptuous manner annoyed me so I had no hesitation about playing hard and taking advantage of his weaknesses. As the match progressed, he lost one game after another. His cronies began to jeer. He got flustered and made more errors. I actually began to feel sorry for him.

"But if you make me mad while playing tennis, watch out," Betty said with a smile.

"I also played tennis in Paris when I was there on business. I played with several French women and had some enjoyable mixed doubles as well. I once had a partner whose last name was "Cochet." He turned out to be a brother of Henri Cochet, one of the famous group of French champions known as the "Four Musketeers" in the late 1920s, early 1930s.

"I have one other international tennis story. When I was a visiting fellow at Wolfson College in Oxford I could easily bike to nearby clay and grass courts. But biking on the wrong side of the road with heavy traffic terrified me. Although I was delighted to accept invitations to play with friends, I was worried about getting there. On one occasion, I was biking into a round-about when I saw a large truck heading toward me. I just stopped and yelled 'help!' before jumping off my bike and walking it around the traffic circle to the other side. I actually thought I was going to get crushed."

"So you've had some pretty exciting times playing senior tennis whether it's in an international tournament or in pick-up games with friends," I said.

"Oh, yes. Senior tennis has been a blessing for me as it is for many, whether they compete in USTA tournaments or not. Our legs stay strong. For someone my age, I'm still pretty fast. It's simply a matter of aging better.

"Senior tennis helps keep us in good health, both mentally and physically. Even if your mind doesn't keep up with your body, you can still play good tennis. I know an excellent player who I've played many times in national tournaments who suffers from Alzheimer's. She can't keep score, but her muscle memory remains quite sharp. We all keep score for her, but not knowing the score can be an advantage in tennis because she doesn't choke on the big points! Everyone's scared to play her she's so good!

"Winning a gold ball is as good as it gets! Sometimes I get in these moods where I think maybe I'll retire, but like an old war horse, I hear the trumpet and I go! As soon as I get an entry form, I forget the agony and all I remember is the fun."

Sadly, Betty passed away in her sleep on January 31, 2016 at the age of 92. I lost a new friend.

CHAPTER 10:

FRAN MEEK

"The most enduring part of tennis is the friends you make," said Fran Meek to me at her charming little white house that sits high above the road in Chappaqua, New York.

Fran is tall and thin with a perfect build for tennis, and she has inspired tennis players in the Westchester area since the 1950s. Fran's strokes are classic and flawless, she's steady as a rock and she knows the game inside and out, singles and doubles. Having played with and against her for many years, I know that to be true.

Fran taught tennis at a small summer swim and tennis club, Seven Bridges, in Chappaqua and at the Saw Mill Club in Mount Kisco from 1978 until her retirement in 1998. In addition to teaching at Saw Mill, she was given the responsibility of arranging leagues, observing new members to assess their games and, unofficially, to listen to member complaints – of which there were many. That, she did well too. Her demeanor is calming. She listens carefully and responds thoughtfully.

Fran was born on December 24, 1932, in Upper Montclair, New Jersey, a progressive, suburban community with the wealthy, blacks, Irish and Italians, all living in separate areas, the children attending their neighborhood schools. It is not until the young people go to Montclair High School, a fully integrated institution, that the community comes together.

Fran's parents, Helen Farnsworth and Howard Schneidewind, were both children of immigrants who sought the American dream. In particular, her maternal grandfather, born poor in the Midwest, came East as a young man, bought two woolen mills in New England, prospered, and, indeed, found that dream.

"I had a very privileged childhood," Fran said, more than once, almost as an apology.

"Every summer my grandfather took the whole family to Point of Woods, Fire Island where he rented a house for all of us. A little tennis club just happened to be within walking distance, and from the time I was 6 or 7, I'd walk over there where they had a backboard, and I'd hit against it for hours.

"Then World War II was approaching, and in 1939 we were evacuated from Fire Island because of the threat of Nazi submarines in the waters off our coast. The summer after the U.S. entered the war, my grandfather rented a beautiful, turn-of-the-century house in Spring Lake, New Jersey. Because it was large, family and friends came to visit, and I can remember my mother clipping food coupons at the kitchen table before going off to buy the groceries.

"The Spring Lake Bathing and Tennis Club was nearby and it too had a backboard," she said. "I was delighted. I'd hit every day against that backboard. On Sundays, the club had its famous luncheon, with linens and fine china and a display of delicious dishes. Ladies came dressed in fashionable dresses, the men in suits, and an orchestra played. One Sunday I was in my usual spot hitting against the backboard, and a gentleman -- I don't remember his name – but I do remember that he had played on the U.S. Davis Cup team, was watching me. He came

Fran Meek

up and said 'let me show you something. You have a very good game and you must continue, but you need some help with your footwork.' He gave me a demonstration, and I mimicked him. 'You keep this up,' he said as he went back to the luncheon."

"Did you play with other people at all?" I asked.

"Oh, I'd play with anyone who would play with me. Mostly boys. By the time I was 10, I was either on a court or using the backboard all day. And I started playing in the club tournaments. I even got to be the club champ in 1948 and 1949."

"Did you play in any USTA tournaments?" I asked.

"When I was 15, I joined the USLTA and played in the Eastern Section's junior tournaments, mostly in Westchester and New Jersey, and the national juniors held at the Philadelphia Cricket Club. I played in the nationals twice, and the second year I made it to the quarterfinals, which earned me a ranking of No. 9 in the country. Because of that, I was selected to be on the Junior Wightman Cup team. The week before the Wightman Cup tournament at Forest Hills, we were given a week of instruction and drills by the top coaches in the country, including Eleanor Tennant, who later became Maureen Connolly's coach. That was such a thrill.

"But, one thing I'll never forget when I was at Forest Hills and the West Side Tennis Club during this time. Althea

Gibson was playing in the main draw, and I couldn't believe how poorly she was treated back then. She just wasn't accepted by the players or the West Side Club, and was always by herself. Even fans avoided her. In 1950, I played at Forest Hills, and my Dad was with me. He was anxious to see Althea play, and fortunately she was scheduled to be in the Grandstand. Later, I looked over toward the Grandstand, and there was my father - the only white face among a sea of black faces.

"That is a good example of how we discriminated back then – sad but true," Fran concluded.

Changing subjects, I said, "Back then there were no indoor courts for players in the Northeast. Did you just give up the game in the winter?"

"You're right. There were no indoor courts, but again I was very privileged. During spring vacations while in high school my grandparents brought the whole family down to Palm Beach, Florida. I played with a pro there who was the coach for the men's tennis team at Duke. During my senior year, my father asked if I would like to take the year off and play in Europe. I told him, 'No Dad. I'd rather go to college. Duke would be my top choice.'"

Fran got her top choice and entered Duke as a freshman in 1950.

"Duke didn't really have a women's tennis team in those days. We had 'play days' that our Physical Education Department organized. The PE teachers picked the girls they thought would be good on the team. One was a friend I knew from the juniors. We'd play other universities and colleges. Again, the teachers arranged all the transportation and the line-ups, but it was all very casual."

I asked, "Did you play any more sanctioned tournaments while you were in college?"

"During the summer of 1951 after my freshman year at Duke, I entered two or three national grass court tournaments, warm-ups to Forest Hills. One was held at the Orange Lawn Tennis Club in South Orange, New Jersey not far from my home. Unfortunately, I lost in an early round. Maureen Connolly, 'Little Mo,' was also in the tournament and made it to the final which was scheduled to be played on Sunday. But heavy rains caused the final to be delayed to Monday. Maureen won, but because of the delay, her travel arrangements to Gloucester, Massachusetts where her next tournament was being held, fell through. The gentleman who ran the Orange Lawn Club knew my father and knew too that I was driving to Gloucester to play in the same tournament. He called my Dad to see if Little Mo could hitch a ride with me. 'Of course" said my Dad.

"So, much to my surprise I'm to be Maureen Connolly's driver! I was nervous. 'What if I'm late or get into an accident? I'd screw up Maureen's schedule and the Essex Club would not be happy.' Anyway, I did drive Maureen to Massachusetts, and it was much easier than I thought it would be. She was a young, carefree teenager who just wanted to listen to the Top 40 hits on the radio!

"We had to drive through Cambridge, and it was getting late, so I decided to stop at a hotel and get us a room. I tell Maureen to stay in the car while I go to the front desk. As I open the door I see two 'Harvard-type' young men manning the desk. I tell them I need a room for the night. They respond, 'We're all full.' I say, 'But you can't be. It's 11:30 at night, and I can't go any farther. And besides I have a very famous tennis player in my car, and I need to take care of her. They ask who, and I say 'Maureen Connolly.' 'Oh sure, Maureen Connolly, come on.' 'No really. And Maureen and I need a room for tonight.'

"The young men bantered with me for a while. Then, I noticed their faces drop in disbelief. They were facing the entrance while I was looking in the opposite direction, but I saw in a mirror on the wall behind them, what they saw: Maureen sleepily walking through the front door wondering what was taking so long.

"The boys conferred and said, 'Well, the only thing we have is the bridal suite. You can have that' which was fine with us. So we slept that night in the bridal suite, and the hotel didn't charge us a dime!" Fran said, chuckling happily.

Even though Fran described Maureen as a teenager, she wasn't that much younger than Fran. Nevertheless, Maureen had already achieved spectacular success in the tennis world. At 16, she won the U.S. Championships (the modern-day U.S. Open), at 17 she won Wimbledon and at 19 she won the Grand Slam, winning all four majors - Australian, French, Wimbledon and U.S. Championships - in one year.

"The next morning we drove to Gloucester, and I didn't see much of Maureen after that. In those days, the players were put up in the homes of the club members, and we went our separate ways. I won my first-round match, and then in the second round who do I meet but Maureen Connolly. Maureen was all business and didn't say a word about our adventure. She won pretty easily as I recall, but after the match, Hazel Wightman, the founder of the Wightman Cup, who had been watching, came up to me. She introduced herself, and I said, 'It's a pleasure to meet you.' And it was! I was delighted. Anyway she said, 'You keep playing your game. You're going to be just fine.' What a thrill that was!"

Not long after the Essex Club matches, Fran and the other top players headed to Forest Hills for the National Championships played on grass.

"I look at the draw and see that I have to play 'Little Mo' again," Fran said. "'On no,' I said to myself, 'Please don't put me on the stadium court! I don't want to embarrass myself in front of hundreds of spectators.'

"Fortunately, the match was played on the Clubhouse Court, the court closest to the West Side Clubhouse, which was bad enough. Again I said to myself, 'Please don't make a fool of yourself.'

"We start playing and Little Mo doesn't seem to be herself. Suddenly the score is 2-2, and then I win three games in a row! It's 5-2 and I'm in the lead. During the changeover, I sit down and the ball boy at the net turns around and says to me, 'Do you think she's sick?' He, too, was surprised at her lackluster play, but I'm not sure his remark was much help to my confidence. So, we go back out on the court, and all of a sudden a light turns on. The true Maureen Connolly was back, and she won 7-5, 6-0.

"But, I was relieved and not unhappy with the way I had played. I have always thought, though I don't know it to be true, that her famous coach, Eleanor Tennant, was watching the match and made Maureen nervous. Actually, she made me nervous too. In any event, those are my 'Little Mo' stories, and neither time when we played against each other did she ever mention our road trip."

While at Duke, Fran met a fellow classmate, Bob Meek. They dated and shortly after graduation in 1954 they were married. Bob entered the Marine Corps, and they lived in Quantico and Camp Lejeune. When Bob was honorably discharged, Fran and Bob moved to Westchester and to Chappaqua in 1957 where Fran has lived ever since.

"I'm still in the same house. It was a great neighborhood for my kids, Leslie and Mike, while they were growing up and it's been good for me all these years."

"Fran, did your tennis background open any doors for you?" I asked.

"Actually it did. I played locally, often with a friend who belonged to Seven Bridges Field Club, a small swim and tennis club in Chappaqua. Bill Dumpke, head of the tennis committee, saw me play and asked if I'd be interested in giving lessons, particularly for the kids. 'Sure' was my response. I started there in 1969 and built up the program through the '70's. Then in the fall of 1978, Curt Beusman, tennis player and founder of the Saw Mill Racquet Club, heard of me and asked if I'd join the teaching staff at Saw Mill. I was the first and only female pro. I grew up at Saw Mill. As soon as I graduated from Duke, I got married, had kids and never really worked. But, at Saw Mill, I had to be organized. I had to have lesson plans. I had to learn to deal with the public. Curt wanted me, specifically, to handle the middle-aged women who were taking up the game in droves and to set up leagues and USTA teams.

"I played on some of the USTA teams too. One team, a 55-and-over 4.5 team, made it to the USTA League Tennis National Championships in Tuscon, Arizona. Well, you remember, Judy. You were on the team and we only had six players - enough for three doubles teams - whereas many of the teams, especially from California and Texas, had at least twelve on a team with coaches and trainers. We didn't do very well in the tournament, but we had a blast. We certainly did have fun despite not winning many games on the court. It was a thrill just being there."

I smiled in agreement.

"What do you like most about tennis?" I then asked Fran and without much hesitation, she responded.

"The camaraderie. I have made dear friends through tennis. I like the social part of the game. You're with people you enjoy, but getting lots of exercise at the same time. I like working on my game too. I never stop trying to improve. Even today, at 83, I'm still working on my game and loving it."

CHAPTER 11:

JOHN POWLESS

John Powless is a hard man to pin down. He travels the world playing in senior and super senior tennis events. However, I finally cornered him at a hotel in Virginia Beach where he was playing the USTA National 80-and-over clay courts in singles and doubles.

Tall, 6 foot, 5 inches, handsome with a shock of well-coifed white hair, and as personable and positive as they come, we found a computer room that the hotel front desk said we could use. Space was tight, but John curled his long legs under a chair, and we began our journey.

John, born on August 24, 1932 during the Depression, was raised on a large farm in the small town of Flora, population approximately 4,000, in southern Illinois. He lived with his extended family of great grandfather, grandfather, grandmother, parents, aunts and uncles, siblings and cousins, all under one roof in a large farmhouse.

"I slept in the attic on a straw mattress," he said. "But when an aunt or an uncle or somebody went away on business or whatever, I'd take up residence on their feather bed till they returned.

"Everybody worked on the farm," John explained further. "We had no running water, no heat and no electricity, and nothing was motorized. When I was nine, I started plowing with a single blade plow pulled by one of our work horses. The farm was large, very large, probably several hundred acres. We grew acres and acres of crops - all kinds - and we'd grow alfalfa for the horses and cows to eat. The alfalfa was harvested and packed into large stacks and left in the fields so the animals could feast at their leisure."

"Did you have a large herd of cattle?" I asked.

"No, we kept the cows just for our own family needs. We didn't sell any milk or dairy products."

"Did the Depression have an impact on your lives?"

"No, it really didn't. To begin with, we didn't have running water, electricity or mechanized equipment. We didn't have anything invested in the stock market. We were hard working farm people. Life didn't change for us.

"But World War II did have an impact," he said. "I was too young to enter the service, but many of my relatives served. I'll never forget one day when I was 9 or 10. I was out by our barn, and I saw a small World War II plane, a P-38 Lightning, heading toward me. The plane flew very low over our barn, turned upside down, and there was my uncle flying his plane, a Pathfinder, giving me a salute! I saluted right back."

John paused and added, "I often wondered if he ever got into trouble for that maneuver."

I asked, "So John, you grew up on a farm, and everybody worked their butts off. How in the world did you get started in tennis?"

"My Dad was a tennis player," he said. "When he was 18 or so, he was hustling this good looking gal who played tennis. She told him that she wasn't interested unless he could beat her. So he set out to learn the game, and a match between them was

John Powless sitting in the computer room of a Virginia Beach hotel, August 2015

arranged. Unfortunately, the young lady beat my Dad, and the romance was over. But not his romance with tennis. He kept at his game and became quite a player."

"You told me Flora is in southern Illinois, but was it unique in any way?"

"Flora was on the Baltimore and Ohio Railroad, and a large, three-story depot was built in the early 1900s to accommodate all the passenger trains that came through every day. And one of the town's annual attractions was a tennis tournament on the 4th of July. We'd have a draw of 128 players coming from all over, even some well-known players, Dick Savitt being one. And my Dad usually did pretty well and became fairly well-known. One day, a gentleman, Louis Roeder, got off the train hoping to play my Dad whom he had heard of. I'll never forget it. He was dressed in a double-breasted suit. I'd never seen such a suit. So he introduces himself to my Dad and says, 'Cecil, so when am I going to get to play you?' My Dad replied, 'You have to beat my kid here if you want to play me.' The poor guy never got to play my Dad!"

John laughed at the thought of one of his early victories on the tennis court.

But Louis Roeder, who happened to be a reporter, first covering the New York Giants and then the New York Yankees, kept in touch with young John, especially when John played in the national tournaments at Forest Hills in New York. Roeder took him out to dinner during the tournaments and continued to be a mentor of sorts.

Continuing in his non-stop, stream of consciousness fashion, John said, "When I was 11, I went to enter a local tournament. I had my racquet, and I wore my usual tennis clothes: bib overalls but no shoes or shirt. The tournament director defaulted me because I didn't have 'the proper attire.'

"While I was still a kid, my father and I built a dirt tennis court on our farm, and folks from all around came to play on it. The court became known as the "Frog Island Tennis Court.""

"How did you come up with that name?"

"Well, every time it rained, the frogs would come out and take over the court. So, we started this tradition that if you wanted to play after the rain you had to catch a frog. And to make it more exciting, you had to catch the frog after dark. Have you ever tried to catch a frog after dark?"

"I can't say that I have."

"It's not easy because if you just go after the frog he'll jump away, and you'll end up with a fist full of mud. What you have to do is shine a flashlight at the frog. Then you've got him."

"You've got some great stories." John just smiled broadly.

"And the best part is, they're true," he said.

"Now, when you got to high school, did your high school have a tennis team?" I asked.

"Oh yes. In our high school, everybody *had* to play three sports, and the only three sports offered were football in the fall, basketball in the winter and tennis in the spring."

"No baseball? America's favorite sport?"

"No baseball. A lot of the people who lived in Flora were oil people from Texas and Oklahoma. Their sports were softball and tennis. So, the school wasn't going to have a softball team because no other school in the area had softball teams. Tennis became the third sport. We'd start football practice in August, and once that started, all the basketball hoops in town were taken down. No sneaking in pick-up games with your buddies on the side. When basketball practice started, the same thing. All the boys in school concentrated solely on basketball. Then came tennis - same deal.

"We'd have our practices after school, and then at 9 p.m. every night the town whistle blew meaning all the kids had to get home and go to bed. That was one way to take care of idle mischief."

"How'd you do on the tennis team?"

"Glad you asked," answered John, grinning. "I won the State Championship my senior year, and that had never happened in little Flora."

"Has it happened since?"

"No, it hasn't. That's a pretty good long-standing record. And it was a pretty good win. I beat the No. 2 player in the U.S. juniors, Al Kuhn from Evanston High School. Over the years we've played against each other many times, and we've become great friends."

After high school, John went to a pharmacy school in Michigan but soon transferred to Murray State in Murray, Kentucky. He played forward on the basketball team all four years and led the team to the Kentucky Invitational title.

"And I set the single scoring record at the time - 34 points in one game."

In tennis, John was equally triumphant, never losing a match in all three years of varsity competition. He also was the Ohio Valley Conference singles and doubles champion all three seasons.

After graduating from Murray State in 1957, Powless taught and coached basketball and tennis for two years at Florida State. He followed that up with three years as assistant basketball coach at the University of Cincinnati under the Head Coach Ed Jucker.

"We had one remarkable undefeated season and compiled an amazing 78-6 record over three years. During those three years, the Cincinnati Bearcats had two back-to-back NCAA titles defeating Ohio State both times, before losing to Loyala University in the NCAA finals in 1963."

John's next move was to the University of Wisconsin where he coached basketball for 13 years and tennis for five. Leaving the University of Wisconsin in 1976, he launched a new tennis career as founder and owner of the John Powless Tennis Center in Madison, Wisconsin. The center opened its doors in 1979, and it's still going strong with eight hard courts and two Har-Tru indoors and four hard courts outdoors.

"The club was recognized by the USTA as Club of the Year in Wisconsin as well as Best Tennis Club in the Midwest and was the finalist for the National Club of the Year contest," John proudly said. "All our programs are very strong, particularly the juniors and the Rising Stars programs. We're helping to get kids off the streets and onto the courts."

"After college, while you were coaching tennis and basketball, did you have a chance to play in any national or sectional tournaments?"

"This would have been in the late 1950's, early 60's," he said. "That was when I was playing my best tennis. Don Dell was a top professional, Davis Cup captain and later one of the first player reps and sports' promoters, and he knew everybody in tennis - well, he was always calling me to come East and play in men's events. So, I did. I'd play at Forest Hills, and some of the other tournaments in the East, and I got into the top 20 in singles and as high as No. 3 in doubles at one point. But, you know, this was all before we had Open tennis in 1968. I still played competitively, but there was no money in the game.

That's why I kept my 'day jobs' - coaching. And, to tell you the truth, I didn't think they'd ever go for open tennis. Boy! Was I wrong."

Changing subjects, I asked, "So how did the idea of senior tennis start?"

"The USTA was never much interested in senior tennis. It actually started with World War II veterans. They fought hard for world peace in the European theatre and occasionally, during leaves, had a chance to play tennis, often with their military counterparts. After the war was over many of them, along with the Canadians, said, 'Let's get together.' They arranged to hold tournaments at a club in Lake Placid, New York every year for years. Draws were established for four singles matches and three doubles. The winner was awarded the Gordon Cup, a handsome gold cup resting on a marble base.

"After a few years as the average age of the entrants was 45, I decided it made sense to drop the 'veterans' title as many of the players were not veterans, including myself - I was only nine when the war started - and rename it 'Senior Tennis.'

"The Gordon Cup is still played the last Thursday, Friday and Saturday of July, alternating one year in Toronto, Canada, and the next in Cleveland, Ohio. The Canadian seniors invite some of their best players, and the Americans do as well. Forty-five matches are played over a three-day period, and the winning country is awarded the Gordon Cup. The Davis Cup, by the way, is the only international team tournament older than the Gordon Cup. I often speak at the dinner given by the host country and have a chance to tell old stories of matches won and lost and of longtime friendships made."

While John caught his breath, I thought I couldn't imagine a better after dinner speaker than John with his endless enthusiasm, good humor and raft of stories.

"We started as a 45-and-over tournament but eventually it grew to a 50-and-over," John continued. The USTA considered the Gordon Cup merely social, so we decided to recruit top players - Vic Seixas, Bobby Riggs, Gardnar Mulloy, the No. 1 tennis player in the U.S. and favorite partner of Billy Talbert, Davis Cupper Tommy Edlefsen, and Lester Sack are just a few of the names I can think of now who played in the Gordon Cup matches. Their participation helped to get the USTA's attention but still no financial support.

"But we kept going. Then, Jay Freeman of Little Rock, Arkansas, an aging player and one of the original veteran players, and Roe Campbell from Knoxville, Tennessee, suggested we expand the senior tennis to 55-and-over and call it 'Super Senior Tennis.' He said 'We can't compete against these 45 and 50 year olds. We have to expand the category to 55s, 60s and even beyond.'

"So, a clubhouse in Knoxville where Roe was a member placed a cornerstone announcing the birth of Super Senior Tennis. Jay Freeman, Van Zerbie, Joe Cullen, C. Alphonso Smith, Roe Campbell and others were the founders of Super Senior Tennis which has now grown to include even 95-and-over.

"We still didn't get any funding from the USTA. They thought we'd never get enough entries to make the tournaments worth it. Van Zerbie, a USTA board member, asked the Board to sanction the tournaments, but when he was turned down, he said 'The hell with you all,' offered his resignation and stormed out of the room.

"After that episode, Van and I talked and settled on a plan. Van was to go back to the Board and ask again for support knowing that the Board would claim we wouldn't have enough entries. Then I was to get up and say, 'Listen, this guy, Van, has done so much for tennis, we'll just hold the tournament anyway.' And that's what we did.

"So we had to go it alone. We bought our gold, silver and bronze balls, the trophies for first, second and third places, and we set up our own tournaments. We had 64 players in each draw. We had so many entries, they were coming out of our ears! And even today, we have 32 players in the 95s! One of them is Warren Webster, a World War II Thunderbolt pilot. What a character he is.

"We established Super Senior Tennis, Inc., a not-for-profit organization promoting tennis opportunities and enjoyment for players 55 and above, and we publish the 'Super Senior Tennis News' sent free to all the members."

"Are you involved in that?"

"Oh yes, I'm on the Board of Directors and Editor of the SST News. And many years later Senior Tennis spread to the women who have their own organization, the National Senior Women's Tennis Association [NSWTA] which has its annual meetings in Houston. I'm a life member of NSWTA and go to their meetings every year. I think we're the only sport now that is totally co-ed with the men supportive of the women and vice versa.

"And we have every combination of play you can think of: husband and wife mixed, father/son, father/daughter, mother/son, mother/ daughter, grandfather/grandson, you name it.

John took a sip of water, and I changed the subject.

"How about your own seniors' career, John?"

"You might say, my seniors' career started early because I played many father/son matches with my Dad. This would have been in the 1950's when I was playing my best tennis. We won the national clay court father-and-son tournament three years in a row! And now I'm continuing the tradition by playing with my son Jason in father/son events. We've won two events and have been the finalists several times.

"But, I really got into senior tennis when I was in my 40's, and I've been playing it ever since."

I asked John how many gold balls he has accumulated, but he didn't give a number.

"I've got a bunch because I've been fortunate enough to win national titles, but I don't keep track," he said. "People always ask me, and I tell them. 'I don't know. You can go over to the trophy case and count them up.'"

Then John changed the subject. "I have to tell you about Charlie Hume. Charlie is 91 years old, and he just won his first gold ball. Now that's what I call 'hangin'' in there. It's remarkable that these seniors persevere, and when they win, especially at 91, it's such a sweet victory."

"That's a good segue, John," I said. "Tell me what you most enjoy about playing senior tennis?"

John replied, laughing, "No match is fun until it's over."

"No, really. What are the benefits of senior tennis, and what do you like most about it?"

"First is the camaraderie and the relationships you develop. I told you about coaching basketball and winning two NCAA titles back to back when at the University of Cincinnati. Occasionally I'll get a phone call from a player, but in tennis I get phone calls every day from tennis players!

"Second, and this is totally unique to tennis - its international aspect. We play cup matches all over the world with players from different nations, and they become friends. I'm leaving to play the Gardnar Mulloy Cup in Croatia. We're playing at a club on the Adriatic which is spectacular! Some of the countries participating are Australia, New Zealand, Japan, Argentina, South Africa, Sweden, Norway and Germany. Many of the players I have played against before. They're already friends, but there will be new ones, and they'll become friends too. This sort of international connection through tennis should be expanded into other sports and activities. Maybe then we'd have more understanding and be more tolerant of foreigners."

"My third reason is personal. I played senior tennis with my Dad in the '50's as I mentioned. Winning the tournaments we did was very special and made our bond even stronger. And the same thing is happening now with my son, Jason. We play father/son tournaments together and enjoy our time working as a team."

Pausing a few seconds to gather himself, John concluded, "And, with senior tennis you stay fit and engaged. You're meeting people all the time and enjoying their company. And, just look at the senior players - particularly the super senior players. They don't look their age and they don't feel it either. I can't think of anything better than that to recommend senior tennis and super senior tennis to all players. They don't have to play at the level of the ranked players to enjoy the benefits. It's open to *all* players."

But John wasn't finished. He had some tips for all senior players.

"First, staying injury free is important. That's not always easy, but we have such advanced medical care that my tennis buddies with bad hips and knees are back on the court with no pain; meds and physical therapy help us heal too.

"Second, you have to play on a regular basis. When Roger Federer hired Stefan Edberg as his coach, Edberg told him that he had to play more as he got older. To keep himself agile, quick and fit, he needed court time practicing and competing. And we see the results of that now. Federer plays more tournaments and is playing his best tennis.

"Third, everyone is different so you have to create your own routine. Whatever it is that works best for you - diet, practice, drills, weights, competition, running, walking - should become your routine.

"And last, you have to be disciplined and tough. When you decide to play competitive senior tennis you must follow your routine and play on a regular basis to be 'tournament tough.' If it's not top level competitive senior or super senior tennis, you still want to win when you go out to play with your buddies and being disciplined is the best way to accomplish that."

John Powless' actions speak as loud as his words.

CHAPTER 12:

ROLF THUNG

Rolf Thung has been one of the Netherlands' top tennis players for years. He has played in all four Grand Slam tournaments, as well as on several Davis Cup teams for the Netherlands and happens to be the President of the Royal Dutch Tennis Association, the Dutch equivalent of the U.S. Tennis Association.

Born on July 27, 1951, Rolf is tall, lean and handsome, with salt and pepper hair but looking much younger than his years. I met him through my friend Linda Thung Ryan, Rolf's sister. He became an instant friend with his engaging personality, big smile, sharp wit and tennis stories to tell.

I had a chance to speak with Rolf while in the car en route to the U.S. Open. I immediately started peppering him with questions during our hour-long drive from Westchester to Flushing Meadows. Fortunately, he was a very willing interviewee.

"How did you get into tennis?" was my first question.

"Because my mother played at Wimbledon," he responded quickly.

That stopped me in my tracks.

"In 1957, when I was six years old, my mother got through to the third round at Wimbledon, an amazing feat in and of itself. But she did have some help from her second-round opponent, who got my mother into the Guinness Book of Records. During their match, the opposing player double-faulted seventeen times in a row, something that has never happened before or since!"

Maria Helena de Amorim of Brazil was Mrs. Thung's record-holding opponent. The record still stands and will likely never be broken.

Rolf continued, "My mother was also the Dutch women's champion for several years in doubles and now, when we have our Royal Dutch Tennis Association meetings in the Tennis Association meeting room, I always see her photos among the Dutch champions hanging on the walls."

"How about your Dad? Did he play tennis?"

"Oh yes. My father was a tennis champion in Java, Indonesia, where he grew up," Rolf said. "He was a Naval Officer by profession, but his passion was tennis. He made it into a science and was actually ahead of his times in many ways. He started with mini-tennis for warm ups. Now everybody starts warming up like that, but certainly not then. He also started the first bilateral tennis institute in Rotterdam in the seventies. Nobody had ever heard about the left and right brain characteristics then. He started with vision tests and mental training long before anybody else did in the Netherlands. He learned himself and taught others to have bilateral tennis strokes - equally good at playing left-handed and right-handed."

After we arrived at the U.S. Open, my husband Gordon and I separated from Rolf and his sister Linda – Gordon and I hitting the field courts while Rolf and Linda headed to the President's Box in Arthur Ashe Stadium. We reunited while

Rolf Thung at the 2015 U.S. Open

watching some men's doubles later and my question and answer session continued.

"So Rolf, tell me about learning tennis from your parents."

"I first started playing tennis with my mother a lot," he said. "She really infected me with the fun of the game. She was the nicest person you could imagine, but I started winning against her. Then abruptly we stopped playing. I never could remember why, but many years later she told me that she didn't like losing to me - or to anybody! On the court, she was as fanatical a competitor as you can be. That must be the reason she had such good results. In my memory, she had a very good forehand, a great forehand drop shot and a great forehand lob. Had I inherited her fanaticism, I also would have had much better results.

"When I showed real interest in the game, my father 'discovered' me. I became one of his tennis pupils, and probably also one of his 'guinea pigs.' Remember the mini-tennis? He started that with me, having me play in the service court all the time. I felt like a fool. We spent hours and hours on the tennis court. Only much later, I realized how much I learned from my father - not only in tennis but also about life in general."

After graduating from high school in 1971, Rolf served for 21 months in the Dutch armed forces, a mandatory obligation for all young men. He joined the select Royal Dutch Marines officer's training school, and of the 22 who entered the program, only 12 finished.

"Very non-Dutch to have such a competitive system," added Rolf. "After nine months of intensive training I became a second lieutenant."

"Nine months is a long time for training, isn't it, especially when you're only in the service for 21?" I asked.

"Yes. That's true. Normally, the obligation is only 18 months, but because of the extensive training, three months was added to the tour. Again, very uncharacteristic for the Dutch. Because I finished among the top five of the class, I was able to choose my assignment. Most 'top per-centers' chose bases on Aruba and Curacao in the Dutch Caribbean, but I chose to remain in the Netherlands instead to work on my tennis as much as possible. I think the fact that the Marine Corps Commander was a tennis-playing fanatic is why I never had to do reserve duty in my playing days. But, as it turned out, while in the Marines, I became runner-up in the National Championships for the first time, and to my knowledge the reputation of the Marine Corps didn't suffer."

In the summer of 1973, Rolf gladly put away his military gear and devoted himself to playing in the small, international tournaments in Belgium and the Netherlands. There, he met an Indian coach, Akhtar Ali, who worked on Rolf's game and encouraged him to join the four-month Indian tournament circuit in the coming winter season. Rolf did just that.

"How was your time in India?" I asked Rolf later that night as the four of us sat down for dinner.

"Very exciting," he said. "After I arrived in India, Indian Airlines, the domestic airline, went out on strike which made travel more difficult for us tennis players who were going from week to week to new locations. Train and so-called ambassador cars were our only options.

"On the Indian Circuit mostly Indians played, and I got to know several who became good friends. One week we played in Amritsar and had to play in Calcutta next. The night before our departure by train, my Indian friends and I ate something from the street that didn't agree with my European stomach, and I got really sick. As we started our journey, I was feeling terrible, and the trip was to take two days and two nights. To make matters worse, the ride was bumpy, jostling everybody left and right and stops were made in every little village. But, actually the rough ride settled my stomach somehow and made me feel better by the time we approached Calcutta. But, I was weak and didn't do well in the tournament.

"Now to the second available mode of transportation: the 'ambassador cars,'" he continued. "They were old, much-used Fords that could carry six or so passengers. We took one trip by ambassador car. Putting our suitcases on the rack on the roof, we started off at 8 p.m. on a 12-hour journey. First, the driver took a detour to buy a cake which he then took to the temple. Coming back to the car, minus the cake, the driver said, 'Our trip is blessed. We'll be safe the whole trip.' At the time, that seemed a quaint gesture to me.

"India is a huge country and the roads, especially off the beaten track, are hardly roads. They're dirt with hairpin turns that take you up high into the mountains. And, they're basically one way. There isn't much traffic, but when there is, what you are most likely to encounter are large trucks. Typically, the trucks do not yield. If you're in a car, and you see a truck coming at you, you pull to the side and get off the road quickly. Not our driver. Maybe it was the blessing, but he'd barrel straight ahead. We passengers were screaming, 'Get off the road. Get off the road please! We're going to die!' Even though pulling to the side of the road and staring down the mountainside to the distant valley below is frightening, it was far better than getting killed! Well, it must have been the blessing, because each time we faced an oncoming truck, our driver stayed on the road, and the trucks yielded. We made it to our next tournament, but never again would we travel by ambassador car."

Linda, Gordon and I were speechless after that story with our mouths wide open. Just then, our dinners were served, but Rolf continued.

"A real plus was getting to know the Indian guys well as we traveled from tournament to tournament. They helped me in so many ways - with the language, with directions, with the culture. And they helped me negotiate with the Indians. The tournaments didn't offer prize money; only appearance money, so learning how to bargain became very important. I learned by watching my friends negotiate in stores. In the store, the shopkeeper would make an offer for a certain product; my friends would keep saying 'no' until the shopkeeper stopped making counter-offers. This meant you were getting closer to the real price. Then they would say how much they liked the product but that it was still too expensive, mention an even lower price and walk out of the store. If the shopkeeper came after them, they knew there was still bargaining room. If the shopkeeper did not go after them, they knew the price they offered was too low and they would go back and buy the product for the last offered price.

"Actually, I sometimes use that methodology now when negotiating," admitted Rolf. "I don't literally walk away, of course, but use a similar tactic."

"Did you stay on the tour after that?" I asked.

"I was on the tour full time for four years. I played at Forest Hills in 1975 in singles and doubles. My doubles partner was John James, an Aussie. He's a great guy. And we took a set from Ilie Nastase and Jimmy Connors!"

"Good for you guys!" I exclaimed. "How about Wimbledon? Any good stories there?"

"I played singles at Wimbledon in 1974, 1975, 1976 and 1977, but I played mixed doubles in 1973 with Tine Zwaan, losing to Billie Jean King and Owen Davidson in the third round."

I asked him if he had any other fun stories from his playing days.

"In the fall of 1975 and 1976 I played in Australia as part of the Asian circuit," he said. "Actually, that reminds me of a story about Cliff Richey. You know Cliff?"

Gordon and I nodded.

"I've known Cliff since he was two years old. The cutest, most rambunctious little red head you've ever met," I interjected about the former U.S. Davis Cup star from the early 1970s.

"We were playing in Melbourne, Australia at the Royal South Yarra Lawn Tennis Club, where the accent is more *English* English than in Britain. On Tuesdays, the ladies of the club were having 'Ladies Day' in the clubhouse, and the chatter was very, very British. Cliff and I were having lunch too, and the chatter was so prominent you could hardly hear. Cliff, with his Texas twang, had had enough of it. He suddenly yelled out 'FUCK!!!' A stunned silence followed."

"I can see Cliff doing that. He's not one to hold back."

Gordon was curious and asked, "Did you play any Davis Cup?"

"Oh, I played on several Netherlands Davis Cup teams. We played Sweden and Bjorn Borg in 1974. I actually played him three times over the years and managed to win one set. We beat Finland that year. In 1979, I played doubles with Tom Okker against France in Amsterdam. We won the doubles, but we lost the tie. Okker lost the deciding match against young Yannick Noah in five sets. Our Dutch fans were crushed."

"So after this amazing, carefree tour, you decided it was time to finish your education and get on with your life?" I asked.

"Yes. You might say so. It was time. I went to the University of Amsterdam and majored in Economics. In 1981, I worked full time but went back to school in 1987 to finish my education with a Masters in Economics. For about 20 years, I was a management consultant. In 2004, I started my present business called People Intouch B.V., which uses a system I developed, the SpeakUp, enabling employees or as you might say 'whistle-blowers' of mostly large international corporations, to report possible misconduct to their own company anonymously and without reprisals."

"That must be a tool that corporations yearn for?"

"I've been very lucky. The concept has caught on, and I have many Fortune 500 and major European corporations signing on."

Rolf and I didn't have a chance to finish our conversation that evening so after he returned home to Europe, I followed up on my interview over the phone. I asked Rolf how the Netherlands organizes its competition and other tennis events.

"It's very different from the U.S.," he said. "First, the most popular sports in the Netherlands are soccer and tennis, in that order. The Royal Dutch Tennis Association has 600,000 members, a large number for a country as small as The Netherlands, because when someone joins a club, the membership fee to the Association is included in the club's fee. It's very inexpensive and automatic.

"We don't have tennis in the schools or universities as you do in the United States, but, like Germany, we have a very active "club" community. To join a club is inexpensive - $100 to $300 for the year - and there is no extra fee to book a court. Public courts are very rare in the Netherlands; actually there are almost none, and we can use our outdoor courts eight months out of the year. However, for indoor courts there is a charge.

"The clubs compete against each other, with players ranked according to their ability, similar to the USTA system of 2.5, 3.0, 3.5, 4, etc. The teams travel, leagues are formed, and the RDTA [Royal Dutch Tennis Association] organizes all this activity.

"For us, if you're a 1 or a 2, you're considered a top player. We have no ATP points, but the competition is intense, and we also have senior tournaments that are arranged according to age as you do. Recently, I played in the 60-and-over world championship in La Baule, France. The Netherlands took eighth place - a reason to be proud.

"The Netherlands also has an I.C. - International Club - as does the U.S. and we compete against other countries for coveted cups and bragging rights. I've been on the Dutch I.C. Board for 34 years, and that's how I met John Powless.

"At the IC Week in the Netherlands in 1991, John gave Prince Bernhard, our Queen's husband, a Prince bag and an USA IC hat. On the day of the finals the prince proudly wore John's hat. He's a good sport."

"Have you won any gold balls?"

"No, the Netherlands doesn't give out gold balls, but I won the 60-and-over national championship in doubles."

"What is it about senior tennis that you enjoy most?"

"I enjoy tennis, period. If I play younger players, they have the speed and strong serves and strokes which make it a challenge for an older player like me. That's fine with me. On our club team, I can play someone as young as 18. And I play a lot of doubles and mixed doubles. Two of my teammates were pregnant when we played mixed together. That seemed to make them stronger!

"Tennis is a game that is so difficult that it never gets boring. You can always learn, and you keep practicing to improve. The types of tennis players you meet are so varied: baseliners, net rushers, pushers, thinkers, strategists. A match is a mental dual between two minds. And it never disappoints, win or lose."

"Rolf, do you have some tips for senior players?" I asked.

"Enjoy the process," he said. "It's not only winning that's important but the play itself - whether you hit a nice backhand down the line or a smart drop shot. How do you foil your opponent's strengths?

"Enjoy your opponents too. I can't say that enough. Often, the late starters have trouble with that. A player needs ambition, but it's important to enjoy the match itself. Federer is a perfect example of someone who enjoys the play no matter who his opponent is. He enjoys the process, the competition itself, the analyzing, the strategizing, the execution."

On that note, our conversation ended.

As I reflected on my time with Rolf, I thought of him as a Renaissance Man – one who is gifted in intellect, business acumen, leadership and athleticism. He doesn't flaunt his accomplishments; on the contrary, he takes them in stride with good humor and humility. I decided his calm equanimity results, in part, from his fascination with and love of the game of tennis, every aspect of which he enjoys.

CHAPTER 13:

JIM NELSON

Jim Nelson, the consummate senior tennis player, has won 107 gold balls and six USTA doubles Grand Slams, three with Bob Duesler in 1982, 2006 and 2008, and three with Len Lindborg in 1990, 2000 and 2005.

"I was on my way to winning a seventh Grand Slam with Duesler in the 75 doubles, in 2011, but when we got to the fourth and final leg of the clay tournament at Virginia Beach, it was rained out and rescheduled for November," he said. "We both had prior cup commitments for November, and we couldn't play."

With a ready smile and devilish sparkle in his eyes, Jim loves to talk about his tennis. He and his wife, Barbara, enjoy the good life of southern California, both playing tennis and some golf. They are blessed with many friends with the same interests. And they like to party too.

Jim was born in Huntington Park near Los Angeles on August 11, 1935. He started playing tennis in high school, and by his senior year he played No. 1 in singles for his team.

"I didn't play any juniors tournaments," he said. "Our tennis coach was also the football coach, so not much coaching occurred. I learned most of my tennis when I played at South

Gate Park where Clyde Walker taught. He later became Billie Jean King's coach. South Gate Park had the fastest cement courts I can remember. I didn't know how to hit ground strokes. The surface was so fast we'd serve and get to the net as fast as we could. Walker thought I had some talent and offered to give me lessons for one dollar. My parents, however, weren't in favor of me spending money on tennis lessons."

I asked, "Did you play in college?"

"After high school I studied at USC [the University of Southern California] as a day student with a pre-dental major," he said. "In 1955, my second year at USC, I tried out for the tennis team and was sure I'd make varsity, but Coach George Toley started recruiting foreign players. He recruited Pancho Contreras and Joaquin Reyes from Mexico and the following year, Alex Olmedo from Peru who later played for the U.S. Davis Cup team and was ranked in the top ten for a while. I didn't make the varsity. I dropped out of school and worked the next year for UPS on the night shift. After the trucks completed their daily routine and came back to the garage I would gas them up, wash them and load them with the packages for the next day's deliveries. My hours were 10 p.m. to 4 a.m. Then I'd drive home to Fullerton -- where I lived with my parents -- to get some sleep. During the day I took some courses at Fullerton Community College.

"By 1957, I was feeling the urge to go back to school but away from home, so I applied to the University of Utah and was accepted. I didn't contact the tennis coach when I got there as I thought I'd have to work, but a tennis friend of mine from Fullerton, who was a student at Utah, insisted that I come out and talk to the coach, a gentleman named Theron Parmalee. He gave me a tryout and set up a match with the No. 2 player from the previous year. I won and was on the team.

"With a really top No. 1 player, Wayne Pearce from Salt Lake City, and a strong squad from No. 2 to 6, we won the Skyline Conference," he continued. "We won all eight team matches and all nine individual matches. Wayne and I were selected to go to the NCAA Championships being held at the Naval Academy in Annapolis, Maryland. We were the first players ever to represent the Skyline Conference in NCAA tennis. Both Wayne and I lost our second round matches, but it was a great experience for a west coast boy to be on the east coast for the first time.

"I left Utah that summer fully expecting to be back in the fall, but when I returned to California, I received a notice from my draft board that I was to report to the U.S. Army for active duty. I wrote the board and my congressman to get deferred because I would lose my tuition, books and housing scholarship at Utah. Deaf ears!

"In July 1958, I reported for basic training at Fort Ord in Northern California. At the end of basic training, I was selected to attend Army Intelligence School in Maryland. After graduating from intelligence school, I was assigned to a CIC [Counter Intelligence Corps] in Pasadena. That was a good post for me. When I was getting my security clearance, a fellow tennis player, Lt. Ken Dillman, told me about an Army tennis tournament at Fort MacArthur in nearby San Pedro. I put in for some time off, and the C.O. [Commanding Officer] okayed it. I ended up winning the singles and the doubles with Ken, which got us in 'the flow.'"

"What do you mean – in the flow?" I inquired.

"The military services conduct a sequence of local, regional and national events leading up to an All Army, Navy, Air Force and Marine competition. They then select a team to compete in the Inter-Service Championships usually held at the Army/Navy Country Club in Washington, D.C. If you do well in the beginning, you are 'in the flow' which means you have an opportunity to continue to the next level and possibly to the Inter-Service event.

"After our victories at Fort MacArthur, Ken and I got orders to report to Fort Ord for the 6th Army District Championships. Dillman and I won the doubles, and I lost in the final of the singles, but winners and finalists were selected to train at the U.S. Military Academy in West Point and to try out for the team representing Army at the Inter-Service matches. My C.O. was not happy about this because it meant I could be away for as long as six weeks. But, he relented.

"West Point's courts were clay, which I had never played on before, but I found it to be a good surface for my type of game. I had some wins and losses but didn't make the final team. The next year the local tournament was at San Pedro again but my C.O. said, 'Not this year.' Not wanting that to be the final answer I spoke to the Head of Special Services, a full Colonel who remembered me from the year before. He cut orders for me to play the 6th Army Championships, straight in. My C.O. was not pleased. This made for a frosty last six months in the Army.

"In 1960, the All Army training was in Denver at the Fitzsimmons Army Hospital. I made fourth man on a strong Army team, and we went on to the Inter-Service Championships at the Army/Navy Country Club. The competition was terrific. Many well-known tennis players, Barry MacKay, for instance, played. And, remember, Arthur Ashe played for Army years later in inter-service matches. I lost in singles to Hank Jungle in a good match, but straight sets."

"You have to admit tennis was taking you away from 'military' responsibilities" I said. "And, your tennis was getting better and better. Army life wasn't bad for you."

"I did have a really good assignment in the service," Jim said. "It was a great location – no hardship there. The chance for me to travel and play some top tennis was fantastic.

"I go back to my detachment, and my C.O., to my surprise, pulls me into his office to be his secretary - to do the typing and filing. My tour was about to end, so I didn't think that assignment would be too bad. Then the Colonel told me that if I extended for three months I would negate my reserve obligations. That sounded like a good deal to me, and that's what I did.

"I was married in 1960 while still in the Army. My wife, Marjie, was getting her masters in library science at UCLA, and I still had a year to go to get my degree. So when I was discharged from the Army I applied to UCLA, majored in psychology and finally graduated in 1962 at the age of 27.

"After graduating, I was hired by Pacific Telephone, later AT&T, for six years. In the meantime, we had two boys - Brian in '64 and Brad in '68 - when I was offered a position as a stockbroker. I stayed in the securities business for 37 years.

"After raising the boys I started playing more tennis – with them too. They're still playing tennis. In 1970, when I turned 35, I had never played any big time tennis, but I entered the men's 35s tournaments, and my career in senior tennis began. My big breakthrough was when I reached the finals of the Men's 45s National Hard Courts at La Jolla Beach and Tennis. I was unseeded but managed to work my way through to the final, where I lost to Jim Perley, a big lefty with a tremendous serve. That's when I really got the bug, and I still have it."

"So, you don't have any plans to quit even though you're in your eighties now," I asked.

"No, if I'm healthy and able, I would love to play the game with my buddies for many years. It's a great life."

"What is your most memorable match?"

"I have two favorite tennis matches, both in doubles and both in the same tournament," he said. "In 1980, my partner Ron Livingston and I were playing in the Grand Masters tournament in Los Angeles. There were big name players in the draw - Neale Fraser, Frank Sedgman, Pancho Gonzalez and Alex Olmedo. Ron and I played in the thirty-two draw qualifier, and we beat Hugh Stewart and Bob Perry in the final, which got us into the main draw. In the quarters we met Pancho Gonzalez and Alex Olmedo. By some miracle, we won the first set 6-0. Gonzalez quipped to the crowd, 'Don't these guys know who we were?' Well, Gonzalez and Olmedo came back in the second set and beat us 6-3. Now to the third – the decider. We won it 6-3. Game, set, match to Nelson and Livingston."

Jim then got up from his chair and led me to a cozy corner where favorite photographs were displayed with him

Jim Nelson(right) and Ron Livingston after their famous win at the
1980 Grand Masters tournament in Los Angeles

and Livingston standing proudly under the score board after their win over Gonzalez and Olmedo.

"In the semis, we faced Frank Sedgman and Pancho Segura, both world class players," he continued. "Sedgman was still a wonderful volleyer and Segura was one of the most clever players I ever played. We lost the match 7-6, 5-7, 7-6, but it was the best match I ever remember playing. Frank Sedgman was one of my idols. What a thrill to play so well against him.

"My second favorite story occurred in the mid-80's," he continued. "Jack Kramer was running the Los Angeles Pro Tournament at the UCLA tennis complex. John McEnroe was the top seed, and his quarterfinal match was to start at 7 PM. By chance, it was a night that the tournament was honoring seniors, and Kramer asked my partner, Bob Duesler, and me to play one set against Ed Kauder and King Lambert on center court at 6:30 as patrons filed into the stadium. So, here we were playing on center court with about twenty people in the stands, but the stadium started to fill up. After half an hour Kramer came over and said, 'Keep playing. McEnroe is having a problem getting here.' So we did. The stadium holds 5,000, and it was nearly full. 'Play another set,' said Kramer. It's after 7 now, and the crowd started booing us. They had not bought their tickets to watch four old guys; they came to see McEnroe. Finally, as the booing got louder and louder, Kramer came out and announced that McEnroe had the flu and wouldn't be able to make it.

"If I ever run into 'Johnny Mac' I plan to ask him for my appearance money," said Jim with a big grin.

Jim is still very active in the super senior program, not only as a player but also as a USTA volunteer and committee member of many senior tennis organizations. In addition, he's especially proud of forming a senior association, separate from the USTA, started in 1973 with seven members which grew to over 800. Its "mission" was to start and direct senior tournaments, publish a newsletter and celebrate victories with an annual awards banquet.

Jim has a bounce to his step, a ready wit and sunny attitude about life. I think it's all because he has found his fountain of youth: senior tennis.

CHAPTER 14:

JOHN JAMES

John James, a tall, fit, unassuming Australian, is one who knows the game of tennis and how to play it. Born on March 7, 1951 in Adelaide, Australia, his parents introduced him to the game at an early age.

"I think I was four or five, and I'd tag along when they played," he said. "The game certainly interested me, and I started hitting tennis balls against the wall of our brick house. But I didn't start taking tennis lessons until I was nine or ten. My first teacher was Clem Teague, who worked at *The Advertiser of South Australia,* but also coached tennis and gave lessons on behalf of the newspaper. He took an interest in me, and sometimes he'd take me with him to give clinics, mostly in schools in southern Australia. We'd travel by plane, a DC-3, all over the Outback to small country towns."

"How exciting was that for a twelve-year old boy?"

"Very… and I remember the kids were jealous that I was able to get time off from school."

I first learned of Australia's vast, remote interior land comprising 2.5 million square miles and very few people when reading Colleen McCullough's fascinating book *The Thorn Birds* many years ago. I don't remember much of the plots, but I do remember the harsh, hot climate, the fires, the infestation of mosquitos, the drenching downpours washing out what roads there were, the isolation, the cattle stations and enormous farms of thousands of acres. Certainly the best and most efficient way to travel was by air.

John went to the Adelaide Boys High School, playing on its tennis team while there.

"The top four ranked junior players in the State of South Australia were at our school, so we had an unbeatable tennis team," he said. "These four players, including me, played for the state team in nationwide Linton Cup competition. With Neil Higgins, who was a high school teammate, we won the Australian Open junior doubles in 1969. Peter Smith was also a teammate on that team, and he later became Lleyton Hewitt's coach."

After graduating from high school, John worked for two years, first for a clothing manufacturer and second for the Royal Automobile Association in the accounting department. On weekends he taught tennis.

"Adelaide wasn't a big tennis center then," John said. "People played a lot but there were few who took it to the international level. In the 1950's, Ken McGregor and Adrian Quist were top international players who called Adelaide their home but no known players after them.

"After the two years of work I had saved up enough money to travel to Europe and England, and I stayed abroad from April through September in 1971. I didn't do too well. I had never played on clay before and struggled. But, I did well on the Australian grass court circuit and travelled back to Europe in 1972 having a little more success this time.

"In 1973, I played at Wimbledon losing in the final of the qualifiers but because of the players' boycott organized by the new players' union [Association of Tennis Professionals]

John James

which I hadn't joined yet, I was accepted into the first round where I lost in five, tough sets to Harald Elschenbroich of Germany. To play at Wimbledon had been a childhood dream. Even though I got into the tournament because of the boycott, it was still a big thrill.

"After Wimbledon, I traveled to the United States," he continued. "Because of my experience playing in Europe I did well on the American clay, even though the U.S. clay was much quicker. In 1973, after the ATP's successful boycott, we saw an awesome change in how players were treated and tournaments were organized. It was all much fairer."

John played in all the majors: the Australian Open twelve times, Wimbledon five times, the French three times and the U.S. Open eight times, playing first on grass and clay at Forest Hills, then on hard courts at Flushing Meadows.

"Did you play some of the top-ranked players at any time?"

"I played all of the top players of that era including Bjorn Borg, John McEnroe, Jimmy Connors, Ivan Lendl, Guillermo Vilas, Stan Smith, Ilie Nastase and Vitas Gerulaitis."

John, in a very laid-back, modest tone, began his tale of wins and losses against the top players in the world.

"In 1974, I played Jimmy Connors at Bretton Woods in New Hampshire and lost 6-3, 6-3 but at the time he was No.

1 in the world. I had never played a No. 1 player before. I had another chance to play him in 1978 in Tulsa, Oklahoma. Again, Connors won, but the score was a bit closer, 7-6, 6-3. And I had a good win over Ilie Nastase at the Queen's Club in the U.K., 9-8, 7-5 in, I think, 1977. The match was played in the early years of the tie breaker which I won at 8-all," John added to explain the strange score.

"I played John McEnroe twice in singles and several times in doubles with my partner, Kim Warwick. Once we played against McEnroe and Peter Fleming in the semis of the Tournament of Champions at Forest Hills after the U.S. Open moved to Flushing Meadows. It was a close, well-played match, but we lost 7-5 in the third set. In 1975 for the U.S. Open I teamed up with Rolf Thung of the Netherlands as my doubles partner. We were a pick-up team, and we had to play Ilie Nastase and Jimmy Connors in the first round. We lost, but the experience was well worth it."

Rolf happened to be visiting his sister again in April, 2016 and had a chance to stop by Chestnut Ridge Racquet Club where John worked to reminisce, particularly about their careers in the 1970's and the match against Nastase and Connors.

"We like to think we gave them a good warm up as Nastase and Connors won the title defeating Tom Okker and Marty Riessen in the final," said Rolf.

"I played Bjorn Borg twice," John continued. "I lost to him 7-6, 6-4 in the second round of the U.S. Open at Forest Hills in 1977, the last time the Open was played at Forest Hills. But I had a win over Borg in Sydney, Australia in December 1974 at a lead-up tournament to the Australian Open. The score was 6–4, 6–3, and all I remember of the match was being very nervous on the final point. I served wide to his forehand into the deuce court, and fortunately, he missed the return.

"After the Borg win, I jumped from No. 220 on the world rankings to about 130. I followed that with some more good results and was steadily moving higher. Later that year, I played at Forest Hills where there's a big board in the men's locker room listing the top one hundred players. I was expecting to see my name, but it wasn't included. I learned later that the Sydney tournament where I had beaten Borg had been removed from the ATP records. The ATP Board had decided that the Sydney tournament did not meet the minimum $25,000 U.S. total prize money requirement to receive points as the Australian dollar had dropped in value at that time, and the exchange rate put it below $25,000 U.S."

John's best year on the tour was in 1979, when he cracked the top 100 in singles and top 50 in doubles. He reached three of his nine career ATP doubles finals also in 1979 and won two ATP doubles titles – Hobart, Australia in 1980 with Chris Kachel, and, appropriately, in Adelaide in 1981 with Colin Dibley.

"I've got a story about when I played Ken Rosewall in Washington, D.C. in the summer of '77," he continued. "Rosewall had announced that he would be retiring after playing in the U.S. Open later in the summer. In recognition of Rosewall's remarkable career, the D.C. tournament director decided to declare the night we played, *The Ken Rosewall Night*. My match was played on center court with a large audience in attendance. Of course nobody wanted me to win, but I gave Ken a good game anyway, losing 6-4, 6-4 in the first round. I saw Ken many years later at the Australian Open, and we had a good chat about the match."

"Do you go to Melbourne often?" I asked.

"I go every year. It happens that my mother's birthday is January 19th, the same time that the Australian Open is being played. My Mom is 102 years old now and doing very well. She lived alone in her home until three years ago when she went into an aged care facility near my sister Jill who visits frequently."

"Any other stories of places you played or players you've competed against?"

"I was in Tehran, Iran in 1979 playing with Mansour Bahrami, an Iranian, just before the Shah was deposed. I didn't see much of the city, but the people I saw were very poor. And we were playing the tournament at the Shah's country club. The contrast was stark.

"And then there was the time I was playing in a tournament in Cincinnati, Ohio, during that summer's worst heat wave. In those days, play was not stopped because of the heat. I play the South African player Bob Hewitt in the second round. He wins the first set 6-2, and I win the second set 6-2. We went right into the third set without a break. I'm to serve first. I towel off, and when I turn around to serve, Hewitt wasn't there. I look over at his bench; not there. Then I see him on the side line, and he says, 'That's it. I retire.'

"In the next round I played Cliff Richey. Cliff is scrappy, has stamina, is always in great shape and never gives up. We split sets, and the same thing happened. Cliff retired! And he's from Texas where it's always hot. I guess that's one way for me to advance in a tournament. I got to the quarters and lost to Harold Solomon.

"One year, to make a living, I played in 33 tournaments, singles and doubles. And, I was playing in weekend things, too. That's not an easy schedule. I was married and when our first child, Courtney, arrived I left the tour, except for some local tournaments in Orange, New Jersey, for the national grass courts, Boston at the Longwood Cricket Club for the national doubles and the tournament in Washington, D.C. I left the tour in 1981 and have been a teaching pro ever since."

"After you left the tour did you play in any senior events?"

"Before I got to the seniors, which starts when you reach the age of 35, I played in lots of little tournaments in clubs like this on weekends. When I turned 35, Lloyd Emmanuel, a local pro, invited me to compete in the Masters Series tournaments that he was promoting. I ended up winning 18 straight singles tournaments."

"That's a pretty good record," I commented.

John smiled and continued, "Then I played in the 45's and did well."

Actually John did very well. He was No. 1 in the Eastern 35s and 45s every year he entered, and he was ranked No. 1 nationally in the men's 35s in 1986.

"It seems that there's a drop off in tournament entries between the 45s and 55s," I said. "Would you attribute that to men having careers and family obligations?"

"It was for me," John said. "I have three children - Courtney, J.J. and Billy. They're grown now and on their own, so it's easier to play in the Atlantic Coast Cup, for instance."

"What is it that makes tennis special for you?" I asked.

"That's hard to answer because there are so many things that I enjoy about the game. First, as the USTA website says, 'It's the game of a lifetime.' And that's so true. As you get older you have to change your game and do different things, but that adds to the mental part of the game. What's my best strategy now? And, the game is more physical too. With the new racquets, it's more of a power game. You have to train harder to be faster and stronger. "

"Are you still playing in the seniors?" I asked.

"Yes, but I don't play in the national events because it requires so much traveling and time, but I love the team events. In the Eastern section we have what's called the Atlantic Coast Cup where we play teams from New England, Middle States and Mid-Atlantic. The tournaments last two days and it's good competition. The Atlantic Coast Cup matches are all played on Har Tru. I stay away from competing too much on hard courts – they're too tough on the body at my age."

"Do you see more seniors playing tennis at Chestnut Ridge?"

"I do. I'm teaching more seniors now. Teaching them is a unique challenge. We work on different things - anticipating where the shots will be coming from, what kinds of shots. I work on seeing things earlier, which is a part of anticipation too. The basic skills are extremely important for seniors just as they are for the younger players. If you don't have the basic skills, it'll be hard. I also teach them new strategies to make up for loss of speed and agility. Today, there are so many seniors who are playing for their own enjoyment, not for competition, and regardless of their skill level, they're having a great time.

"We also have a lot more seniors' activities at Chestnut than we did in the past - doubles leagues, mixed doubles leagues; USTA-sponsored 8.0 teams, 9.0 teams. It's all good for the growth of tennis."

"Do you have some tips for senior tennis players?"

"First, the basics are most important: watch the ball, move your feet, prepare the racquet," he said. "If you can do those three things your tennis will improve. Of course seniors have trouble with movement, but they develop shots that are useful such as the drop shot and lob or the slicing and dicing that throws opponents off their games."

I've known John for many years and knew that he played some big time tennis, but I never recognized the full extent of his career. He has always been too modest to go into any detail. I'm glad I got him to open up.

CHAPTER 15:

HARLAN STONE and JONATHAN BATES

"I was a tennis rat when I was a kid," admitted Jon Bates of his early days in the sport in New Canaan, Connecticut. "My mother would drop me off at the courts in the morning with $1 to buy a coke and a sandwich, and I'd stay well into the night to watch the men when they'd come to play after work."

Jon's inspiration during those early years was Keith Jennings, who was an assistant pro at the New Canaan Field Club, where he and his family were members.

"The assistant pros - I think there were two or three - didn't give many lessons, but they were available to hit with us kids, and I remember every day asking Keith, 'Will you hit? Will you hit?' Keith was amazing. While he was at the Field Club in 1965, he played at Forest Hills at the U.S. National Championship and got to the third round. We all went down to watch the third round match against Charlie Pasarell. Pasarell beat him 6-2, 6-3, 6-2, but it was a good match, and he ended up being ranked in the top 20 in the country that year."

Born July 7, 1953, Jon first became interested in tennis through his mother, Marcia, still active and healthy at 94. Marcia happened to be the granddaughter of the 10th Governor of Washington State, Roland Harley, and she began playing tennis on the court at the Governor's mansion. Tennis became her passion and while a student at Whitman College in Walla Walla, Washington, she was No. 1 on the women's tennis team.

Jon, looking somewhat skeptical, added, "At least, that's the family story. Not many colleges or universities had women's teams back in the 1940's."

Marcia remained passionate, and when the family moved to New Canaan in 1955, she was a charter member of the New Canaan Field Club, played on the women's team, headed the junior tennis program and started Jon playing the game when he was five.

"Fortunately she didn't teach me her strokes as she was a one-sider and couldn't hit the low balls to her backhand."

But still, Jon wasn't totally committed to tennis when he was nine or so. He loved baseball too, and played on a Little League team and on an All-Star team that almost made it to the Connecticut World Series finals. His first sanctioned tournament was a 14-and-under New England tournament, where he nervously lost 9-7 in the third set. Of course he was disappointed, but a gentleman who had been watching the match came up to him after and said, "You're just as good as he is, but you played too tight."

The tournament, however, helped him become more committed to tennis. As a freshman at New Canaan High School, the home of powerhouse tennis in the area, he made the freshman team - "freshmen couldn't try out for varsity," he explained.

But the match that convinced him that tennis was his sport came during a 16-and-under New England junior

Harlan Stone (left) with Jon Bates
at Stone's offices

tournament played at the Longmeadow Cricket Club in Massachusetts. Jon wasn't seeded and had to play the No. 3 seed, Jeff Smith, in the second round. Jon was down 6-0, 5-1, 40-15. His opponent had two match points, and Jon was a whisker away from defeat. Chances of pulling out the game were next to zero. But, Jon decided to concentrate on one point at a time. One by one. He broke serve, then held serve and continued to grind. His opponent began to choke, missing shots he usually handled well. Finally, Jon prevailed and won the match.

"That's when I knew I was a player," explained Jon.

He lost in the semis to a top junior, Fred Steiner, but that year he was ranked No. 8 in New England 16-and-under, a proud accomplishment. Back at New Canaan High School as a sophomore, he made varsity. The team was unstoppable and won the Connecticut State tournament. Jon graduated in June of 1971 and that fall, he entered Amherst College as a freshman – the same time that his future senior doubles partner Harlan Stone was making New Canaan's freshman team.

An economics major, Jon not only played on the freshman tennis team, but he also played soccer. He decided not to go out for basketball at Amherst, but to spend "the winter working on academics." However, his gym teacher, Coach Ed Serues, who watched him play squash for the first time, had other ideas. "Play on our freshman team," he encouraged, and Jon agreed. So much for working on the academics. He started the year at No. 9 and worked his way up to No. 1 by season's end.

"The varsity squash team was No. 2 in the country my sophomore year when I played at No. 5," Jon said.

By his junior year, Jon whittled down his athletic activities to tennis and squash. During the summer of 1974, between his junior and senior years at Amherst, Jon joined his good friend Randy Adam, who had left New Canaan High School for Colgate, and together they traveled to Europe to play tennis. They entered a couple of tournaments, first in Great Britain. These were pre-satellite days, but the young Americans were welcomed warmly by Brits and others, who opened their homes in Liverpool, England, Oslo, Norway, Copenhagen, Denmark and elsewhere.

Of course, early July brings Wimbledon to the world, and Jon and Randy had tried to notify the tournament committee to announce their availability to try and qualify. But, sadly, they never heard back from the committee. Undeterred, they arrived at Wimbledon in their jeans and T-shirts and tried to convince the committee in person.

"Sorry, boys. You can't play in the qualifiers. But how about trying to qualify for a linesman's position?"

"Sure," they said.

After one day of training, Randy and Jon were welcomed to Wimbledon as official linesmen. In their blue blazers and official badges, they were given five pounds a day to spend - but only on the Wimbledon grounds. They were sent off to the back courts to call lines – Jon, however, did make it to Court No. 3 and later was to call lines on Centre Court, but rain destroyed his chance. He remembered calling the service line for one of

Ken Rosewall's matches on Court 3, and Rosewall giving him a dirty look. Jon was mollified by a spectator who said, "Don't worry. You were right."

He remembered, too, calling lines for one of Tom Gorman's matches. At one point, Gorman gave him a quizzical look, but later confided in him "I was just trying to intimidate you so you might give me a good call the next time."

Actually, the Wimbledon tournament committee was delighted to have Randy and Jon calling lines, as many of the linesmen/women were quite old. During one match, Jon noticed that an elderly woman calling the center service line had fallen asleep.

"I don't know how long she had been asleep, but when I approached to wake her up, it was obvious she was in a deep sleep."

After the first week of Wimbledon, Randy went off to play in a tournament in Belgium, and Jon had made arrangements to meet his girlfriend, Abby, a junior at Smith College, who was singing with the Smith Chamber Singers in Paris. After the week's separation, Jon and Randy caught up with each other in Copenhagen, Denmark, for a tournament. Then they went on to Hanko, Finland and Oslo, Norway to enter tournaments, finishing their odyssey in Great Britain for one final chance to win a trophy. And, to his surprise, Jon won. Not only that, but there was prize money - 50 pounds that kept him solvent until returning home. What a grand way to travel throughout Europe with homes opened by gracious hosts, reasonable expenses and weeks of competitive tennis to hone their skills.

Back at Amherst for his senior year, Jon was captain of both the squash team and the tennis team. Under his leadership, the squash team was ranked No. 8 in the country, and though his tennis team didn't fare as well, Jon was undefeated at No. 1 singles going into the New England Intercollegiate Tennis

Championship. He made it to the final in singles, losing to Harvard's No. 1, Gary Reiner.

"It was a disappointment, of course, but I won the 'inner game,'" summed up Jon, referring to a phrase made famous by Tim Gallwey's book *The Inner Game of Tennis*. If you play your game, and you play it well, you've triumphed mentally despite a loss.

Jon and Abby both graduated in 1975; Abby started law school at Northeastern University and Jon became a history teacher, which he loved, at Applewild School, a small, independent school in Fitchburg, Massachusetts. And, in June, 1976, they were married in Gladstonen, New Jersey, with the reception following at Abby's home in nearby Califon. In the fall, the young couple took advantage of the faculty housing at Applewild, and spent their summers at the Oak Hill Country Club, where Jon was the tennis pro.

Wanting to try something different, Jon left Applewild after three years of teaching and joined the Merchants National Bank of Leominster in Leominster, Massachusetts as assistant to the President. However, he realized that teaching was his true passion.

"What do you most enjoy about teaching?" I asked.

"Many things. I enjoy working with and simply being around 12 - 15 year-olds. Helping students to understand new concepts, or to overcome areas of trouble, or to become better athletes, is rewarding. I treasure the freedom and trust to plan my own classes and practices. I appreciate and thrive on being able to work with motivated and dedicated colleagues, many of whom are also good friends. And I particularly love the academic year - the beginning and end of each school year. What could be better than having the summers off to play tennis!"

With that in mind Jon left the Leominster bank, and, in the fall of 1981, joined the faculty of the Greenwich Country

Day School as a math teacher in the 7th, 8th and 9th grades, where he continues to teach today.

As Abby's practice as a real estate and trust and estates lawyer grew, and Jon continued his teaching, the family grew too. First came Robert, born in 1981, then William in 1984 and Elizabeth in 1987.

Jon's long-time senior doubles partner Harlan Fiske Stone, was named after the 12th Chief Justice of the U.S. Supreme Court, but he's not related to him. Harlan's father and mother decided their new son, born on August 27, 1957, needed a name of distinction and Harlan Fiske Stone fit perfectly.

Harlan started playing tennis on a regular basis in the fifth grade, when he often rode his bike four miles after school to the Kings Highway tennis facility in Darien, Connecticut, where Craig Mielke, a well-respected tennis and paddle tennis player and professional, was in charge. At first, Harlan was torn between tennis and the other sports he loved - baseball and basketball - like so many boys that age.

"But when I turned 12 or 13, I fell in love with tennis," explained Harlan. "I really got into doubles, which is unusual, as most kids start out with singles and stay there. But I met up with Phil Dukes, a player two years older than I, and we clicked."

Phil, tall and lanky with a mass of curly hair reined in by a bandanna, had a home-grown, unorthodox game, but he was an All-American in college at the University of South Carolina.

"He and I played almost every day for four years, and as we got better in high school, we became regulars in a men's doubles league that Craig Mielke started."

Their doubles skills were so good that in 1981 they were ranked No. 2 in New England men's doubles. Harlan also played tennis for New Canaan High School's formidable team.

"When I was there the team never lost," Harlan said. "We might lose an individual match, but never a team match. All of us went on to play Division I college tennis."

After graduating in 1975, Harlan chose to attend the University of Virginia.

"UVA is excellent academically, and I wanted a warmer climate. And, the University gave me a full scholarship. I played tennis all four years, starting at No. 7 in singles, but worked my way up to No. 4 my senior year. UVA was good but we never won the ACCs [Atlantic Coast Conference]. North Carolina always came out on top. During the summers, I played with my good buddy, Craig Mielke, and we won some invitationals together. But the best invitational was the Manursing Island Tournament in Rye, New York. The competition was always excellent, pulling in college players and recent graduates still playing top tennis. At Manursing, I played with Jon, winning three times, in 1974, 1976 and 1978. This was the beginning of our doubles career together. And I won again in 1982 with another good Connecticut player Jay Gepfert.

"I know how to pick good partners," added Harlan with a smile.

The Manursing tournament was the brainchild of Alby Collins, a longtime member of the Manursing Club and a tennis player himself, who started it in memory of Tommy Richardson, the younger brother of Ham Richardson. Tommy, dying too young from diabetic complications, was an excellent player but not as good as Ham, who won the NCAA singles twice in the early '50's while at Tulane, became a Rhodes Scholar and studied at Oxford in England while he managed to find time for tennis and achieved the No. 1 ranking in the U.S.

The tournament is still played and is open to all, gathering entries from college players, ranked players, seniors and others. Ham often played in the tournament and served as the main speaker at the Saturday night dinners.

After graduating from UVA in 1979, a serious job search began for Harlan.

"My Dad was a TV commercial cameraman and director and got to know Joe Cullman, an avid tennis player, and also the CEO of Phillip Morris, the cigarette manufacturer," he said. "My Dad thought he could get me an interview with Mr. Cullman. Sure enough, he did, so I went on the interview thinking it was for a job at Phillip Morris, which I wasn't too excited about. But I wasn't going to turn down an opportunity like this. So, I go to the interview and after introductions Mr. Cullman pulls a tennis racquet out of his desk drawer. He stands up and starts swinging the racquet and asks, 'How do I get good top spin on the ball?' The rest of the interview was all about tennis with me showing him how to get top spin and other finer points of the game. Mr. Cullman was great and easy to talk to. Out of the blue he says, 'How would you like to work for me? I'm chairman of the International Tennis Hall of Fame, and we need a good fund raiser. You would work here in New York City in our Phillip Morris offices.'"

Harlan accepted the offer and worked for the Hall of Fame for a year. Harlan's most striking memory of his time with the Hall of Fame occurred when he and his future wife Susan, his girlfriend at the time, had to dress in 1890's tennis attire and hand out flyers in front of Madison Square Garden for a tennis event going on inside.

"It was two degrees outside, and we were freezing!" Harlan said. "We'd run into the Stadium for hot chocolate whenever we could."

Harlan then joined John Korff, a tennis promoter, who ran women's tour events, most famously in Mahwah, New Jersey.

"I stayed with John for 18 months and then started my own business, Stone Sports."

Harlan, then only 24 years old, convinced the owner of the New Canaan Racquet Club, an indoor sports facility in New Canaan, to give him court time and seed money to promote a senior tournament featuring tennis greats, Rod Laver, Stan Smith, Ken Rosewall, Ilie Nastase, Roy Emerson, Bob Lutz, Cliff Drysdale and others. Harlan named the event the Merrill Lynch Tennis Classic, and for 14 years Harlan ran it, adding the Saw Mill Racquet Club, another sports facility in Mt. Kisco, New York, as a second venue. These players, enjoying center stage again, showed the crowd how senior tennis should be played. And, in the relaxed atmosphere, the players entertained their audience with friendly wisecracks about their opponents' games and other highjinks. The Aussies, once the matches were over, settled down with 32 ounce cans of Fosters beer. I remember the events well, having enjoyed being a spectator many times. And what *hutzpah* Harlan had to put this all together at the mellow age of 24.

In 1985, Harlan sold his business to *Golf Digest-Tennis* and subsequently joined *Octagon,* a global sports and entertainment marketing company, rising through the ranks to become its president, then switching to *Velocity,* another sports marketing firm for six years, before taking a position with the USTA in 2008 as Chief Business Officer.

Once again, in 2011, having the urge to own his own business, Harlan started *SJX Partners, Inc.,* a sports and entertainment marketing firm.

"We represent properties - the U.S. Open, Cirque de Soleil, the Ryder Cup, Little League Baseball and Lincoln Center and others. Basically, we find corporate sponsors for their events. My partner, Jeff Jonas, was my right hand man at Octagon. He moved with me to Velocity and came with me when I started SJX. Jeff and I are now 50-50 partners at SJX.

"Actually I've really been lucky with long-term partnerships. My partner in marriage, Susan, and I have been married 31 years; my business partner Jeff and I have been working together for more than 25 years, and my tennis partner, Jon Bates, and I have been playing together since the late '80's."

Harlan and Susan's three children, Zack, 28, Sam, 25, and Leanne, 23, all play tennis, but only Sam played tennis in college at Franklin & Marshall. Zack played baseball at Williams, and Leanne was an All-American lacrosse player at Washington & Lee.

"I'm very proud of them. Now Zack is a music agent in California, Sam coaches tennis and squash at a prep school in Connecticut, and Leanne teaches with Teach for America in Charlotte, North Carolina."

I asked Harlan to tell me about his senior doubles career.

"I found my tennis soul-mate, Jon Bates. We have great fun together, and our skills mesh well. Jon's really better than I am - always consistent. I'm a little streaky, but I have a good return of serve, overhead and volley, all so important in doubles. Over the years, we enter as many as eight to ten tournaments a year; currently we're No. 1 in New England in the 50's and 55s. We've played some 20 - 25 national tournaments - in the beginning we were just cannon fodder for the early rounds, but more recently we've managed to get to some quarters in big events and won several national category II tournaments."

Category II tournaments are a level below the national tournaments. If you do well in these lower-level tournaments, you can usually get a good seeding for the national events. Then you avoid meeting the first seed in the first round.

On June 7, 2015, I was at a Category II tournament in New Haven, Connecticut and watched Bates and Stone play the final in the 50 & over against Jeff Clark from Lancaster, Pennsylvania and Al Hernandez from Yardley, Pennsylvania. The tournament director seeded Bates and Stone No. 1 in the 50s draw. Interestingly, they weren't even seeded in the 55-and-over draw. Go figure.

As I was watching, Bates and Stone were down 2-5 in the first set. I heard Stone yell out in frustration, "I'm missing everything!"

Jon quickly, but calmly, replied, "Good return though."

I thought 'That's a good team.' When one player is not playing his game, the other offers encouragement by mentioning what he did well.

Bates and Stone won the second set, but lost in a tight third set. Then, after a short break, they were back on the court playing the final of the 55s, which they won easily.

After the match, I arranged to meet with them together at Harlan's office to learn more about their doubles career.

Jon and I arrived at Harlan's office at about the same time, and we were escorted by one of his assistants, a very attractive, young black woman, who led us to a conference room.

"Harlan will be right here."

Shortly, the door opens and a burst of energy in the form of Harlan, dressed in jeans and a polo shirt, sails through. A big smile on his face, he was eager to talk about his and Jon's tennis exploits.

"Remember the New England Open doubles tournament we played a few years ago?" Harlan asked Jon to start their remembrances of their doubles career.

"It was 2009, and we played some college kids, I think, from Sacred Heart in Fairfield," said Jon. "I was 57 then and Harlan was 52."

"We were playing indoors in the finals, and the lighting was pretty bad," Harlan said. "Every time our opponents served, their ball toss was lost in the lights. We never saw a serve. Not one! These boys were licking their chops thinking 'These old guys don't have a chance.' But, somehow we got enough serves back by just blocking the ball, and we took over from there. The kids didn't know doubles strategy, got frustrated and we won the match."

Without prompting, Harlan and Jon went on to another story.

Jon asked, "Remember the National 45-and-over Hard Courts? We played in Westlake Village, California."

Harlan nodded.

"We flew in that morning, rented a car and drove to the tournament, arriving two hours before our first match."

Harlan continued, "We're always arriving at the last minute. But, we play the match. We're down two breaks in the first set, but we manage to win in straight sets. We were finally warmed up. In that tournament, we got to the quarters, and we're serving for the match at 5-4 in the third set. I hit a volley crosscourt right on the outside line. The fellow at the net who was right there when the ball lands starts to walk to the net with his hand extended when we hear his partner, who was standing in the far back court, yell 'Out!' We couldn't believe it. And the guy at the net backed up his partner. I think he did it reluctantly because the guy in the back court was one of the top players, better than he was, and he felt he had to support his partner's call. We were livid and finally called a referee who had us play the last game at deuce. We did, and we lost both points and ultimately the match."

Jon added, "What a disappointment. Generally, line calls in senior tennis are good, but apparently this fellow had a reputation."

Continued Harlan, "So a few years later we play the USTA National 50s tournament in Santa Barbara, and this guy is in the tournament. He and the same partner are on our side of the draw, and we think, 'Ok, now we will get our revenge.'"

"Unfortunately," Jon continued. "Harlan pulled a calf muscle, and we lost."

"Have you ever won a gold ball?" I asked.

"No. We haven't even won a bronze ball," said Jon. "But every time we've played in Philadelphia - we've played four or five times there - in both the 45s and 50s, we've lost to the winning team. Bad draws I guess. You know we have our day jobs, both are demanding, so we don't get to play as much as some of these other guys, who can get away and spend more time on the courts. But once, we thought we had the perfect draw."

Jon continued, "We were playing in the National 55 clay courts in Savannah, Georgia. We check the draw and notice that on our side of the draw we had beaten every seeded team, so we thought this is our chance! We're gonna win this tournament - or at least get into the finals."

Harlan picked up on the story: "So the No. 1 seed in the tournament calls the tournament director a half hour before he's to play and says he can't make it. Unfortunately for us, the USTA rule is that if no matches have been played and the player pulling out of the tournament is seeded in a national tournament, which this was, the draw had to be redrawn! We didn't know this call had been made. We're just waiting at our court to start when one of the volunteers comes to the court and removes the names of the players about to step on the court. 'What's going on?' we ask and learn about the rule and the need to redo the draw. Can you believe it?"

Jon, good humoredly, ended the story. "The new draw couldn't have been much worse for us, and we lost in the second round to the best team in the tournament. But, we won five games, which was more than anyone else got against them."

Laughing, they continued.

"Here's another good one," Harlan chimed in. "Jon and I were playing in the finals of the 45 doubles of the National Public Parks Tournament, a category II, in Stamford, Connecticut. It was 2004, and we're in the finals playing against the No. 1 seeds, Paul Moss and Michael Curry. They hit a lob deep, and I turn to chase it down, running at full speed, but I totally forget about the light poles that were positioned near the back of the court. I'm like a cartoon character banging into the pole, saying, 'Ok, bring it on. The more you hit me the better I am.' We beat them in straight sets anyway, and they ended up No. 1 in the country that year."

Harlan and Jon then recalled a Category II 50s tournament in Wheeling, West Virginia.

"We made it to the finals, but because of rain delays we didn't play till late Saturday," said Jon. "The problem was that the next day was Father's Day, and we *had to* get home to celebrate 'our day' with our families."

Fortunately, they focused on their game during the match and didn't worry about the logistics of getting home. They won, but realized they had missed their plane and would have to make other arrangements.

"We decide to rent a car," Harlan said. "We leave Wheeling at 9 pm, we take turns driving and listen endlessly to WFAN on the radio to keep awake, finally arriving home at 4 am, but in time to enjoy being spoiled by our kids."

The boys seemed to be enjoying themselves as they recollected some of their favorite stories, laughing and bantering as they went along.

"One other story," added Jon. "Back to 2010, I played with Wade Frame in the National 55 grass courts at the West Side Tennis Club in Forest Hills, New York, because Harlan was not old enough. In the quarterfinals, we were in a third set tie-breaker when a massive storm with menacing dark clouds appeared out of nowhere. Perhaps trying to get the match over quickly, we end up losing. As we were in the showers, we heard thunder and crashing trees and rattling windows as a microburst struck. The wind caused total devastation in a short five minutes - windows were blown out, trees fell onto the courts, furniture flew about, courts were destroyed, and we were stranded at the club until midnight."

Harlan added, "It was fortunate that the U.S. Open had been completed. Even so, the storm caused over $1 million in damage to the USTA National Tennis Center.

"Once in a while we're held up by injuries," Harlan continued. "Actually, Jon never gets hurt, but I manage to slam into poles and things like that. So, I've had three neck fusions, a left shoulder arthroscopy, a left knee arthroscopy and a left hip replacement."

"Don't forget the cramping," said Jon.

"Right. Three years ago we were playing in Concord, Massachusetts, where it was brutally hot, and I went into a full body cramp. The pain was excruciating! We took a break in the match, and another player in the tournament - who happened to be a doctor - recommended that I drink pickle juice. I was willing to try anything, so I drank the pickle juice and 20 minutes later I was back on the court, and we won the tournament!"

I interrupted and asked, "With all the injuries and problems with draws and missing flights, what is it that keeps you playing senior tennis?"

Harlan didn't hesitate to answer.

"We love playing together. We match up well. Jon's the steady one, and my return, volley and overhead are very effective in seniors play. We encourage each other. I can't ever remember having a disagreement."

"I can't either," said Jon. "We encourage each other all the time. And I love that people enjoy watching us play because we know doubles and we know how to play. I probably wouldn't play if I didn't have Harlan as my partner. We have some kind of chemistry. And we're not hyper-serious about the matches. Sure we want to win, but if we have a loss it's definitely not the end of the world."

Harlan continued, "And we really like to compete. We like the exercise and the challenges of the game. You know, Jon and I play singles against each other to get ourselves ready for a tournament, and we don't give an inch. We're fiercely competitive even against each other. And the camaraderie is important, especially in the team matches. Our favorite tournaments are the team matches. During the Nationals, we don't seem to have time to socialize, but the team matches are different."

Harlan said that his favorite event is the "Play in May" event that he started in the 1990s, to benefit the Norwalk Grassroots Tennis program in Norwalk, Connecticut.

"It's the largest inner city program for kids in Connecticut, and every May we play the 'Play in May' event," Harlan said. "We always have eighty to a hundred teams enter; the teams are divided into flights according to the team's ability, and we make a lot of money for the kids."

"And you know, there's another plus to senior tennis," Harlan interjected. "It's not something we generally think about, but I have a friend who is the pro at the Longwood Cricket Club in Brookline, Massachusetts, who told me about this very good senior player at his club. The man is being overtaken by dementia, but that doesn't stop him from playing tennis. He may forget the score, but his partner helps him with that, and his strokes, strategy, finesse and athleticism are still fine."

As we concluded the interview and I prepared to leave, Harlan, pushed back his chair to stand and said, "You know. I don't care if this never gets published, but I've had a helluva time remembering all the fun we've had playing together."

Jon nodded in agreement.

CHAPTER 16:

CHRIS and BILL DRAKE

The energy level was soaring. Nine college tennis teams were participating in the Dartmouth Invitational tennis tournament - Yale, Brown, Williams, West Point, Middlebury, Buffalo, Fairfield, Amherst and the host, Dartmouth.

Belly bumps, high fives, shouts of encouragement, hand slaps, fists, blistering serves down the T, fast feet, deep, precision shots – it was all happening on the six courts of the Boss Tennis Center in Hanover, New Hampshire. Testosterone was flowing freely, and Chris Drake, Dartmouth's men's varsity tennis coach, was in total control patrolling the courts, offering advice to his players, encouraging each Dartmouth team member, watching closely from the visitors' section and finding time to write down all the scores, getting the next match out on the courts and finding time to see his top player, senior Dovydas Sakinis, playing in another tournament in Tulsa, Oklahoma via live stream on the internet.

Chris has been the Dartmouth coach since the summer of 2010. He and his father Bill are one of the best father-son doubles teams who compete in USTA father-son tournaments. We found a quiet spot in the stands where we could talk, and Chris could keep his eye on his players. We didn't have much time for small talk.

"So, Chris, when did you start playing tennis?" I asked.

"I guess I was about five when my Dad started me playing tennis," he said. "He was the pro at The Country Club in Brookline, [Massachusetts] and I'd hit with him when the courts were free. Or we'd go to the local public courts. And I went to the club's summer camp and got some tennis instruction there as well. But, I liked other sports too - baseball, soccer, basketball, golf. We lived in a great neighborhood with lots of kids in Needham, Mass., so we had no trouble getting pick-up games."

"When did you become more serious about tennis?"

"I was really small for my age but entered some of the New England junior tournaments anyway. My first big tournament was the National 12-and-under zonal tournament in Indianapolis. We played in the big RCA stadium out there, and my Dad and my opponent's Dad were the only two people in the whole stadium. But it was exciting, even if I did lose.

"I'd say when I got to high school, I began to grow a bit and focused more on tennis," Chris continued. "I played freshman and sophomore years, and during the summer between my sophomore and junior year, my mother drove me all over the country. Or at least that's what it seemed to me. I played in St. Louis, in Washington, D.C., then back to St. Louis, and I can't remember if there were other stops. But, I never even won a match. My poor Mom. We joke a lot about it now - the winningless journey - but it must have been pretty grueling for her.

"Despite those losses, with the good competition, my game was actually getting better. By the time I was in the 18's, I was among the top three in New England. So, junior

Chris Drake at Dartmouth

year I didn't play for the high school team because I was playing in national tournaments during the college recruiting season. Fortunately, I did well enough and got recruited by Brown. I was planning to rejoin my high school team for my senior year, but broke my arm playing hockey."

"Darn. Bad luck," I interjected. "Tell me a bit about your Brown years."

"I had two very good tennis friends from New England who had chosen Brown - Ben Brier and Jamie Cerritani - so that was a good start," Chris said. "Brown had a new coach, John Choboy, and we all worked well together with him. It was a fun team."

"How were your stats?"

"I started at No. 4 singles and No. 2 doubles, and my senior year I was No. 1 doubles and No. 2 singles. But, more important, during my junior year, Brown won the Ivy League title for the first time in the history of Brown tennis."

"Good for you and your team. And after college?" I asked.

"I didn't know what I wanted. But I decided I wanted to be involved in tennis, so I took a job at the Junior Academy of Tennis in Natick, Mass. I lived with some of the other young pros in Boston, but I was itching to play more competitive tennis. So, I went back home to save money and joined the satellite tour in 2003. My first exposure to the tour was a month in southern California sleeping on a friend's couch the whole month. I didn't have any ranking at the time, so I couldn't qualify for any tournaments. Finally, there was a tournament with 128 *pre-qualifiers* entered - pre-qualifiers, not qualifiers! You had to get through the pre-qualifiers before you could enter the qualifiers. I was one of the 128 pre-qualifiers and got to the semis where I lost, but I did well enough to qualify for my first qualifier tournament. Finally, I was making some progress. But I lost in the first round and headed home again.

"But I didn't give up on the satellites. My next quest took me to Ecuador, where I stayed for a month. I earned my first ATP points in singles and doubles and was off and running! First, we were in a big city, Guayaquil, and the second two weeks we were in the poorest place I'd ever seen. The poverty was everywhere, but I spent time meeting the 'locals' and had a chance to practice my Spanish. Two other players and I rented a hotel room for $12 a night. It was tight, and it was hot! Everything was hot in that little village. The temperature and humidity were in the 90's, if not more. We befriended the cab drivers and one took us to the local hot spots. The place I remember most is going to this little shanty to see a cock fight. Cock fights were really popular with the locals - probably their only entertainment. The whole experience opened my eyes as to how people live in such poverty but seem to survive.

"The tournament itself was in a new resort in the next town, and I won some more points. What I liked about satellite play was that you could enter both singles and doubles draws in the same event. I always did better in the doubles."

"Where did you go next?"

"To Ourense, Spain in the northwestern province of Galicia, just north of Portugal. I went by myself, but thankfully I had family friends from home who sponsored me without any expectation of being reimbursed. There were two tournaments, each lasting one week. Andy Murray was in both."

"Did you get to play him?"

"No. I wasn't on his side of the draw, but Andy won both tournaments. The best I did was losing in the quarters in one of the tournaments. But while I was there I recognized a kid from junior tennis, Zack Dailey, so we palled around together.

"In all, I played in Israel, Venezuela, Mexico, and many countries in Western and Eastern Europe. The competition was really good, and I could see that my game was improving. The whole experience matured me. I was living on my own. I had to arrange my schedules and learn how I would get from here to there. I had to watch my pennies for sure. And I got to meet lots of people - not only Spaniards but also young players from all over the world. Sometimes we stayed in people's homes, but mostly in hotels. My ATP points in doubles got me to No. 350 in the world, and that's when I decided to pursue doubles play."

"How long did you stay on the tour?"

"Probably two and a half to three years when I realized it was time to get serious about my future. While on the satellite tour I missed college tennis, and that's what prompted me to enter a four week 'bridge' business program at the University of Chicago. The program was designed as an introduction to business school, but it gave me enough information about running a small enterprise that when I learned that Northwestern was looking for an assistant tennis coach, I applied."

Our interview was interrupted briefly when Chris, always vigilant, looking from court to court said "Excuse me," got up and leaned over the railing to shout, "You can get errors from the other guy by hitting deeper and harder through your shot and playing more aggressively."

Not losing his train of thought, Chris continued, "When I started, the team was 0 and 11, but by the second year our record was 6 and 4, and we made it to the NCAAs. Arvid Swan was the head coach. He was very supportive, and I learned a lot from him.

"I stayed at Northwestern for three years, and in the spring of 2010 I learned that Dartmouth was looking for a head coach because Chuck Kinyon, Dartmouth's longtime coach, was retiring. Again I jumped. "

Chris got the job and started in September of 2010. He and his wife Eliza and two boys, Miles, and Theo, bought a house and began to put down roots.

"When you came to Dartmouth, what kind of shape was the team in?"

"During the period, 2000 to 2008, Dartmouth's team struggled, but in 2009 it began to improve," Chris said. "My first year the team worked hard and made it to No. 3 in the Ivy League."

"What's your teaching philosophy?" I asked.

"Getting the guys to buy into the team and working together. When a player struggles, he gets in his own way. I find that when they realize it's a team effort and that they're a part of it, it makes a difference. Also, conditioning is key. I have the guys working out on the courts. It's agility training and sprints, a strength program and balance and coordination of the various muscle groups. Proof to me that that makes a difference occurred recently at the Princeton Ivy Plus Tournament in Princeton, New Jersey. The Dartmouth players had twelve three-set matches, and we won them all. That's a pretty impressive showing."

"What about recruiting?"

"Recruiting today is, of course, very competitive. But fundraising for recruiting and other expenses has increased three times since I've been here. You were watching Roko play. He is a freshman from Zagreb, Croatia. He went to a top school there and actually reached out to us. He contacted many of the

Ivies and I think some other top universities. I knew a Croatian, Lovro Zovko, a former opponent of mine in a challenger tournament, who knew Roko. He spoke very highly of him. Roko fit the model of who did well here, and I offered him a spot on our team.

While talking, a player from one of the visiting teams was watching Roko play. He yelled to Chris, "Where'd you find this guy?" Chris joked, "Under a rock in Croatia."

"The tennis world is definitely global, but actually, it's a small community as well. You know someone who knows someone, and you make your connections."

"Tell me a little about playing father/son tournaments with your Dad?" I asked.

"I guess we started playing them when I was twelve or so," he said. "I was so small then, and he was the better player. I learned a lot about doubles from him. But by the time I was in college, the roles reversed. I had gotten bigger and better, and he relied on me rather than the other way around. We only played in the National Father/Son Grass Courts which were always held at the nearby Longwood Cricket Club. We lost to Charlie Hoeveler and his son Charles twice in the finals. You know them."

"Sure. Charlie is a Dartmouth grad."

"My biggest regret is not winning the finals for my Dad. We came close but never got the gold."

I had an appointment to meet with Chris's father Bill at The Country Club in Chestnut Hill, Massachusetts, one of the most famous clubs for golf in the United States, where Francis Ouimet famously won the 1913 U.S. Open and where the United States won the Ryder Cup in 1999.

The club's long driveway wound around the golf course, up a slight hill and led me to the courtyard with the large, wood-frame, yellow and white trimmed clubhouse its spacious porches, enclosed and open – a welcoming sight with its elegant, old school charm. I found the indoor tennis facility, a building almost one hundred years old, and entered and walked down a long corridor with off white walls that, I don't think, have ever been updated. I ended up at the tennis shop overlooking the four indoor Har-Tru courts, where Bill was busy with a women's clinic. After he was done, we sat down in his office and talked about his life and tennis career.

Bill was the son of a Navy Commander and pilot and moved all over the country in his early years, but in 1960, when he was 14, the family settled in Hanford, California, a town in the San Joaquin Valley, south of Fresno and surrounded by farming communities.

"I was always good in sports and played football and basketball in high school at Hanford High, but I had a friend, Dennis Kemble, who suggested I take up tennis," he said. "Tennis to me was a sissy sport, but I was small for football and basketball and decided to try tennis. I was introduced to the coach, Jack Sanford, and to his method of teaching tennis which was quite unique. I was hooked. Jack taught me so much about tennis, good sportsmanship and respect for the game.

"Tennis was popular at Hanford, and we had 60 boys and girls go out for the junior varsity and varsity teams. There was no girls' tennis team so they played with us on our teams, and they were good. Jack started his practices with 45 minutes of exercises: jumping rope forward and backward, jumping double ropes, running a mile, doing pull ups and pushups. The girls did everything we did, except their pushups were from the knees. Then he'd give us a 10-minute lecture about some aspect of tennis: respect for the game, certain rules, stories of the great players of the day such as Rod Laver and Ken Rosewall.

"Next came warm-ups when the varsity players went to the courts. There were six of them, all lighted. The JV players went

Bill Drake

to this massive backboard, a two-sided cement structure that ran the length of the six varsity courts. Junior varsity players never got on to the tennis courts until they made varsity, but the drills against the wall were the same: deep shots, overheads, volleys, serves - all the strokes. Practices would go on for two hours. And at the end of each school year we faced a two-hour written final exam on the rules of tennis.

"After one year of hitting against the backboard, I made varsity as a sophomore - at last, a chance to play on the courts. By junior year, I was No. 1, and our team never lost a match, in large part because the girls were so good. Our boys were good, but our girls were better. One girl, Vicky Thomas, was No. 8 in northern California, and I could never beat her until my senior year.

"We got so good that we got cocky, including me, throwing my racquet against the wall. Jack yelled out, 'Drake! Go!' which meant I was to run a mile around the school. Not only was it humiliating but while I'm running someone else takes my spot. That was the end of my racquet throwing. With Jack, sportsmanship always came first, and as a result we all became better competitors.

"We also had challenge matches every day after the drills. If you wanted to play in a higher position, you needed to win your challenges. Whoever won would get the higher seeding.

"And I have one more story about Jack Sanford. The team was preparing for the conference championship, and I had to write a paper for my history professor on *The Federalist Papers*. I hadn't finished it and told the coach that I needed to miss practice. 'Bill,' he told me, 'You can't miss practice.'

'But coach, I've gotta go work on my paper!'

'Bill. You can't miss practice.'

"I left and went to my buddies on the team and told them the situation. We agreed to confront the coach. If I couldn't play they would not play either."

"Sounds like a boycott to me. Did it work?"

"You'll see. Coach says to me, 'Bill, if you miss practice, you're off the team. If anybody misses practice, they're off the team too. I'll play the remaining games with my junior varsity if I have to.'

"I went home and told my parents. They supported my decision to miss practice. Jack was unmoved. I was out of the line up if I missed practice. So, I went to my history teacher, Mr. Christianson, a tennis groupie, and told him my dilemma. He decided that I could hand the paper in a day late. What that experience taught me was that everybody crumbled but Jack. If you're going to maintain the respect of your players, you cannot back down, no matter the consequences, if you feel you are in the right. That was another lesson for me in respect, discipline and principle.

"My senior year I really got good, especially considering I never held a racquet and didn't know how to keep score until three years before, but when you spend massive amounts of time practicing, you improve. By chance I entered the National Hard Courts in Burlingame, California, and got to the third round, where I beat Terry Neudecker, which was a huge victory.

Neudecker had a high ranking in the state and was expected to win. After the match the University of Minnesota's new tennis coach, Joe Walsh, who was scouting Neudecker, came over to me instead and offered me a scholarship to play for Minnesota. Was I interested? Of course I was interested. I lucked out, accepted his offer and went to the University of Minnesota in 1966, graduating in 1970.

"I loved Minneapolis. It's cold - really cold - in the winter, but the school had an underground tunnel system, so we never had to go outside. Dave Cross, from Rockport, Maine, was my roommate and doubles partner. We became great friends.

"During the summers of my freshman and sophomore years, I was on the teaching staff at John Gardiner's tennis facility in Carmel Valley. That was an amazing opportunity. Not only did I learn from Gardiner's way of teaching, but I also got to teach some of his star-studded clients, like Janet Leigh and Tony Curtis' daughter, Kirk Douglas' son, and Senator Perry's son. He was a senator from Illinois, and while his son was at our facility his sister was kidnapped. It was in all the papers, and we had to give extra protection to young Percy for fear of him being kidnapped too."

"Did you get to know any of the other instructors?" I asked.

"Oh yes. There was lots of camaraderie. One instructor was Vijay Amritraj, who became a top international player.

"Then for the summers following my junior and senior years, Dave and I decided to tour Europe and play some high level tennis. The first summer we toured Holland, Denmark and Germany. For the second, I contacted a European organization affiliated with the Spanish tennis circuit and learned that, if we entered pro tournaments there we could get appearance money, laundry money and free housing.

"Yeah. We can do that! So I pieced together an eight-week itinerary taking Dave and me from Barcelona down the eastern coast of Spain to its tip in the Mediterranean. What a rich experience that was. We were housed by gracious Spanish families, learned about the food and culture of Spain, cherished the girls on the beach and understood that the tennis fans' enthusiasm for their Spanish players was relentless. Even when I didn't have a prayer of winning a match against a Spaniard, the fans cheered and stamped their feet in support of their countryman. But, we got in all the tennis we wanted, had our expenses paid and forgave the fans."

Back at school, Bill captained Minnesota's team and was voted most valuable player his senior year.

"Between Joe Walsh, Jack Sanford and John Gardiner, I learned from the best and adopted much of their teaching philosophies," added Bill. "After graduating from Minnesota in 1970, I went back to California to be near my parents and to attend San Jose State for a Masters in Clinical Psychology. But, after a year and a half, I decided to move to Massachusetts where Dave Cross lived.

"It's 1972, and the tennis boom in the U.S. was picking up steam. I applied for and got the Head Pro position at the new Longfellow Racquet Club in Wayland, Massachusetts. Because the club was an indoor facility, it was only open eight months of the year. That was perfect, as it gave me four months every year to play on the tennis circuit."

"Any good stories of matches you played then?" I asked.

"In the mid 70's, I played in the U.S. Pro Championship at the Longwood Cricket Club in Chestnut Hill, Massachusetts against Bob Lutz, a top U.S. player. I was confident that I could beat him because he had bad knees. So, I win the first game - I was serving - and think 'This is my moment.' Lutz serves, I send back a good return and run to the net and hit a great volley.

Lutz runs half way across the court, hooks the ball around me for a winner just inside the baseline. I say to myself, 'That wasn't luck. This guy is really good.' I lost the match 6-1, 6-0. That's when I decided I'd have better luck playing doubles.

"Not long after that match, I was playing at Forest Hills. We're in the beginning of the Open Era, and tennis is becoming very exciting. My wife Pat and I, and my partner Bill Crohn and his wife, drive to Forest Hills on a great adventure. Bill and I sign in, and we find out that if we want to play doubles together all we have to do is sign up. We had some doubles points so we did. We were the last team to get in, and we made the cut. The next day I was sitting on the terrace in front of the West Side Tennis Clubhouse and overheard Fred Stolle, the wonderful, high-ranking Aussie, ask, 'Who the hell are Drake and Crohn? They beat Laver and me out of the draw.' I felt pretty guilty especially since we lost in three sets in the first round to Butch Seewagen and Terry Moor.

"A lot of life is just being lucky. The Boston Lobsters - owned by Bob Kraft who now owns the New England Patriots - was forming a team of Bob Hewitt, Ion Tiriac, Kerry Melville Reed, Wendy Turnbull and some other really good players, but they needed a few more and since I was local, I was picked. But, they were all far better than me and I only played when the team was either so far ahead or so far behind that my contribution wasn't going to matter.

"But, one day after practice, a team of people came up to me and said 'Bill, how would you like to do a 30-second commercial?' I was stunned but said, 'Heck yes, I'd like to do a commercial.' I spent a day in Rye, New York where 'Painted Shoes,' a thirty-second commercial for Fred Perry's tennis shoes, was being filmed. That was the most lucrative day of my career. For one day's work, I earned over $35,000 from residuals that ran for the next three years.

"Another lucky break was getting to know Fred Sharff, a sports agent for Phil Esposito, the hockey player. Fred represented some of the players on the Lobsters and I got to know him. I was a hitting partner for some of his female clients, and he suggested I get into professional coaching. Of course, this was a new venture for me, but I decide to give it a shot. My first major student was Marise Kruger from South Africa, who was the No. 1 junior player in the world. After I took her on, her ranking shot up to No. 20 in the world, and in 1975 she beat Virginia Wade, Britain's favorite women's tennis player. But, Marise got homesick, didn't like all the travel and decided to go home to South Africa to get married and have a family. I was heartbroken.

"Next Fred introduced me to Barbara Potter, a sixteen-year old from Connecticut. I gave her a week of lessons and realized she's got it. She's going to be good. And she was. I was with her for six years. She shot up to the Top 10 and got to the semis of the U.S. Open in the early 80s. The WTA [Women's Tennis Association] awarded her the most improved player, and she was chosen to play on the U.S. Fed Cup team. But being a professional coach isn't easy. You can have differences of opinions on strategy and technique, and if I'm not the boss, I can't coach. We parted ways."

"Let's talk about your senior tennis," I suggested.

"Sure. Through the 45s I played a lot of senior tennis - all the national tournaments. In 1994, when playing in the 45s, I got as high as No. 7 in the country in singles and with Doug Barrow to No. 3 in doubles. I played some, too, with Peter Bromley in the 45s, particularly on grass. Peter Bromley and I are playing in the early rounds of a Category I tournament, and Peter's pretty excitable - very competitive but excitable."

"I know Peter," I interjected. "He's like Peter Pan - always a kid and totally lovable."

"Right. So Peter and I aren't doing so well, and he says, 'Bill, we've gotta hit the ball harder.' So, I agree, and I go for my shots but they're missing long. Pete then says, 'Jesus Bill, we gotta keep the ball in play.' Our strategies didn't work very well in that match.

"Then I was playing with Doug Barrow. We both had high rankings, he in the Eastern Section and me in New England. Every time we played, we'd lose in the semis, so I said to Doug, 'We gotta split. We're just not winning together.' Doug didn't like that, but he agreed and found another partner. I did too. The next tournament, Doug and his new partner win! Doug couldn't wait to get back at me for a good ribbing, 'The minute I drop you, I win.'

"But it was said with good humor and no malice. That's what's special about senior tennis. You bust your chops to win, but when it's over, it's not competitive. It's laughs and a few good beers. We've known the other players since the juniors, we interact, and our lives are enriched."

"Now how about playing father/son with Chris?" I asked.

"I loved playing with Chris. In the beginning, in the early 1990's when Chris was only 12, I was the captain of the team. He was tiny for his age, but he was a good listener and did as I told him. Then he grew and morphed into a very good player. That's when he became the captain. We're very close as you can imagine, and it killed him when we lost three times in the finals of the father/son.

"Chris is a terrific young man, and to spend time with him, my son, playing a game we both love, is remarkable. And all the men in the tournament are experiencing the same thing - a special bond and social attachment."

With Bill turning 65, he and Chris are now in the "Super Senior Father/Son" category, which provides a new challenge.

"My goal is to get in better shape after retirement," Bill said. "Chris always stays in good playing condition especially since he gets to play with his Dartmouth team."

"What is it about senior tennis that draws the players to the game?"

"Tennis has found the fountain of youth! Really. And senior tennis is the vehicle to get you there. When you are playing good tennis at an advanced age, you feel younger. With each new body part – knees, hips – you get a new lease on life. You're reborn! And you're constantly being re-born as you advance into a higher age category. It's truly phenomenal. The genius of tennis is also the great friendships you make over time. Decades of matches and experiences you all have in common.

"With all the pressures of today's society, tennis offers a healthy outlet to relieve stress and anxiety," he continued. "The game is rewarding. It brings joy to people, especially those who improve. At whatever level or age, tennis brings youthfulnes, health, companionship and a positive attitude. I love teaching the five-year-olds, and telling them, even though it probably goes in one ear and out the other, 'You're gonna love this game forever.'"

CHAPTER 17:

MAS and SUSAN KIMBALL

Mas Kimball served a near ace wide and rushed the net to hit the winning volley when he saw the return whiz by, out of reach. The returner noticed his surprise and displayed a wide smile on her face. Yes. Mas was playing mixed doubles in a winter mixed doubles league that gathered on Sundays at Hastings-on-Hudson's courts overlooking the Hudson River in New York, just north of Manhattan. I don't know what happened during the rest of the match but Mas had decided, "I have to meet this young woman."

Meet Susan he did, and a three-year relationship followed with lots of tennis and also some skiing.

"I wasn't much of a skier until I met Mas and started skiing with him," Susan admitted. "He is an excellent skier, even a certified ski instructor."

In February of 1990, Susan and Mas treated themselves to a skiing vacation at Park City, Utah. On the third day of soft, Utah powder and bright skies Mas said, "Let's get married."

"Here?" asked Susan.

"Sure. What could be a better place?"

Susan agreed. But how does one get married in Park City on short notice? They started investigating and found that two people could marry them: the Mayor of Park City or the Justice of the Peace. The Mayor wasn't available, but they met with the Justice of the Peace.

"I can't do it tomorrow," he informed Mas and Susan, "because I promised Mrs. Kelly I'd plow her driveway. How about the day after?"

"Friday?" asked Mas looking at Susan for approval. When she nodded, he responded, "Yes. Friday is fine."

On another gorgeous "Utah day," February 23, 1990 to be specific, Mas and Susan met the Justice of the Peace at his office before their morning runs. Dressed in their best ski outfits, they stood before the Justice, a giant of a man, said their vows and were pronounced man and wife. And without hesitation they were off to the slopes.

Mas was born in Tokyo, Japan on July 14, 1949, the son of a Japanese mother and American father serving in the U.S. Army's occupation forces.

"Japanese women who married American men were not well accepted by their families and friends, but my father was enamored with the Japanese culture, and soon he, too, was welcomed. Only Japanese was spoken in the home.

"From the time I was 2 ½ to 5 ½ I was raised in a Buddhist monastery. After the war, the Buddhists provided daycare centers in many parts of Japan until the government was able to re-establish daycare centers. Many of the children lived at the centers 24/7, and I only saw my parents once or twice a month.

"We meditated twice a day, learned martial arts and developed a keen sense about how to approach life, the calm, no-frenzied way of the Buddhist monks.

Susan and Mas Kimball

"And the martial arts gave me an 'in' when my family moved to Bedford-Stuyvesant, Brooklyn. I was 6 1/2. I couldn't speak a word of English so was put into kindergarten, but I had a special skill that made me feel a bit more comfortable among so many strangers: my martial arts. That was something my classmates had never seen before, and they were in awe. I picked up the language pretty well, sailed through first grade, skipped second and was put into the third grade. From then on I was fine.

"We lived in an integrated neighborhood, which helped me fit in," he continued. "The only thing was that there were no Buddhists or Buddhist Temples, but my father was a Presbyterian, and he started taking us to his church. We went faithfully every Sunday with my sister, who was also born in Japan, and me going to Sunday School. Then as two sisters and a brother, born in the U.S., came along, they too trundled off to Sunday School. Now, I'm not a part of any organized religion, but I still follow many of the precepts of Buddhism."

"Tell me a bit about your family," I suggested.

"Well, my Dad was in the Japanese import-export business, and my Mom was a 'stay at home' Mom. She was a super talented seamstress and made *all* our clothes. She was also a gifted knitter. Two of my sisters had significant careers as ballet dancers, first with Alvin Ailey Ballet Company and then branching off to Broadway, movies and Europe. And my mother became a costume designer for Alvin Ailey as well as for some Broadway shows."

Mas excelled in high school at Brooklyn Tech, one of two schools in New York City, the other being Bronx High School of Science, that required passing an examination before entering. They were also the first schools in New York City to have computers available for the students. Computers became his passion.

"I went to City College of New York [CCNY] after high school and majored in math, the only avenue - there was no computer science degree back then - to computers. IBM had a summer program, specifically for minorities, for two summers. I went both summers. The first three weeks was class work but the rest of the summer I was out in the field. I learned so much in the field - how the computer worked, its glitches and how to fix them.

"At the end of the second summer, I got married. My wife, Ruth, was 19; I was 20. I actually needed permission from my parents in order to get a marriage license as I wasn't 21 yet. Ruth's parents were Ester and Ira Gollobin. Ira was an immigration attorney, and they were both Jewish activists. They had to testify before the House Un-American Activities Committee in Washington during Senator Joseph McCarthy's heyday, and many of their friends were blacklisted. I remember looking through a family scrapbook one day, and there, folded, was a picture of my mother-in-law on the front page of the *Daily News* with the headline, 'Ed Markey names the Gollabins the No.1 Communists in New York State.'

"That was a difficult time in our country's history," I added.

Mas nodded.

"Did you finish college?"

"Well, after the summer programs at IBM, I got a part time job with Crompton-Richmond, manufacturers of corduroy and velveteen, and began to learn the garment business. I continued to go to CCNY, but Crompton-Richmond wanted me to work full time. I took the job and went to CCNY part time, but after one year of that I dropped out, only 14 credits short of graduating.

"At Crompton-Richmond, I was first a part-time programmer starting work around 11 or 12 midnight when no one else was in the office. All the paperwork had been done and entered into the computer so I was able to finish up my projects without interruption.

"I had been managing Crompton's data processing department and decided I wanted to start my own business. I spoke to my boss, who encouraged me to stay, and even offered a good bonus. But I had made up my mind. I learned of a company that was having problems with its systems. This was just what I wanted to do: write software programs for small companies. I was about to set up my business when I got an offer from one of the leading upstart jeans companies. It was owned and run by three crazy Jews of Syrian descent whose business was going wild, and their computer system couldn't handle it. They knew they had a good product, their business was growing fast, but they were constantly putting out fires. Employee turnover in the computer department was 90%, and the office was in total disarray with the owners contributing to the chaos. I had an interview, and told them that I'd take over the computer department but that they could not set foot in my department.

"One of them says, 'Ken [CEO of Crompton-Richmond] tells me you're the best. How much do you want?' I knew that the first six months were going to be hell, probably working 18 to 20 hours a day, so, not really wanting to take the job, I came up with an outrageous salary, a car and parking privileges. 'That's a lot of money,' my future boss exclaimed. 'Well, you want the best, right?' was my reply. Without hesitation, he made his decision saying, 'You can start tomorrow.'

- "I started the next day, and over time hired new employees, fixed the software that was crashing every day and after six months stabilized the software and the department."

I asked, "Would I know the company?"

"I think so. *Bonjour Jeans*.

"With the company's continued success, it came time to start thinking of replacing our current system with one that would support a company which was growing like crazy. At that time, IBM had subcontracted a Philadelphia software company to write a system that would be the holy grail of the garment industry. My crazy boss and I drove to Philadelphia to see this developing system, but I could see that it was not going to work and told him we should write our own. But, when he decided to go with IBM, I told him I could not be a part of this going forward. I was not prepared to go through another six months of hell. The new IBM system was installed without me, which ended in a disaster with lawsuits hurled back and forth.

"That's when I decided to branch out on my own, but I needed some computer consulting experience first. I worked for a firm specializing in computer consulting for a little less than two years. Then I was ready.

"My first customer was a referral from my Syrian friends - Seruchi Sportswear. The owner, another Syrian Jew, as crazy as the others, was desperate with business way up or way down, no inventory tracking, eight typists entering data as best they could and total confusion. I said, 'You pay me $5,000 per month consulting fee for nine months. You buy the equipment and I'll write the software. When I sell the software to others I'll give you your money back.' I ended up doing the job in six months. Senuchi got its money back in four months and within two years I had licensed the software to over 300 companies.

"About this time I went to a *Bonjour Jeans'* Christmas party. Even though I was no longer an employee, I remained friendly and on good terms with everyone. My old boss said, 'You were right to go out on your own.' I agreed. Within two and a half years of starting the business, a company came to me and offered to buy my systems and my customers. The deal was very attractive, and I accepted."

"Did you just retire then?" I asked.

"No. PCs were out now, and networking was the next big thing. Novell, the first big networking company, in Provo, Utah, captured the field, and I became an independent consultant working with them and others."

"So, where does tennis fit in here?" I wondered.

"I didn't start playing tennis until I was 29. I was a part of the big tennis boom of the 70's. By that time, I was living in Mt. Vernon, New York, in an apartment complex that had two hard courts. Some of my neighbors and I thought 'Well, we've got these courts. We should learn how to play tennis.' And that's what we did. We read up on the rules, bought books on how to play tennis and went out and started playing. We started the *Westchester Plaza* - the name of the apartment complex - *Racquet Club*, and before too long we had 300 members. We organized tennis parties, and in the winter found an indoor tennis facility, a converted warehouse, with six courts to hold our parties. Remember how popular tennis parties were back then?" Mas asked.

"Oh, yes," I agreed. "Whatever happened to them? They were such fun."

Mas continued, "We even organized outings, one I remember in particular in New Paltz, New York. We contacted the Town to get permission to use the public courts, and whole families drove there for the day of tennis, kid's games, cards, backgammon, whatever. We even had a newsletter so the members were informed of all the activities."

"Did you ever take formal tennis lessons?" I asked.

"When I was 45, I took a year of lessons from a black tennis pro Jerry Alleyne. He was an older gentleman who had been a member of the ATA [American Tennis Association], and a world class player. But the USLTA banned African-American players from their tournaments, and he never got to play in USLTA events during his prime."

The ATA was established in 1916 to organize tournaments for black players; finally, the color line was broken in 1950 when Althea Gibson was allowed to play at the U.S. National Championships in Forest Hills. Then, of course, Arthur Ashe broke through as well.

Mas continued, "Alleyne taught at the Hudson Valley Tennis Club, and he transformed my game. He was an incredible person - very kind and giving. He was actually ahead of his time with a different way of teaching the mechanics of tennis. First, he'd toss a tennis ball and ask you to catch it; then he'd move farther away and ask you to catch it. This routine continued. Then, he'd give you a racquet, but asked you to grip it very close to the racquet head and to imagine the racquet was an extension of your hand. Once the student got comfortable with that maneuver, he'd say 'Now as the ball gets to your racquet, swing and put your racquet on your shoulder.'"

Susan who had been listening to our conversation and had been one of Alleyne's students added, "He'd say 'when you want to hit a ball that's a few steps away, think of opening a door. Would you stretch your upper body to reach the door? No. You'd move closer to the door and turn the knob. So that's what you do in tennis. Don't stretch for the ball that's out of reach; move your feet to get closer to the ball.'"

"He made tennis understandable," said Mas. "When I turned 50, I retired from my consulting business and concentrated on playing and teaching tennis. I taught kids as well as adults, and used Alleyne's methods. It seemed to work."

Susan got started in tennis much earlier than Mas, being introduced into the sport when she was 11, despite the objections of her mother.

"My mother tried desperately to make me into a graceful, dainty, proper young lady," she said. "She made me take ballet. I hated it. She made me take piano lessons. I hated it. All I wanted to do was read, do jig saw puzzles, walk on the stilts my father made or get on my bike, and, later, play tennis. One day I was roller skating, fell and broke my front teeth. I think my mother finally gave up.

"Our school had sports, tennis being one," she continued. "I played tennis. One day I was playing and the coach for the junior county team saw me play and asked if I'd like some lessons. Of course I joined the team, and every time I played for the county I got free lessons!"

Susan was born on April 6, 1945, in Birkenhead, Great Britain, located on the peninsula that sticks out between Wales and Great Britain. An only child, her father was a customs and excise officer, her mother a teacher. She was sent to an all-girls private school, took the A-level exams when she was 18, and her score placed her in the top three percent of those taking the exam.

"In England, if you do well on the Level A exam, you are permitted to go to University. And it's all free. I chose to go to Manchester University and majored in mathematics. But I hated school. I never felt challenged.

"When I was 21, I married a gentleman named Barry, and we both went to teachers' training college. I never wanted to be a teacher, but I applied for a vacant teacher's post in Devon at a tiny country school. The town was full of sheep and local farmers. But I loved their clotted cream with strawberries. We stayed there only one year, and I took a teaching position at a private boarding school for girls in Kent in the south-eastern part of England. One rainy July weekend when Barry and I were in our subsidized housing with no money and a fire blazing to keep us warm, I saw an ad in the *Times Education* section about full-time teachers' positions in the Bahamas. The pay was good, a 7% gratuity was added, there were no income taxes but there were lots of palm trees, beaches and warm sunshine. We both applied, Barry was accepted, and the annoying rule back then was that once the husband is accepted, the wife is also. He got the contract and I was allowed to tag along - I didn't like that arrangement, but, of course, I took the job.

"I had been teaching in a girls' private school, and the first day of classes in The Bahamas was a disaster. I couldn't understand a word my students were saying. There were 100 kids in each class, and we had desks and chairs for only 30. I hated it. I had nightmares. I hated the sameness.

"We teachers, all recruits from England, were wild. For the first time in our working careers, we had disposable income. We were in our 20s, and would go to the local pub for lunch and have a beer or two. And the drinking would continue in the evenings.

"The school was terribly disorganized, and I was quite discouraged, but I stayed there 11 years and had even applied for Bahamian citizenship. Tennis was my savior. I had an opportunity to play in local tournaments and met many local players who asked me to join in their games.

"Barry and I took on a position of caretakers at the Coral Harbour Hotel, which was in bankruptcy. Life there was great – we had a full-time maid, 20 acres of property including two tennis courts, a beach, docks. We really didn't have to do anything. And we lived there rent free. It was an incredibly beautiful spot, but at some point Barry and I got divorced.

"In 1979, my citizenship papers hadn't come through. I didn't want to return to England, I had broken up with my then boyfriend, so I decided to go to America to live with a family friend in Sparta, New Jersey. My 'aunt' was very generous to take me in, but I needed money fast, so I took a crash secretarial course at Katherine Gibbs and became a secretary. That was the last thing I wanted to do, but I got a job with Paine Webber. I loved my first boss, an Egyptian Jew whose father was the biggest importer of toothpicks. I liked him from the first day we met. He was fun to work with, but he left Paine Webber to join his father's business.

"Within two years I was working as secretary for the head of the municipal finance department, but even that bored me. I thought I should go back to University and get a masters degree in computer science, but my boss suggested that I move over to the analyst program. I did and stayed with Paine Webber for 25 years, working with municipalities in the financing of mortgages for lower income clients. I enjoyed that, but didn't like all the office politics. I couldn't be bothered; didn't play the game, but I did keep my self-respect and, at the end of the day, could look myself in the mirror and be pleased with my performance.

"I retired in 2005, and haven't worked a day since. I enjoy waking up in the morning with a day to do whatever I please - garden, cook, read, travel and play tennis."

One can say Susan has her opinions and is difficult to please, but she found her mate when she met Mas.

"What is it that you most like about senior tennis?" I asked Mas and Susan.

"I'm more relaxed," said Mas. "I'm willing to share information about how to play your best tennis and beat other players. I've been lucky to be injury-free, but with today's medical wonders, many injuries can be repaired."

Susan added, "The tournaments we play in are great, especially the husband and wife tournaments. We have developed close friendships with other married couples."

Mas and Susan played in the 120's (the team's combined age must be at least 120 years) of the National Husband/Wife Championship in March of 2016 at Mission Hills, California.

"We lost in the semis in three sets to a new team," said Mas. "But, next year we qualify for the 140's, and we'll be ready. More important, we're playing really good players who were top players in their youth. I couldn't keep up with them then, but now I can because I stay in shape. I stretch. I see a chiropractor for re-alignment, and I get frequent messages. I'm a strong competitor. When I play against a former top player and he hits a drop shot, I can get to it, especially if we're playing on red clay.

"And I enjoy giving back to senior tennis by running some of the tournaments, in particular, the Caribbean tournament held in the Bahamas and the Brandon Veterans' Championships held in May. Players come from all over the world. We have men's singles and doubles, women's singles and doubles and mixed doubles with age groups from 40 to 80."

Susan concluded, "Seniors have to know that they can get better, especially in doubles. It's never too late, and after the great competition, there's eating, drinking and good fellowship. Retirement for us has made us wonder how we ever had time to work."

CHAPTER 18:

THE SAW MILL BOYS

For years I've known Dick Parsons, a retired social studies teacher and a regular tennis player at the Saw Mill Club in Mount Kisco, New York. We often bumped into each other getting on or off the tennis courts. He often played in the middle of the day with a group of men, and I thought they'd be an ideal example of older players who don't enter sanctioned tournaments but love the game and play their hearts out.

"We have a group of approximately 20 to 25 men who play faithfully on Mondays, Wednesdays and Fridays," said Dick. "We lose five or six in the wintertime as they go south, but they return to join us in the summer."

"How did this group get organized?" I asked.

"Well, about ten years ago, when I retired and had some free time on my hands I'd go to the club mid-afternoon to practice my serve. I noticed that many of the courts were vacant and those that weren't, were being used by guys also retired or about to retire. And they were complaining about having to pay the full-court fee. 'Hey, we're doing Saw Mill a favor. If it weren't for us the courts would be empty and Saw Mill wouldn't make a dime.' So Larry Lippman, one of the players, and I decided to meet with the General Manager. We told him – not that he didn't know it already – that the courts mid-day are open and that the club should make them available to us older gentlemen at a reduced rate. The manager got back to us and offered the courts between noon and 3 pm at a nominal rate. We had to be of a certain age, but we would have unlimited use of the courts during that time, as long as we signed up and didn't interfere with players paying the full fee. We were delighted and started out with four or five players, but gradually more joined us, and now we're up to 25 or so. The 'nominal fee' has escalated to $350 per semester, but that's still a bargain."

The following week, I attended the playing session of the "Saw Mill Boys" to soak in the atmosphere and get to know these senior athletes better. The "boys" started arriving well in advance of the noon starting time, not wanting to miss a minute on the court. They were definitely a congenial crew, all anxiously organizing their teams – who'd they play with and on what courts.

I asked as many of them as possible what they most enjoyed about senior tennis.

Jerry Robinson, 76, jokingly said, "It gets me out of the house and it's a lot more fun than the treadmill!"

Roger Hendricks, 76, in a more serious vein said, "I love tennis, and I'm getting better because of these games. It's a great group of guys and lots of fun."

Jon Gordon, 67, said "Boredom is the worst form of torture." I think he meant that as a positive statement about playing tennis.

Ron Tobias, 73, said, "I'm constantly learning and by practicing I learn even more."

Ron and Les Vissers, 69, who started playing tennis only two years earlier, use the Monday, Wednesday and Friday sessions to practice.

The Saw Mill Boys - kneeling, left to right: Dick Parsons, Ron Tobias, Les Vissers, Standing, left to right: Joel Wolf, George Von Dung, Howard Patron, Alain Sasson, Jon Gordon, Larry Lippman, Jim Mann and Ken Legun.

"We'll play doubles occasionally, but we practice our strokes and we take lessons together," said Ron. "Two years ago when Les started, he couldn't even hit a backhand. Now he has a great backhand!"

Les added, "I never played this game before in my life. And I know there's been significant improvement."

Later, I got to watch Les and Ron practice their games out in the bubble. They kept the ball going without any breaks, and occasionally gave helpful advice to each other.

Lippman, 69, said, "I love the exercise and the camaraderie. When I was working I always felt anxious about my responsibilities and what I had to do the next day. I have anxiety playing tennis, but it's not work. It's fun. It's healthy anxiety."

Alain Sasson, 72, said, "Tennis keeps you young and healthy both mentally and physically."

George Von Dung, 73, added "It's not giving in to our ailments. We play through them and feel better for it."

Howard Patron, 73, anxious to get on the court just yelled, "Tennis is the best!"

Gil Goldman, 80, likes the competition. "And then after we play we go up to the café and enjoy some wine."

Lippman adds, "And George is our social chairman. Every six weeks or so he organizes an outing. We'll meet for pizza or hamburgers at a local restaurant."

Ken Legunn, 59, a dentist and natural left-hander, had to learn to play right-handed because of an injury to his left arm. He's quite proud of the progress he's making as a "rightie."

"In the beginning I couldn't even make contact with the ball, but now I'm doing pretty well. And they say that relearning the sport is good for the brain. That's another reason why I love the game."

A 75-year-old retired college chemistry professor who only wanted to be referred to publicly as "Nathan," was very anxious to talk with me, but away from the other players. I was taking pictures and talking with Nathan's doubles mates, and he kept saying, 'Come on, Judy. Let's go outside. I want to tell you something.' I wasn't quite sure why he wanted to talk in private, but I followed him to the lobby where we sat on the lone sofa.

Nathan began. "I've played sports all my life and when I turned 60, things started to happen. First, I had to have knee arthroscopy, then both shoulders needed repairing and I lost muscle tone. Then I had skin cancer plus the usual high blood pressure and blocked arteries. And I have peripheral arterial disease. Do you know what that is?"

"Not really."

"It's a chronic circulatory condition that narrows the blood vessels reducing blood flow to your limbs and can last your whole life. I am taking six medications a day. I had two hip replacements, both with titanium. And I had bladder cancer. I play with a wrist brace, an elbow brace, a knee brace. But I can still run!

"Some play for enjoyment," Nathan continued. "Some play for skill. I play for my life. I have difficulty with my secondary circulatory system but the more exercise I get, my body builds more alternative vessels so more blood and oxygen get to my arms and legs. My health is improving because of tennis. I used to play racketball and paddle, but both sports are too taxing for the body. That's why I play tennis. Plus, I enjoy the game. I play three times a week, singles and doubles, and I go to the gym two or three times a week. But, I have the most fun playing tennis. My father and two brothers never lived past 63. I'm 75 and feel great."

I was glad Nathan was so insistent to talk with me. His story is one I won't forget.

My second question of the boys was "Have you had knee or hip replacements or orthopedic procedures performed in order to continue playing tennis?"

Some of the boys had already left to play their matches, but clearly, modern medical treatment and procedures have enhanced their lives.

George, the party organizer and formerly in the construction business, talked about his lower back problems that did not need surgery. Alain, formerly a teacher of French, had a left knee replacement. Parsons had a right knee replacement, and Jim Mann, a former history teacher who is now a philanthropist and member of several corporate boards, had a left hip replacement with a right hip replacement scheduled for the near future.

Joel Wolf, a 68-year-old retired mathematician from IBM, had four knee meniscus surgeries. Tobias, a focus group facilitator, had one hip replacement, and Lippmann, now in the first year of his retirement from *Business Week*, had undergone shoulder surgery and meniscus surgery on both knees.

Only 70-year-old Bill Shekalus, a former financial advisor, said, "I haven't had any injuries, not even a sprained ankle."

But, clearly, today's physicians, especially orthopedic surgeons, have brought new life and vitality to "The Saw Mill Boys." They are a contented, happy group of older men from varied backgrounds loving their weekly games and feeling no need to enter competitive senior tennis events. We can all hope to follow their example.

CHAPTER 19:

BERNICE MYERS

On a sunny spring day, I found the home of Bernice Myer atop a small hill in Cortlandt, New York. Driving up the narrow driveway, I noticed Bernice's car facing me in the carport. I wondered how in the world she could drive backwards up this narrow, steeply inclined driveway - but I hadn't met Bernice yet.

After ringing the doorbell, I heard a cheerful, "Come in. Be right there."

Soon, out popped Bernice from her studio, thin but obviously athletic and in superb shape. She walked with a fast gait without any hitches. Wearing jeans, sneakers and a white tennis shirt, with her short, white, curly bob and a ready smile, she offered me lunch.

"Thanks so much, but I just ate."

She led me through the foyer, and I was immediately struck by all the art on her walls. Many featured landscapes, scenes of Paris, all colorful and inviting. One painting was obviously a younger version of Bernice.

"Who is the artist? The paintings are wonderful!"

"That's Lou, my husband."

I didn't get to ask much more about the artwork, as she was anxious to offer more refreshments.

"How about some ice cream. Chocolate?"

She could tell I was a hard sell and continued, "So I have it on a stick. It's really skinny."

Still not selling me anything, she suggested, "Water?"

"Sure. That would be good."

We then settled down where I had a chance to learn a bit more about Bernice. She was born in the Bronx on April 17, 1925, and lived on Grand Avenue with her parents, immigrants from Hungary and Germany. After high school, Bernice met Lou Myers, a young U.S. Navy sailor, and they were married in 1947.

Lou was a cartoonist, and during his stint in the Navy during World War II, he became well known, drew for *"Stars and Stripes"* and met some stars including Marlene Dietrich. After being discharged, Lou and Bernice lived in Paris for several years, where he continued to freelance as a cartoonist. Bernice, too, was a talented artist and began writing and illustrating children's books, many of which are still in print.

When she was a young woman Bernice was told by a physician that because of a "turned womb" she may have difficulty having children, but while still in Paris she suggested to Lou that they at least try. Nine months later, having returned to the United States, Lou and Bernice became the proud parents of their first son, now a writer, and a few years later, they welcomed their second son, now an artist. Like father/mother, like son.

Upon their return to the United States, Lou took a job with *The New Yorker*, where he remained for many years. His passing nine years earlier was a great loss to Bernice.

Bernice preferred not to discuss her private life in detail, which I respected, but with an eagerness, she said, "Let's talk

Bernice Myers with two of her children's books

about tennis. That's what you're here for, right? I love my tennis."

The young family moved to Cortlandt, New York in 1970 where Bernice continued to live. Now, out in the country with her boys a bit older, Bernice took up tennis, and she has played ever since.

"I took a lesson or two, but mostly I learned by watching the really good players," she said. "Billie Jean King was my inspiration. When I had trouble with my game, I'd get some professional help, but I never took lessons or joined clinics on a steady basis. But you should see my slice."

Bernice started playing at a popular tennis club in Cortlandt and on the Lakeland High School courts, also in Cortlandt.

"I play only doubles now and only twice a week," she said. "I have my regulars. There are four or five of us. It's like a sisterhood. We've become good friends. We don't play with women who are so competitive that if a shot is missed they sigh or give you a bad look. No. Oh, we're competitive, but if you try for a shot but miss, that's OK. You tried. But when you hit a winner, oh, that's great and it's OK to strut a little. And we like to laugh. We don't take ourselves too seriously."

I know a tennis-playing buddy of Bernice's, Sara Cook, who is two decades younger and raves about Bernice's tennis.

"Bernice is fast on the court," Sara told me. "She places her shots beautifully, and she hits shots that are tough to return. She may be 20 years older than the rest of us, but she's as good as if not better than we are."

I asked Bernice if she played in any USTA senior tournaments.

"No," she responded. "I just enjoy playing a lot and playing with my friends."

"Do you think tennis keeps you young?"

"Probably," she said. "You know I play with women who are not in my age range. I like that. It's invigorating. And being with friends, getting out of the house, doing something together that's so much fun, keeps my spirits up. I don't really think about old age. I'm healthy. I eat a good diet - vegetables, fruits and chopped meat only once a month. I got a prescription for reading glasses three years ago, but I don't use them much. I do my exercises. You know, I get on the floor and stretch, touch my knees to my head, things like that. I see my heart doctor on a regular basis, just to make sure everything is OK. I did have lymphoma 12 years ago - had chemo, lost my hair. But, I'm fine."

Indeed, Bernice is fine. Watching her dash around her house, seeing how limber and flexible she is, suggests to me that Bernice is one helluva 90-year-old lady.

Her story is important because she represents many players who may take up the game later in life and may not have had much training or classic strokes, but who cares? They enjoy the game as long as they can, which can turn out to be a very long time!

CHAPTER 20:

JULIE VERRONE

J ulie Verrone greeted me at the back door of her house in Bedford Hills, New York with her contagious, enthusiastic smile that spread across half her face and welcomed me with her lilting Australian accent. I knew Julie through tennis, and, among other things, she is known for her withering forehand. Do not serve there!

We settled down in her living room on a comfortable sofa and she launched into her personal story with tennis.

"I was born in Sydney, Australia, on June 26, 1947, one of five children," she said. "I was in the middle, two brothers, two sisters. My Mum, Dorothy, died two days shy of her 87th birthday. She never went past high school but always worked. The job I remember most, I don't know why, was in the office of a businessmen's club. That sounded intriguing to me. My Dad, at 46, while walking across the road, was hit by a car driven by the son of a police sergeant who didn't even have a license. He died instantly, and no charges were ever brought against the boy. The whole thing was a shock to everyone. My Dad was well liked in the community and loved his family. And, he was a terrific athlete in rugby, cricket, tennis and boxing, what you might call a 'typical Aussie.' For three years in a row he was his school's top athlete.

"My parents were grandchildren of immigrants to Australia who came from Scotland, England and Ireland, and we lived in a four-family house in Bondi Beach, very near a little tennis club and the beach, which was only a half mile away. My brothers, sisters and I would walk to the beach, totally unsupervised, much of the year as the Sydney climate is very mild. But when I was seven or eight, I started going to the tennis club. Mr. Ferguson was the pro, and I just started to pick up the balls for him. He must have been pleased because he gave me one lesson a week and I didn't even have to pay. Then I graduated to sweeping and watering the club's six courts. Every day after school I'd go there all year round.

"We kids pretty much raised ourselves as both our parents worked," she continued. "But, that wasn't so unusual back then in Australia."

I asked whether she had entered any tournaments.

"Yes, as I got a bit better, but I had to find out where the tournaments were being played and how to get there. I'd take the train mostly though sometimes I'd hitch a ride with another player. I'd bring my racquet, of course, but that was about it. Nobody in the family came because they were working, but I knew they were proud of what I was doing.

"I remember playing mostly with Karen Krantzcke and Patsy Turner, Lesley Turner's younger sister. You know Lesley Turner became a world class player. Patsy wasn't quite as good, but she had quite a good game.

"Once I was playing Karen in the finals of a tournament, and I was ahead 6-0, 3-0. At the next crossover she says to me 'Give me a break.' I don't think she was being mean or anything, but after that comment my play went downhill, and I lost the match."

Julie Verrone

Julie is too modest to explain who Karen Krantzcke was except that they were tennis buddies. Karen was among the world's Top 10 singles players in 1970, having gotten to the quarterfinals or better in each of the Grand Slam tournaments. She is also credited with helping Australia win the Federation Cup that year. Sadly, while playing on the Challenger Circuit in the U.S., Krantzcke died of a heart attack while jogging at the age of 31.

"Another time I was playing a really good Australian player, though for the life of me I can't remember who. We were in the finals of the New South Wales 12-and-under at White City. And I won! That was a big deal. You know, New South Wales is a state in Australia - actually the most populated, so there were lots of entries. But, only my uncle came to watch, though my parents wanted to be there but couldn't because of work."

White City Stadium and Tennis Club was the premiere tennis facility in Sydney until the Sydney Olympic Tennis Park was built for the 2000 Olympics. It hosted many major tournaments and was the home of the Australian Tennis Museum with life-size photographs of Australia's tennis greats on the walls: Rod Laver, Lew Hoad, Ken Rosewall, Roy Emerson, John

Newcombe, Margaret Court, Evonne Goolagong and many more. The final of each important tournament was played in the White City Stadium. That's where Julie defeated her forgotten opponent.

In the seventh grade, Julie went to St. Vincents College Potts Point, a catholic secondary school, where she joined the tennis team, not to play tournaments but interscholastic competition among the other secondary schools in the area.

"But our team did well," she said. "I boarded at the school my last two years, and when outstanding students or athletes entered the dining room after achieving a victory, the whole school clapped. I'll never forget the thrill of this recognition. But I have to tell you, our tennis dresses were not very stylish. We had to put our dress on, kneel on the floor, and if the hem touched the floor, the dress was okay. Otherwise, it was in for a remake.

"I graduated from high school when I was 16 and stopped playing tennis. I think I just lost interest, and, more important, I had to get a job. Secretarial school, I thought, would prepare me, and I went for one year to get my degree. At 17, I starting working as a secretary at the Australian Broadcasting Commission for two years, then I went to a public relations firm for a year and finally to RCA, the Radio Corporation of America, where I stayed until I was 21. That's when I decided I'd go to England and travel for a year, but I met a gentleman, 20 years my senior, who changed my plans. Perry Verrone was an auditor with RCA and traveled all over the world doing audits. His tour in Australia was coming to an end, and he said to me 'If you're going to England, come to the United States first.'

"That didn't sound like a bad idea, so I headed for the U.S. and stayed with Perry's parents in Sleepy Hollow, New York. They were fabulous to me. I think they may have been relieved that Perry found a 'woman of interest' and they showered me with kindness. I was loving it. But after about six weeks I said to myself, 'You better get a job.' My best bets were with the United Nations or the Australian Consulate. My typing and shorthand skills were excellent and I had several years of work experience. I ended up with a good job at the UN.

"And all this time I'm living with Perry's parents! Until 1970! Perry had asked me to marry him, but I wasn't sure. I just didn't think I was ready. And actually, I got myself worked up about it. So, I decided to take some vacation time from the UN - you got 28 days a year - and I went back to Australia to try to figure things out.

"First I asked my Mum who said 'Oh I don't know. He's a good man. He'll always take care of you, but I'd love to have you here in Australia.' That didn't really help, and I remained very confused. I was making myself sick! I had never had a boyfriend and really didn't know what love was.

"I went to confession and asked the priest, 'Father, what should I do?' After hearing my story, he said, 'I don't think you're in any condition to make this decision.' And he was right. I was a mess, but I didn't take his advice. Then Perry called from the States and asked me to come back. I told him I was sick. I couldn't. He said, 'If you don't come back now, don't bother coming back at all.' With that ultimatum, I went back to Sleepy Hollow, and we were married on May 16, 1970. I got pregnant right away but had a miscarriage, then got pregnant again, and my first son Christopher was born on November 11, 1971. One year later, on November 21, 1972, my second son Perry was born.

"From the time I left high school, I hadn't touched a racquet, but the next summer, while visiting Perry's parents in Sleepy Hollow, Perry asked me to play some tennis with him. There were school courts nearby, and it felt terrific to be out on a court. And I thought I'd like to start playing again.

"About this time we bought a house in Mount Kisco, and one day, while playing at Leonard Park, the town's public park with two tennis courts, a gentleman, Archie Fournier, saw me playing. He was a member of the Mount Kisco Country Club and he asked if I'd like to teach at Mount Kisco. I said 'Sure.' Within no time, I met with the tennis committee and was hired.

"I taught at Mount Kisco for six years," she continued. "And I helped out a fellow Aussie, Alan Lane, a well-known pro who was going out on his own. Alan was injured, and he asked if I would feed balls during his lessons. Also helping out was Fran Meek, who has become a very dear friend, a fellow lover of tennis.

"About this time, Perry left his job and tried his business skills as an entrepreneur. It didn't work. We were struggling financially, and I realized I needed to get a full time job with benefits. I was hired by the newspaper, the *Christian Herald Magazine,* which was headquartered in nearby Chappaqua. A couple years later, I'm reading *Time* magazine. On the cover is a picture of John Opel, CEO of IBM, and the featured story is all about IBM.

"I tell myself I need to get a job at IBM. How can I do that? I don't have any advertising or marketing or finance experience. I'm 36 years old, but I don't care if I have to start at the bottom. Well, I had an interview, was hired, and started at the bottom.

"It's 1983, and I'm earning $12,800. I have very generous benefits and a retirement plan and I'm loving my job. I slowly worked my way up the ladder. In 1994, I became the team leader on the executive floor at 590 Madison Avenue in New York, and in 1996 I was transferred back to Armonk as manager of the secretaries in the Human Resources Department.

"Louis Gerstner, in 1993, was named CEO of IBM, the first CEO hired from the outside and hired to turn the company around. He succeeded John Akers who was Opel's successor.

Gerstner, for his first three months in office, studied the workings of IBM, its corporate structure, its workforce of 350,000, its research and development, its sales operation - everything. He was tough, but he was in control and totally focused. After his investigation he addressed the employees and said, 'We're hemorrhaging. But we're going to keep the company together.' Many thought parts of the company should be sold off, but Gerstner disagreed and actually saved IBM as a result. 'We have to cut costs, and we have to cut jobs,' unpleasant news for his employees, but he was right, and after some cuts and layoffs, the company began to turn around. But it was a difficult time for everyone.

"Mr. Gerstner's secondary office, on the Executive floor at 590 Madison Avenue, was a busy place with executives and customers coming and going. I was there at the time and made a number of contacts. One was Heidi Terens, Vice President of Communications.

"Despite being happy at IBM, I was getting tired of managing secretaries. I needed something different to keep me from becoming complacent.

"My timing was actually just right, as IBM was the technology sponsor for the upcoming 2000 Summer Olympics in Sydney. Plans were beginning to take shape. I contacted Heidi Terens and said, 'If you need me to work in Sydney, I'm very interested.' Terens said she would get back to me.

"I didn't hear anything for six months. And out of the blue I got a phone call from Terens. She wanted to know if I was still interested. Of course I was! She told me that the Australian counterpart would be visiting in the States in a few weeks and could I meet with her. I was planning a trip to see my family in Australia at the same time, but we had one day that overlapped. We met in a bar and hit it off immediately.

"The next two years - 1998 to 2000 - was a dream. I was named the Asia Pacific customer coordinator for the 2000 Olympics and met with all the general managers of our Asian officers in China, Japan, Malaysia, Singapore and Korea. I'm thinking to myself, 'These people don't know what level I am at IBM. They don't know I'm just a staff person, and yet, I'm giving my power point presentations to them, and they listen carefully.'"

I interjected, "But Julie. You weren't just a staff person. You knew what was going on in the company. You knew Sydney, and you knew how to deal with people from top executives to customers."

Julie didn't say anything, but she didn't disagree.

Julie added, "And by then I had gotten my undergraduate degree from SUNY, thanks to IBM's generous tuition plan for employees. The second year I lived in Sydney. IBM provided me with an apartment overlooking the harbor on Kent Street near the Opera House and the Quay. The views were spectacular. I was right in the heart of Sydney and only a short walk to my office. And I had plenty of room for my Mum to live with me while I was there. I thought I'd died and gone to heaven. But I worked hard, long hours during that year.

"At the end of the Olympics, I would be going back to Armonk and knew that IBM would assign a career manager to help me transition back to a job in the States. But that wasn't going to be necessary. During the Olympics I saw Mr. Gerstner, and he said to me, 'I'm willing to wait for you to come back from the Olympics. Then I want you back in my office.' And that's what happened."

Then Julie said something quite perceptive: "Mr. Gerstner is very creative, but he likes sameness too. He's comfortable with the people and workers he knows. In 2000, I became Mr. Gerstner's Operations Manager for his corporate offices, stayed with him until he retired in 2002 and continued with his successor Sam Palmisano. Palmisano was very personable but 'tough with the big guys.' But, he was always very good to me and didn't put on any airs - just talked like a regular person."

By this time, Julie had earned a masters degree in Organization Development from Columbia Teachers College, thanks to IBM's tuition plan, and she appreciated all that IBM had done for her. And what a ride it was!

"I was very lucky, but I was given opportunities, and I seized them."

Nevertheless, in 2007 Julie decided it was time to retire. So, now it was time for tennis - senior tennis. Perhaps, not quite yet.

"I had played very little tennis except for 'hits' with Fran at Seven Bridges during the summers and at Saw Mill, where she taught part-time for a while. But, then my son Perry asked if I would help him in his business. How could I say 'no' to my son?

"So, I helped him out for 3 1/2 years and then said, 'It's time for me to leave.' My work for Perry was totally the opposite from what I was doing at IBM. I'm very organized and efficient at work and Perry's style is very different. I love him to death and didn't want our work relationship to spoil our mother-son relationship.

"And it's really Perry who got me back into tennis. One day he asked if I'd hit with him. 'Nothing would be more fun,' I thought. We started playing mixed doubles, getting involved in mixed doubles leagues, and meeting women players that were at Saw Mill where I was a member. That led to playing on Saw Mill's women's doubles team as a part of the Westchester/ Fairfield League. In the league we practiced one day a week and played matches with other teams once a week. The competition was very good - all 4.0 and above players. I'm still doing it.

All the players are much younger than I which makes it even more fun. I played too in MITL [Metropolitan Interclub Tennis League] for Saw Mill, another good league that has been around for years. Again, we'd have one day of practice and one day of matches. Saw Mill was always in the top flight so the competition was excellent."

"Did you play any USTA matches?" I asked.

"Yes. I played in many USTA matches, and one, in particular, sticks in my mind. Fran Meek and I were playing at Concordia College, and we were both much older than our opponents. During practice the young women are blasting balls at us and feeling confident. They watched Fran who was then well into her 60s if not her 70s, walk slowly to pick up a ball, back slightly bent. She'd return the ball with classic strokes but without much pace. Our opponents were ready for the kill. But after the match started they got a lesson in how to play doubles!"

"Julie, what is it that makes senior tennis special for you?" I asked.

"You know, I don't really play in USTA senior tennis tournaments, per se, but I am a senior - actually a super senior - and to me just playing as a senior is what's important.

"First, I like that I can still play!" Julie said with her broad smile and hearty laugh. "And I like the people I play with - or most of them anyway. I actually prefer doubles. Singles is too lonely. I've made so many good friends through tennis. And you feel so good when you play well. Sometimes you don't play well, but when you do, it's euphoric! I hope to be playing forever! And why not? It keeps me healthy. Tennis is a lifetime sport whether you're playing in sanctioned tournaments or not. You can enjoy it forever."

CHAPTER 21:

DAN WSZOLEK

S warthy, laid back with a full white, well-trimmed beard and mustache speckled with black, Dan Wszolek is unmistakable to his many tennis friends as he usually wears his Marine Corps baseball cap or an Aussie outback hat.

Dan's parents were Polish immigrants who came to the United States before World War II to Amsterdam, New York, a manufacturing town that did well with its carpet mills, especially Mohawk Carpet. During the war, the U.S. government needed tarpaulins more than carpets, so Mohawk converted its production to the needed tarpaulins to help the war effort. After the war, however, the mills didn't recover as workers moved south where work was more plentiful and taxes were lower. The population of Amsterdam decreased from 40,000 to 25,000. Nevertheless, Dan, an only child, and his parents stayed.

In high school during the late 1950s, Dan was first introduced to tennis by the father of his girlfriend. He started playing and enjoyed it - that's one way to win over the parents. But Amsterdam High School didn't have a tennis team, so Dan concentrated on football and track.

"Senior year," Dan told me, "a friend of mine was applying to college. Most of my friends either dropped out of high school or went to work after graduating, but I thought that if this guy could go to college, maybe I could too."

Dan's friend suggested talking to the football coach, who had helped him get through the application process.

"I didn't know anything about colleges, nor did my parents. If I were accepted at a really good school, like Harvard, and an okay school, I wouldn't have known which one to choose."

After Dan told the football coach that he was interested in potentially becoming a gym teacher someday, the coach helped set up an interview at Plymouth Teachers College in New Hampshire. In May of his senior year, Dan took the bus from Amsterdam to Boston. From Boston to Plymouth, he hitchhiked. Plymouth was a small college - only 500 students - even smaller than Amsterdam High with its 600 students, but Dan liked it, and apparently Plymouth liked him. He entered as a freshman with a plan to major in physical education in the fall of 1960.

"Plymouth had a tennis team. If you showed up for tryouts, you were on the team. If you had a racquet you were captain," quipped Dan.

"Did you have a racquet?" I asked.

"No. The coach wasn't a tennis player, but he knew how to coach. He had lots of practice. Being a small school, he coached J.V. basketball, soccer and even gymnastics."

"Did you get any tennis instruction?"

"Have you seen me play?" asked Dan. "My game is very unorthodox, but it works."

And Plymouth did well in the newly created New England Teachers College League.

After graduating in 1964, Dan stayed on at Plymouth for one year to get a Masters in Education, but before he finished, he and a friend moved to Fort Lauderdale, Florida for

Dan Wszolek

warm weather and adventure.

"I had lots of jobs there: bar tender, cab driver, short order cook and selling Kirby vacuum cleaners door to door," he said. "It was not exactly what I had in mind, but they were jobs. But, I did get a chance to meet Wayne Sabin, a tennis player and pro, who had a roving tennis camp. That year his camp was in Miami Beach. Sabin happened to see me playing and asked if I'd like to work for him."

Dan was only too happy to, but he only did odd jobs maintaining the courts, driving the bus and doing errands. However, he did get a chance to hit with the kids and watched some of the better players - Chris Evert and Eddie Dibbs. Dan never had a lesson as he was not a paying customer, but he learned vicariously.

"How long did you stay in Florida?"

"After a year of too much drinking and not enough vacuum cleaner sales, I enrolled in the U.S. Marine Corps OCS [Officer Candidate School] in Quantico, Virginia."

"That was quite a switch," I offered.

"It was, but it was just what I needed. After 16 weeks of instruction I was commissioned a Second Lieutenant in the Marine Corps. Immediately after graduation, I stayed at Quantico for six months of intense training at the Basic School."

Pausing for a minute, he asked me, "Do you want to know about my class?"

"Sure."

"I was a member of the fifth class of 1967, known for one of its graduates, Jim Jones, who later became Commandant of the Marine Corps. A book was even written about the Class 5-67 entitled *The Boys of 67*."

Dan showed his pride in being a part of that team. From there, Dan was sent directly to Vietnam with the Third Battalion, 9th Marines, where he was a platoon commander with Kilo Company in I Corps, along the DMZ (Demilitarized Zone). Dan doesn't talk much about his year in Vietnam.

"That was then. This is now," he said.

In 1968, Dan was sent to Camp Le Jeune, North Carolina, where he stayed for two years. "I separated from the Marine Corps in 1970, moved to Lodi, New York, got a job as an eighth grade teacher of science and math and bought an old fixer upper - a farmhouse built in 1791 which in its former life was a tavern and stagecoach stop on the route from Elmira to Geneva, New York."

"Another big switch in lifestyle," I interjected.

"You might say so, but working on the old farmhouse and teaching school for the first time were good for me."

Between work and his house, Dan had little spare time and didn't return to playing tennis until 1975 or '76 when he entered some 35-and-over Eastern Sectional tournaments.

"In 1978, I accepted a position at Cornell University as administrative executive officer in the Department of Economics, where I remained until my retirement in 2013. And I finally had many more opportunities to play tennis with experienced seniors who knew the game."

Dan entered some senior tournaments himself, first at the section level, then at the Eastern and national levels. He captured the No. 1 singles ranking in the 45's in the Eastern Section and the No. 2 spot in the New England section. Subsequent rankings have been No. 1 in New England's 60s and 65s as well as national rankings in all of the age divisions he entered - all in singles. Dan kept getting better and better. His old coach at Plymouth Teachers College would be very proud.

"So Dan, what's so special about senior tennis?"

"Senior tennis is like going on a mini vacation," Dan explained. "Recently, I was playing the finals in Hartford in the 70s against Paul Fein of Agawam, Massachusetts. Two weeks before that, I was in the finals again against Paul in Concord, Mass. Paul got the best of me both times but I'm ready for our next encounter. And this week I'm playing in the Atlantic Coast Cup in Manchester, Massachusetts. The competition is always good. It keeps me in shape and away from the booze. I'm not a heavy drinker, but in the winter I like a rye Manhattan, in the summer, margaritas, and red wine all year around. But when getting ready for a tournament and when playing, all drinking gets cut out.

"The friends I've made - I can't tell you what great guys play senior tennis," he continued. "We see each other over and over and remain good friends when off the court. But on the court, it's all tennis and tough competition."

When I asked Dan if he had any new body parts, he responded, "All original body parts though some cease to function."

I think I should have phrased that question a little differently.... But you get the picture, and Dan was not the exception. A good sense of humor, often self-deprecating, was clearly evident among these gentlemen who enjoy their senior tennis - it brings them good friends, good health, healthy habits and "mini vacations."

CHAPTER 22:

TOM BRUNKOW

Tom Brunkow, a retired Methodist minister, relishes his time on the tennis court, particularly with his 12-year old grandson, Gianluca. As well he should. He and Gianluca played in the National Grandfather/Grandson Grass Court Championships at the Longwood Cricket Club in Chestnut Hill, Massachusetts during the summer of 2014.

"We played five matches in a round robin format among eight teams, winning two," said Tom. "One of our losses came at the hands of last year's champions in a three setter. But what was even more remarkable was that we were playing against grandsons who were in high school and college! And, at the same time, Gianluca was playing with his Dad, Ben, in the Father/Son tournament, winning the first round, losing to the No. 5 seed but winning two matches in the back draw. He played eight matches one day and four the next. The kid's a player!"

Since 2014 when Gianluca played with his father and grandfather, the rules have been changed. Now both tournaments are held at the same time so Ben must choose whom he'll play with, either Gianluca, or his other son,

Lorenzo. Tom gets to play in the grandfather/grandson with the son not chosen. Either way, he wins.

Tom, a left hander, began playing tennis at the famed River Forest Tennis Club in River Forest, Illinois, a suburb of Chicago.

"It all started because I had a bad birthday," Tom said as he started his personal story of tennis. "I wanted to be a baseball player. I was a southpaw pitcher with a good curve ball, but when Little League came to town, the coach said, 'Sorry, Tommy, you're too old. You'll be 13 in May.' I was devastated. But my older sister's boyfriend got me a job at River Forest, and I became the ball boy for the lessons given by Cap Leighton, the legendary pro who taught generations of players in the Chicago area. Cap took me under his wing, taught me everything I know and launched me into the sport that has lasted a lifetime."

Tom played throughout high school and later at DePauw University, where he played No. 1 singles and doubles for three years and led his team to many victories in the Indiana Collegiate Conference.

During Tom's senior year, a young woman named Kathy Ault entered DePauw as a freshman, but they never met. After graduating from DePauw in 1961, Tom went to Yale Divinity School in New Haven, Connecticut. When he was in his third year and Kathy was a junior at DePauw, she was invited by another divinity student to a party at Yale. Tom had a date, and the two couples spent some time together. Kathy, apparently, wasn't too crazy about her date - nor was Tom with his - so he was prompted to get in touch with Kathy. The perfect opportunity occurred when he was heading up a voter registration drive in North Carolina. Shortly before her spring break in 1964, Kathy got a phone call from Tom, asking whether she would be interested in joining a group of students he was organizing to participate in a voter registration drive in Greensboro, North

Tom and Kathy Brunkow at Atlantic Coast Cup Dinner, July 2015

Carolina. Kathy was eager to be a part of the Civil Rights Movement, and the timing was right. She could do it during her spring break.

The students stayed at NCA&T (North Carolina Agricultural and Technical State University) which held a prominent place in the civil rights movement of the 1960s. Four of its students, later known as the "Greensboro Four," held a non-violent sit-in at a Woolworths lunch counter. Their efforts led to a broader protest against discrimination, and the university supported the movement. Because of NCA&T's commitment, it offered housing to Tom's team. In addition, Tom's group received a day of training at the university. The team was told over and over again that they were not to go into the black neighborhoods without a partner. The black communities were suspicious of white people – all white people. Following that advice, Tom divided his group into twos, and not surprisingly, he chose Kathy as his partner. The students spent their days walking up and down the streets of Greensboro's black neighborhoods to register new voters.

"I was surprised how often I heard, 'Why bother to vote? The same old white guys will get elected.' We learned a lot about the political realities," said Tom.

"And," Kathy added, "We learned a lot about each other."

Tom was more explicit when he said, "That's when we fell in love."

Kathy graduated from DePauw a couple months later in 1964 and desperately wanted to join the Peace Corps. She was turned down because of a medical condition, a heart arrhythmia that was corrected many years later.

"That was a very hard time for me, but Tom helped me through the disappointment," Kathy said.

As an alternative to the Peace Corps, Kathy was accepted into the French Literature graduate program at the University of Michigan. Meanwhile, Tom was completing his studies at Yale, expecting to graduate in 1965. But Kathy and Tom were spending so much money and time travelling between Ann Arbor and New Haven that one night when Tom called her he said, 'Let's get married.' She didn't hesitate to accept. Kathy finished the semester, left the program and joined Tom in Connecticut. They were married on January 30, 1965. Not a minute was wasted, and while Tom completed his studies, Kathy taught French.

When I asked Tom what led him to the ministry, he replied, "God." I didn't dig any further.... He became a Methodist minister and served six Methodist churches in the Washington, D.C. area until his retirement in 2006. Living in the Washington area gave him easy access to a host of top level tennis players at the Kenwood Country Club and neighboring clubs in inter-club matches. And Tom and Ben played in national father/son tournaments as Ben had become quite a serious player in his own right.

"Now Ben is the director of tennis at the Toluca Lake Tennis Club outside Los Angeles. For some 18 years we played father/son tournaments achieving the ranking of No. 1 in the senior father/son in 1999 by winning both the National Hard Courts and the Grass Courts."

Meanwhile, Kathy continued her teaching but became passionate about mental health issues. She received her MSW in clinical social work and advanced training in psychotherapy. And where did she work? For 30 years she served as a mental health consultant for the Peace Corps, achieving her longstanding wish to "join the Corps."

In an essay Tom wrote for his 50th Reunion from DePauw, he said:

> *My life-long vocation has been that of a United Methodist minister… preaching the gospel and building communities of faith were my passions till the day I stepped down from the pulpit. But all along the way I harbored another passion that fed my soul – the game of tennis…."*

And in a speech he delivered at DePauw's Alumni Tennis Association banquet in February 2011, Tom said:

> *Tennis is indeed a sport of a lifetime. It has been for me…. In my career as a Methodist pastor, tennis played a crucial role. A minister is expected to be kind, gentle, compassionate, and non-violent at all times. You have to sit on all your frustration and anger. As a result, burn out is a serious problem for the clergy. Tennis was my saving grace. It gave me an acceptable outlet for my aggression. The intense focus and concentration demanded on the court was mind-clearing for me…. The stresses of parish life were lifted which allowed me to return to my vocation with new energy and fresh insight.*

Later in his tennis career, Tom concentrated on doubles. In 2011 and 2012, he and his partner Bob Anderman had a good run in the 70s, winning the National Indoors in Houston, Texas twice and the National Clay Courts once at Pinehurst, North Carolina. Now that Tom has turned 75, he's the rookie in the field and either winning or coming in second in all the 75 tournaments he has entered.

"Being a lefty is an absolute advantage," he said. "I'm sure it contributes to my success so far."

Last summer, he and Kathy traveled to Poertschach, Austria, a charming Alpine resort nestled at the base of the surrounding Alps sitting on the shores of a pristine lake. The first week, Tom played doubles as a part of the U.S. team in the European Championship. The second week was devoted to individual competition in both singles and doubles.

Tom explained, "It's 18 days of paradise. The tennis club, as old as it is, has all the amenities and fine dining, and the tennis couldn't be better. Kathy enjoys it too. She loves watching the matches, but more important, as an amateur but gifted artist, she relishes the magnificent scenery as subjects for her water color and pastel paintings."

As Tom and his family so amply show, three generations enjoy and play the sport together. Tennis is indeed a sport of a lifetime. But Tom's story tells us more. Not only does tennis keep him fit physically, but during his career as a minister, tennis also provided the outlet that soothed his soul so he could soothe the souls of so many others.

CHAPTER 23:

TOMMIE WALKER

Tommie Walker looks like he does not have one gray hair, not one wrinkle and not an ounce of fat.

"Not many gray hairs and not one *deep* wrinkle," said the 70-year-old Tommie.

Maybe he's right, but only on very close inspection would his version be noticeable.

I've known Tommie for decades - since the late 1970s. He looks exactly the same as he did then, moves on the court exactly as he did then, and his mind is as sharp and well-oiled as ever. Oh, there might be a tiny bit of balding, but balding is not a part of the aging process; it's genetic.

Born on December 4, 1945, in Berkeley, California, Tommie was the oldest of four with two brothers and a sister. Most of his childhood, however, was spent in North Chicago, "a town completely separate from Chicago itself, near Waukegan and the U.S. Navy's Great Lakes Training Base," Tommie explained.

Tommie had started playing ping pong at 11 and was pretty good at it, but his dad who played some tennis, thought it was time to introduce him to the game when he was 12 or 13.

Tommie remembered three days of hell: "The July temperature and humidity were so high, that my feet were on fire, my head was on fire, and I just hit balls over the fence to get rid of them."

Tommie's dad tried again the next year, this time for a week. Same result. But the next summer, when his father gave it one more try, he decided August might work better as the weather was cooler. Tommie, suddenly, took to the game with enthusiasm and has loved it ever since.

Now, there weren't many tennis players in North Chicago, but "there was a little club of about a hundred members in the South Side of Chicago which we joined," Tommie explained.

"Nobody would play with me, and there were never any courts available. But one day a member, Alphonso Robinson, took me aside and led me to a spot I had never seen - a big wall to practice against."

Tommie spent hours practicing against that backboard. After a while, he decided it was time to enter "the club's ladder," a challenge match format where if you win a match you go on to the next level - or higher step - and work your way up; if you lose, it's over. Tommie went from No. 100 to the top five in short order.

"I didn't care about the ranking," he said. "What was most fun was the playing. I remember Clyde Jeffers. He was fast and had a forehand that he hit so hard, I lost one and one. But, my Dad never had any trouble playing Clyde. I couldn't understand that for a while until I realized that my father saw the whole court, stayed away from Clyde's forehand and used his head when he played."

Within a few weeks, Tommie was beating Clyde.

Tommie attended North Chicago Community High School, but the school did not have a tennis team.

Tommie Walker

"The school claimed to have a tennis program, but the coach was also the baseball coach. He knew a lot more about baseball than he did tennis, and the only courts were three miles away at the town park."

The school did have track and baseball teams, and the coaches were very anxious to have Tommie join their teams - he was fast, athletic, competitive. He played his freshman year but didn't give up on getting a tennis team started. He hit against the school's long, flat wall. In the winter, he went into the gym, placed chairs in the middle of the gym floor to replicate a net and hit away. He got other boys to join him and soon a tennis team was formed with a coach. The coach didn't know anything about tennis, but that didn't matter to Tommie.

"The coach didn't know how to order the balls," he said. "He didn't know the difference between playing on clay versus hard courts. He didn't know how to set up the team or how to arrange the schedule. He had us playing really hard teams in the beginning, rather than having us work our way into the tougher competition. So I kinda took over. And we had a great place to get in shape, Waughegan Park which was in the next town. By the way, Waughegan Park was the home of Nat King Cole. It was also near the Great Lakes Training Base with its tracks and open areas. I rearranged the lineups, the schedules, the practices, and we ended up doing pretty well."

I asked, "Tommie, did you sense any racial discrimination when playing as Arthur Ashe had in Richmond, Virginia where he grew up and later on as a college player and professional?"

Tommie responded, "No matter where you are there's prejudice, but I didn't have a problem as long as folks let me play. There is a certain ethic in tennis. You learn a lot about people on the tennis court, and if you don't like their behavior on the court you don't play with them. It has nothing to do with color. My Dad grew up in the 1930s, became a chemical engineer and served in the Army in World War II. He was a member of the ATA, the American Tennis Association, an association exclusively for black players. When Ashe won the nationals at 17, he was a member of the ATA. Althea Gibson was the first black tennis player to come from the ATA and play as a member of the USTA. They were trail blazers, but I never felt I suffered because of my color."

During summer vacations while in high school, Tommie tried to obtain a job in Chicago with a few companies, and each time he was told, "You're too young." His dad offered to loan him $50 to start his own business selling tennis shoes and stringing racquets. Tommie was only too happy to accept the offer.

"After all," Tommie went on, "I thought it was better than not working at all."

After high school, Tommie attended Central State University in Wilbur Force, Ohio, where he played on the tennis team his freshman and sophomore years, playing at No. 2 and No. 3 singles the first year, No. 1 and No. 2 the second year, and No. 1 in doubles both years. The tennis coach was a good player but not a good coach, according to Tommie. He remembered a tournament in Cleveland where Tommie and his partner, Melvin Searles, beat the No. 1 seed, the No. 3 seed and then lost to the No. 2 seed in the final because the coach had already packed his bags, left the courts and didn't give them money for food after the first two matches. To Tommie, that wasn't a good way to coach.

Tommie stopped playing tennis his junior year. With an academic and a sports scholarship, he had to spend more time studying. But he did manage to make some money stringing racquets for pocket change.

"And I even sold Kool Aid in college," he said. "A glass cost me five cents; I sold the glass for 15. You know, if you want something, you have to pick yourself up and go after it because there's plenty out there. Don't blame others. Just get out there and do it yourself."

And Tommie did just that.

In 1967, he was graduated from Central State University with a B.S. in Physics. After graduation, he enrolled in the University of Connecticut's Masters program in Nuclear Physics which he completed in 1969. During the summer, he had an internship but realized that "a limited number of grants are given out, so you have to be somebody's assistant. That wasn't necessarily what I wanted to pursue," Tommy admitted.

"The other problem is you need to know how to get the grants, and my advisor was too occupied with his own grant application, so I didn't pursue it further."

After obtaining his Masters, Tommie taught high school physics, earth science and chemistry at Plymouth-Carver Regional High School in Plymouth, Massachusetts.

"I never took chemistry so I read the chapter assigned to the class the day before they did. It worked."

But his course changed when he met Ron Rebhuhn at a tennis tournament in New Hampshire in 1972. Ron was a tennis pro on Long Island, and they became fast friends. Ron suggested that Tommie contact the owner of an indoor tennis facility named Shore Tennis in Port Washington, New York. He followed up with an interview and was stunned that with 13 indoor courts they had only six members, but he agreed to take on the task of building up membership, which he did within the first few months. He stayed there for three years and then took a job at the Saw Mill Club in Mount Kisco, New York in 1978.

"It really is a lifetime sport," Tommie said of more seniors taking up the sport. "Tennis is one of the few sports where you can remain competitive throughout your whole life. Your competitive juices flow and you never stop playing. I never have. I was No. 1 in the East in the 60s and 65s and soon I'll be the rookie in the 70s."

Tommie continued, "Not only do I enjoy playing competitively with older players but I enjoy coaching older players. Right now I have three women in their 60s who have been playing the game for years but want to get better. And they are getting better. They're moving better, hitting harder and playing smarter on the court.

"You meet the best people in senior tennis and at the events they hold," he continued. "All over the world you get to know players you've seen or heard of before. It's clear that your reputation precedes you, the good and the bad. But, poor sportsmanship and cheating are not tolerated in the senior events. If one gets the reputation of being a poor sport or a cheater, word gets around quickly, and the player is no longer invited to play in the events. You don't find many cheaters in senior tennis.

"And of course, exercise like biking, healthy eating, prayer and rest are what works for me. Once you're out of shape, it's deadly."

Nutrition is also a passion for Tommie. When in his late 20s, he met someone in a health food store who challenged him to change his diet and to read books on good nutrition. A few years later, he dropped red meat and fish.

"I follow a vegan diet."

Some may say he is a fanatic, but the results for Tommie don't lie.

By chance, when I was editing this story of Tommie, the phone rang. It was Todd Gordon, a player local to our area and good friend of Tommie who was calling for my husband.

"Tommie and I have been playing together since 1985," Todd told me of his history with Tommie. "Tommie is tireless. Tommie and I have played for years together, at least three times a week, sometimes more. And when we play it's not just a set or two. It's at least three sets, and usually five. And I've even seen Tommie play five sets with me and later that day play five sets with someone else! I don't know how he does it!

"And I can truly say this," Todd continued. "Tommie is without sin. He has strong convictions and does what he thinks is morally right all the time. He never does things against others' interests. I mean, he'll honor others' interests before his own."

That is indeed a fitting tribute to Tommie, his character, his intelligence and his tennis skills. I couldn't agree more.

CHAPTER 24:

CHUCK NIEMETH

One morning when Chuck Niemeth was a senior in high school, his principal called him into his office. At first, Chuck thought 'What's this about? I haven't done anything wrong, have I? Maybe it has something to do with student council.'

"To my surprise the principal started asking me questions about college," Chuck said. "I hadn't given it much thought, but I knew I wanted to be a lawyer, so I figured college was something I should consider. It's funny. I never knew what lawyers did, but what I heard of them I thought was good.

"So the principal asked if I'd thought about college, and I told him my tennis story. I had just won a local tournament in Pennsylvania and was feeling pretty good about my tennis, so I entered the Eastern Ohio Championship. In the first round I met the top seed. During the match, I noticed a gentleman watching our match pretty intently, and I thought it was my opponent's father. Well, I won the match pretty easily, and when the match was over the gentleman came up to me. It turns out he was the tennis coach at Kent State and said that he'd love to have me on the team. So, I told the principal 'I think I'll go to Kent State.'"

The principal responded, "That's nice but I think you can do better."

"What's better than Kent State?" Chuck asked. "The coach was a really nice guy."

"You can do better," replied the principal.

Chuck asked, "What's the best school I could apply to?"

"Harvard" was the principal's answer.

"I had never heard of Harvard. I told the principal, 'OK. I'll apply to Harvard, and if I get in I'll go there, but otherwise I'm going to Kent State.' "

What Chuck didn't know at the time was that the principal had recently learned of his perfect SAT scores, 800 in math, 800 in English, and decided Chuck needed some direction. And that was probably good because college was not a major concern in his family.

"My older sisters never went; my Dad didn't go,' said Chuck. "Only my mother went to Kent State for two years to get a certificate in teaching."

Chuck grew up in Lorain, Ohio, a town 30 miles west of Cleveland, with a population of about 60,000, where most men worked in the local steel mill. His paternal grandparents, German immigrants, arrived at Ellis Island in the late 1800's and headed west to Newark, Ohio. Chuck's father was a master mechanic for the railroad and worked mainly in the roundhouse where repairs were undertaken, and his mother taught school for some 25 years.

"I loved sports - still do - and the competition that goes with them. In Lorain, that's what all the boys did. We played football, baseball, basketball. No one ever studied. It was all sports. I was 6 foot, 2 by the time I was in ninth grade, so the coaches were happy to have me on their teams. Football and basketball were my favorites. I was a pitcher on the baseball team, but I was the No. 3 pitcher, and the team only played

Chuck Niemeth awaiting a match at the Atlantic Coast Cup in Bethesda, Maryland, 2015

two games a week. I quickly figured out that I wasn't going to get any playing time, so I decided to try tennis for my spring sport. I'd never played it before, but I made the team at No. 5. Not bad for a beginner. But, I have to say, our coach was the basketball coach and only one fellow on the team had actually taken a tennis lesson.

"I got to be half decent in tennis. At No. 5, I won all my matches, and my second year I played at No. 2 and did very well, also winning all my matches. But, in truth, the Lake Erie League that we played in was far from big time."

During the summers, Chuck worked at the town park for 88 cents an hour, doing whatever odd jobs were given to him. But, his favorite assignment was running the baseball program for the campers.

Chuck did get into Harvard. As the summer of 1958 wound down, he packed one bag of all his belongings, took the bus to Cleveland, then another bus to Boston. When he arrived at Cambridge, he asked the police officer directing traffic, "Where's Harvard?"

The officer responded, "Come on. Where's Harvard? Are you kidding me? It's right here. You're on the campus."

Chuck found where to register, found his suite in Massachusetts Hall, the oldest building on campus and met his five roommates. Their suite was directly above the President's office.

"We made all the noise we could," he joked.

Now the shock of being at Harvard, a world totally foreign to him, hit.

"One of my roommates was John Foster Dulles' grandson," says Chuck in disbelief.

"He lived on the Main Line outside of Philadelphia, which I had never heard of. He went to Exeter, which I hadn't heard of either. He wanted to write the great American novel, but that never happened. The last I heard is that he has a chicken farm in North Carolina.

"But it was more than the privileged background of many of my classmates. It was the academics. I had never studied in high school. I didn't know *how* to study. How was I ever going to get through, I often wondered. I majored in Math, and had to study all the time. Actually, I never felt comfortable at Harvard."

"Did you have a chance to play some tennis at Harvard?" I asked.

"I didn't play much tennis at Harvard either. I made the freshman team but was at the bottom of the ladder and only played once in a while. But I got to know Tim Gallwey a little. Tim quit tennis for 25 years. The pressure was too much, and he wasn't enjoying it. Years later he started playing again and felt little pressure. He was fascinated with the change in his attitude and wrote a book, *The Inner Game of Tennis*, explaining to players how to play tennis without feeling debilitating pressure."

Chuck did well enough academically to get a scholarship to Michigan Law School. He described it as "the best place in the world."

"By this time I was ready. I knew how to tackle the books, but more than that, I loved the enthusiasm, the Big House, the Big Ten athletics. I felt at home."

Graduating from Michigan in 1965, Chuck took his first job with O'Melveny & Myers, a leading firm in corporate and securities work in Los Angeles.

"I had never been west of Ann Arbor!" he said. "I loved LA. Then, it was the land of opportunity. Even newcomers were welcome and had a chance to succeed."

In 1967, Chuck met Anne Meckes of Pelham, New York, who worked as a secretary at O'Melveny.

"Secretaries back then did much more than typing and taking dictation. They worked more as paralegals as we know them today. Anne and I dated and were married in October, 1968. We will soon have our 50th anniversary."

Chuck paused a minute before asking, "Can I tell you a story? It's a little off the subject but it does involve an anniversary of sorts?"

"Sure. Tell me the story."

"One day 25 or so years ago I got a telephone call from a *Boston Globe* reporter. He said to me, 'there are seven billion people in the world, but only two graduated with math degrees from Harvard in 1962 and went on to Michigan for their graduate degrees.' I wasn't quite sure where he was going with this. He continued, "Do you know who they are?' I knew I fit that description but I had no idea who the second person was. He enlightened me, 'You and the Unabomber, Ted Kaczynski.' He was fishing for some information about who he was back when we were in school, and asked if I knew him at Harvard. I said, 'No' and was glad when the conversation ended. But two years ago I went to my 50th reunion, which is really an anniversary, and the class published a book with classmates commenting on their 50 years since graduation. Ted Kaczynski was one of them.

And actually, there was some dark humor in his story, starting with the basics: 'address: cellblock 04475 Florence Penitentiary; occupation: Prisoner, awards: eight life sentences.'"

"What is it that causes bright people with, potentially, good futures, to go so awry?"

"Clearly, he was mentally disturbed," concluded Chuck.

Chuck stayed with O'Melveny & Myers for 40 years when he succumbed to the mandatory retirement age at 65. For 18 of those years he was in Los Angeles and when he was asked to open a new office in New York City, he was more than happy to oblige as he and Anne are both Easterners and they were ready to come home. The couple first lived in Manhattan for ten years, then moved to Greenwich, Connecticut in 1990. But Chuck wasn't ready to put an end to his legal career completely, despite his age. He joined Baker & McKenzie and continues even now to commute into the city three or four days a week.

"Law is a challenge, and I like challenges, similar to the challenges of competition. Competition is in my DNA," he said.

Before moving to Greenwich, Chuck had played only a little tennis.

"It was next to impossible to get a court in the city."

At the age of 60 he decided it was time to take up the game seriously again.

"This was the beginning of my tennis career," he said proudly.

By moving to Greenwich he had ample opportunity to join a tennis club, arrange games and hone his skills. He was still very fit at 165 pounds on a 6 foot, 2 inch frame and fast on his feet. Greenwich for years had a town tournament, a very popular event.

"For ten years I won the 50 and over category more often than not. It's always a great opportunity to meet other tennis players in the area, who are usually eager to play when called. I began playing for a USTA doubles team in Connecticut. We had a terrific team with Roy Anderson and Walter Beatty and some other good players and managed to be No. 1 in Connecticut for years. But our nemesis was Massachusetts. They always won."

Chuck entered all four of the national championships in 2015 for the first time and won two of the Category II tournaments, finishing the year ranked No. 7 nationally in the 75 singles.

"It is always good to be the youngest guy in an age group," he noted.

"What's better for your psychological well-being than to win a tournament? That's one reason why I love senior tennis. Of course, there are times when you lose, but you're out there getting good exercise, getting good competition. Your adrenalin kicks in, and you can win some points you never thought you could. You're on a high - a great feeling for a 75-year-old!

"And the friends I make are very important to me. That's why I especially like the team tournaments like the USTA matches and the Atlantic Coast Cup matches. Your teammates are there for you, win or lose. The arm around the shoulder and the 'tough match Chuck' gestures help to get you ready for the next round. And sometimes they'll offer advice which is helpful. You may not have noticed something that was happening during the game, but they will because they're on the sidelines or sitting on the grass watching - and they'll let you know.

"I guess you could say we're a bunch of old men who stay young, active and engaged!"

Lorain, Ohio would be proud of their native son's many accomplishments, including his mastery of staying young and engaged with the lifetime sport of tennis.

CHAPTER 25:

GREG TEBBE

G reg Tebbe, tall and lean with dark brown hair, gleaming white teeth and a ready smile, is a very young senior! But, already he is giving back to the game he loves.

Born March 15, 1963, Greg grew up in Santa Barbara and graduated from its public high school. Greg didn't take up tennis until he was 13 or so, and when he entered his first junior tournament at 14, he was outplayed by most of his opponents, who had been playing the game much longer. Nevertheless, Greg made the high school tennis team, though not earning one of the coveted top spots.

Greg's father, an attorney, was working in Washington, D.C. for a year on the savings and loan crisis in the early 1980s. The family moved with him to D.C. for the year, and a young associate in his father's office, Danny Waldman, a tennis player who had recently graduated from Harvard, watched Greg play one day and got in touch with Coach Barnaby, Harvard's tennis coach. Soon, Greg was recruited by Barnaby and joined the varsity. Harvard's team, always formidable, then included Howard Sands, one of the top college players in the United States. The Harvard team went to the NCAA's and was ranked among the top 20 college tennis teams in the country. His second year, another stellar player, Larry Scott, joined the team. Greg never played higher than No. 8, which certainly wasn't chicken scratch, but he decided to make a change. He and a good friend and fellow tennis player Mark Goodman took a year's leave of absence and traveled to Europe to enter tournaments in France and Sweden.

"The French system was the best," explained Greg. "They rated each player, and luckily I had a good rating, which entitled me to free housing which was amazing. We'd stay for a week in these gorgeous homes with people who loved tennis and especially loved American tennis players. I kept in touch with some of them for many years.

"And there was prize money," he continued. "Not a lot, but between $500 and $1,000 which was enough to cover our expenses."

Greg and Mark's modus operandi was to study a map of France, choose the destination they'd like to visit, sign up for a tournament in that area - there were tournaments all over - and make their way to Normandy or Nice or Bordeaux.

"This way we got to tour the whole country. But, we had a cranky car. We rented a Citroen, not that old, but just not very reliable. And it looked like it would fall apart if we were in an accident. So we were in Lyon, and Mark was driving. We got sideswiped. It wasn't a strong impact, but for the Citroen, it was enough to do significant damage. The rental company replaced the Citroen without charge and gave us an Opal which was a huge improvement."

After France, Greg and Mark took on Sweden.

"The Swedish system was quite different. There, each tournament continued for a month, not the customary week or so. And the tournaments were organized around ability, not age, so at 20, I could be playing someone 35, as long as our skill levels were similar. Each tournament would start with the

Greg Tebbe

'unknowns' playing in the early rounds, the winners going on to the next. Then, better ranked players were filtered in when the tournament reached the quarters. Actually, the system was somewhat akin to a ladder."

"Housing wasn't provided in Sweden, but we stayed with friends," added Greg.

"So how about your success rate?" I asked.

"Mark and I did pretty well. We got to the finals of a lot of the tournaments, and we won one. It was a men's open, and the prize was $500 or $1000, I forget, but they gave us a gift too. The Swedes commonly gave a financial reward plus a 'gift.' Well, our gift was this huge tube of toothpaste! I thought 'What the heck are they giving us toothpaste for? And why in such a big tube?' It turns out, the tube was filled with caviar!"

Greg returned to Harvard for his junior and senior years, but he didn't rejoin the tennis team. Division I sports take up an inordinate amount of time and effort, and he thought it was best to concentrate on studying. After graduating in 1986, Greg accepted a summer job as a tennis coach, touring with eight promising juniors in the 16s and the 18s. A private company initiated the program whereby Greg made all the travel arrangements, coached the kids and shepherded them throughout the summer. One tournament he remembered was in Germany at the German junior open. Michael Stich, who would later win the men's singles title at Wimbledon in 1991, played in the tournament and won.

When Greg's job ended as summer waned, he applied to Goldman Sachs for a job.

"I think it was this experience I had touring with eight kids and managing their lives for several weeks that got me the job," he said. "I specifically remember two of the senior partners who interviewed me being impressed by that."

Working at Goldman took its toll on Greg's tennis. For ten years, he didn't play, but gradually he got back into it playing with some of the top players in northern Westchester and entering local club tournaments and such.

After 21 years with Goldman working as a trader, Greg retired in 2007, left New York and returned to his roots, his hometown Santa Barbara. It took Greg no time at all to make his way into coaching - at his alma mater, Santa Barbara High. From 2008 to 2011, he was the assistant coach of the boys' varsity tennis team. Since then, he has been the head coach of both the boys' and the girls' varsity teams.

Coaching is not easy, but it's definitely a challenge that Greg sought out.

"The challenges are many," he said. "First, you have the administrative responsibilities - arranging matches for the season, organizing the trips to the different schools all over southern California, deciding what level each player should be assigned to, making sure supplies are available - to name a few.

"And then I plan out the practices. I'm very organized and don't want any dead time. Each drill has a purpose, strategies are learned through specific drills, warm ups are very regimented. Each player does the same warm up. Then I have challenge matches which are an important part of organizing the team. And finally, I'm strict about conditioning and stretching.

"During each practice I spend most of my time observing; watching the kids play their challenge matches, watching their skill at mastering the drills. Occasionally if we have an odd number of kids at practice on a particular day, I'll fill in but that's rare."

"Do you have any assistants?" I asked.

"I have one part time assistant, but I invite all the local pros who work with these kids privately to come to my practices. This has worked really well. The pros like it, and I not only get help, but I also get some good ideas from them.

"Of course, another challenge is working with egos. I always push the team concept. From the first day of practice and throughout the season, I let them know what I expect about their behavior: respect for all their teammates, good sportsmanship, and I dwell on how they're their school's representatives and how they present themselves at other schools is significant. Rarely have I had a problem with my kids, though I've seen plenty of slammed and thrown racquets and bad language from other kids.

"My players are at an age where they're impressionable," he continued. "I hammer home the importance of these life lessons, and I'm happy to say it seems to work. We have 20 matches a season, 10 home, 10 away, plus all the practices every day when not playing matches. So, I spend a lot of time with my players and have an opportunity to mentor them.

"But you know what my biggest challenge is? Parents. Most of my players' parents are terrific, but a small minority is very vocal. Their kids are great. I don't have a problem with them, but in a 'high achieving neighborhood' as Santa Barbara is, I have a few very demanding parents, and, quite simply, I hate to deal with them."

"Why doesn't that surprise me?" I asked rhetorically. "So how about the rewards?"

"One of the rewards of coaching, aside from developing a winning team, is guiding my kids toward colleges. Many of them don't have a strong feeling about where to go; most consider only west coast schools, but, when I think it's appropriate with a particular player, I ask them, 'Would you consider a school in the east?'

"I had a girl on my girls' team, Rachel Dicker Sadowsky, who was not only a top player but also an excellent student. I encouraged her to consider an Ivy League school. She was recruited by both Harvard and Dartmouth. She chose Dartmouth.

"And, of course, having a winning season, seeing your boys and girls improve at all levels from the top to the bottom, is rewarding. When I see my No. 20 player improve I know I'm making progress. We've had a great record. We play in the top division being a large school, so we meet the toughest and best competition. The boys' team is ranked No. 10 in Southern California, which is no easy feat - California is the apogee of junior tennis in the United States.

"My most successful graduate so far is Chase Melton, who played for Cal Berkeley. But, you know, most of the really good players aren't going to high schools any more. They're being home schooled so they can spend more time on their games with private coaches and trainers and tournaments, literally, all over the world."

In July, 2014, Greg played in his first senior event - the 50-and-over National Hard Court Championships held in Santa Barbara. Playing doubles with Will Davies, they lost in the main draw but won the consolation or "back draw" tournament. And, much to his surprise, that one victory won them a national ranking: No. 20 in the country.

Being married with three kids at home, Greg said he was not inclined to play that many senior events, but he said he would leave that option available to him down the road.

"While the kids are home I won't be playing," he said. "Maybe in the 55s.

"Right now I'm playing a lot of USTA league tennis: men's 4.5 and mixed doubles in a 9.0 league," he continued. "Both teams play out of Santa Barbara, and we've done well, winning our flight but losing in the finals of the regional tournaments."

"How do you like playing mixed?" I asked. "I've found a lot of men who don't like it that much."

Greg was quick to reply. "I love playing mixed as the level of play is very competitive and the strategy is much different than in men's doubles. In the mixed, there is much more poaching and movement. I find there is much more discussion of strategy with my mixed partner than in men's doubles, and I really enjoy that aspect of it. I find the women are, generally, more competitive than the men, which makes it even more fun."

I asked, "If you start playing some more 50s tournaments in the years to come, will you play singles as well as doubles?"

"It'll be in doubles. That's the game I love."

"Why?" I asked

"First, I enjoy the team aspect - working together with a partner. There's a lot of strategizing in doubles. It's a bit like the trading skills I used at Goldman - it's fast paced; instant decisions have to be made, and it's always better if your partner knows your strategy before the point begins.

"Tennis keeps me in shape. I don't enjoy running. I like games where I can work toward a goal - winning. For me it's a stress reliever. I concentrate on the moment and forget about other issues facing me.

"I love the competition. We're playing high level tennis, and there's nothing better than playing a long-fought point successfully. I feel like my game is as good as it has ever been, and I have found spending more time on training off the court has been a big factor in keeping my game strong, as well as my body healthy. I work out with a trainer at least once a week where I can focus on keeping my core strong and my body as flexible as possible. I guess it's making a difference since I just went up to a 5.0."

"Congratulations Greg. But, to me, that's not a surprise."

Greg accepted the compliment with a grin and continued, "I also try to bike as often as I can. I probably play twice a week on average and almost exclusively doubles. I find playing singles puts too much strain on my body, and I am convinced I will be able to enjoy tennis for many more years if I limit my singles play. I also happen to enjoy playing doubles much more than singles. Doubles is becoming very popular too with the spectators. The television coverage of doubles matches is much improved. Spectators enjoy the fast play, the net play, the strategizing, the excitement.

"Last, I guess I'd say, tennis is a social game. It's a great way to meet people. And you learn a lot about people on the tennis court. If they have some issues calling lines correctly, that's a clue about their character. If they blow up after losing a point, that too, tells you something about character."

But beyond that, Greg has given back to the game of tennis by coaching his local high school team. In addition, he uses his free time productively to find other projects where his organizational skills and financial know-how can be of use. He has spearheaded a fund raising campaign to improve many of the facilities at Santa Barbara High School.

Greg is an extraordinary young man – modest, bright, organized, energetic, engaged, personable, caring. I could go on and on, but tennis is fortunate to have Greg as a devoted tennis player who looks for opportunities to improve his own and others' games. But more importantly, he personifies what's best in a tennis player who is generous with his time and his talents.

CHAPTER 26:

ROB LABRIOLA

On a rainy April Fool's Day, I drove down a country road, characteristically dirt for the area in northern Westchester County, New York, an area known for its attractive, up-scale homes. I turned into Rob Labriola's driveway and was met at the front door by Rob dressed in his tennis clothes, eagerly looking forward to his lunch-time game. A cappuccino latte was offered and we settled down in his home office where he works three days a week.

Born on April 29, 1966 in White Plains, New York, Rob grew up in Armonk, the son of Michael and Patricia, part of a closely-knit Italian family of successful landscapers. When he was seven years old, he was having trouble seeing the black board in school and not doing well academically. His mother took him to an ophthalmologist, who discovered Rob was almost blind in the left eye and had a stigmatism in both eyes. The doctor suggested that, in addition to glasses, Rob take up some eye/hand coordination activities. His Mom said, 'Well, I've just started playing tennis. Would that be good for Rob?' The doctor said 'Perfect.'

At seven, tennis became Rob's passion.

"I loved it," he told me. "I couldn't get enough of it. I started taking lessons from Craig Sauce when I was seven or eight at the Banksville Racquet Club, and later at Whipporwill Country Club from the head pro Lane Pettibone. These guys were the world to me. I'd have a half-hour lesson for 12 dollars and practice all day long if I could on a court somewhere or against the garage door of our house.

"Lane taught me the fundamentals and Craig focused on topspin. I had to hit the ball six feet above the net and keep it in the court. That got me hitting the ball hard and deep, and even today I hit the ball deep.

"When I was 11, I started entering 12-and-under tournaments," he said. "I loved the competition. I was even ranked No. 22 in the Easterns. That was such a thrill for me - an actual ranking. When I was 12, I started bugging my Dad to put a tennis court in our back yard. He said, 'No. It's too expensive,' but I didn't let up.

"It so happened that my father had a contract with Union Carbide at the time to maintain the corporate grounds and Union Carbide asked him if he could put in two tennis courts. He thought he could. He had never done it before but learned on the job. With that behind him, he finally said, 'OK, I'll put in your court, but only if we can get Uncle Carmine [Michael's brother] to pay for the fence. This was the most expensive part of the project. Uncle Carmine's business was doing very well, and he agreed.

"We put in a Har-Tru court," he continued. "It wasn't the best Har-Tru, but to me it was gold. Maintenance of the court was a family project. My brother Michael and sister Christine, my parents and I rolled the court with a hand roller. We put down the calcium and nailed down the lines."

As Rob talked, I could feel the enthusiasm of this little 12-year old boy totally entranced by his new sport, his new life.

Rob Labriola (right) and his former rival now doubles partner John Dokken

"I didn't care that the kids in school teased me for wearing thick glasses and playing a nerdy sport.

"The court was down a long hill and we had to put in a retaining wall. The area was wet and the bugs were thick - real pests - but I didn't pay attention to them. I had a ball machine, a relic by today's standards that would only hold about 40 balls, and couldn't be adjusted for speed or oscillation. But none of this mattered to me. I was obsessed. I lived on the court practicing my serve, hitting with the ball machine and making sure the court was well maintained."

"A silly question," I said, "but did you play on the high school team?"

"I was a scrawny little kid with thick coke-bottle glasses and I was playing this faggie sport. I was 5'1" and weighed 130 pounds. I got a lot of razzing and bullying, but yes, in the eighth grade I made varsity and played No. 1 on the team. And one match I'll never forget is playing against John Dokken from John Jay High School, one of our rival schools. John and I are partners now in the 50's, but then he was a giant to me. He was 6'2" and weighed 200 pounds. He never lost a high school tennis match and won the state title twice. He crushed me. I might have gotten a game or two, but I didn't care. It was just great to get a chance to play against him.

"In high school I did grow. I still wore the coke-bottle glasses, but I put on weight and reached 5'9" and I was playing tournaments every weekend all over Westchester, Long Island and New Jersey with some nationals sprinkled in, like the Easter Bowl in Miami. I continued to play in tournaments until about junior year. Then I began to think I was missing parties and girls. One of the girls I kinda liked was Sue Lascari, but she had a boyfriend. Anyway, because her last name started in 'L' like mine, our lockers were near each other. And she wore these tight velvet pants. She had two pair - one pair was black, the other was electric blue. She definitely turned my head."

"Which pair did you like best?"

Rob paused a split second, grinned, and said, "The electric blue ones."

So, Rob stopped playing in tournaments, and when it came time to apply to colleges, his ranking that year said "insufficient data." But Rob was accepted by Furman University in Greenville, South Carolina, a small liberal arts college with 2,700 students. Furman was Division 1 in tennis, and the tennis coach was Paul Scarpa, who at the end of his career was one of the winningest coaches in NCAA history.

"Scarpa had almost no scholarship money to offer. The college gave him $4,100 to divide among six players. I had a decent freshman year, so Scarpa offered me a $1,500 scholarship, but I asked if I could talk to my parents first. Scarpa didn't have a problem with that. I called home and spoke to my mother. I asked my Mom, 'Is it OK if I say no?' My parents were doing pretty well financially then and could handle the $8,000 tuition. Mom said, 'Why say no?' I told her that all the guys who had said 'Yes' to Scarpa were now doing all kinds of things for him - picking up his dry cleaning, doing shopping, walking the dog, washing his car. I didn't want to have to do that. Mom said 'Whatever you think is best,' so I thanked Scarpa for the offer, turned it down and suggested he give it to another family who needed it more. Scarpa looked at me like I had two heads.

"After that, our relationship changed a bit. Then for my junior year, I wanted to study abroad. Scarpa said that if I went abroad he wouldn't let me back on the team, so I didn't go, but I went the fall semester of my senior year and when I got back Scarpa kept his word and he didn't let me back on the team and I was done.

"Shortly after quitting the team, I gained 18 pounds and thought 'I gotta do something about this.' I took up jogging and fell in love with it. The jogging got me back into shape at my normal weight of 155. I also took a health and nutrition class, and the professor, Dr. Molnar, said, 'If you want an 'A' in this course, you have to run 13 miles up Paris Mountain.' I did, and I got an 'A.'

"I graduated from Furman in 1988, missed my tennis and traveled to play some tournaments. I really wanted to play on the satellite tour, but my parents, who did not go to college, were disappointed. I felt pressure to continue with school and do graduate studies. I had worked every summer starting at 14 sweeping courts and stringing racquets at the Canyon Club in Armonk for the pro, Peter Fiore, eventually giving lessons for $15 an hour when I was in college. Later, I started my own business *Home Court Advantage* – even had business cards made up – and taught some of the top business executives in New York City who had summer homes in the area. I charged

$75 an hour and loved making money. In 1991, I sold my business to the Ivan Lendl Tennis Center, who wanted my business name and my client list."

You may be getting the picture now that that little kid with the thick glasses transformed his mojo from a scrappy tennis player into an astute businessman with a 'You don't tell me what to do' attitude.

During the summer of 1989, Rob left for four weeks of satellite tennis in Austria. The satellite tour at the time consisted of four one-week tournaments in different locations. The courts were red clay. Rob had to develop a slice backhand so he could extend the points and had to learn to be patient on the clay.

"Jimmy Connors was my idol, so I liked to hit a hard, flat two-handed backhand," he said. "Instead, I had to learn to play like Guillermo Vilas, the left-handed top player from Argentina. I was surviving and got to the third week of play. I was in the third round, and a little crowd of my friends was watching. I got impatient and played my preferred hard, flat game and lost the first set. So, I went to looping balls and slowing the game down and won the second set. In the third set, I lost the first couple of games, lost my patience too and went back to playing my game. Then, I had an impulsive moment. I went up to the net, shook my opponent's hand and defaulted.

"After I defaulted, I went to Venice to see a girlfriend and didn't pick up a racquet for ten years. I thought I'm too old to do this."

Yes, Rob can be impulsive. But, he also has a clear picture of what he wants to do, when and how.

"When I got back from Austria, I decided I wanted to make my parents proud. I went to graduate school for my MBA in finance at Pace Business School full time and graduated in 1992.

Remember Susan Lascori? Susan and Rob became a couple. She graduated from Providence College in 1988 and went to work for First Boston in New York City.

"In business school I started studying the markets," he said. "They fascinated me. Sue was familiar with them, too, and suggested that I go to this open interview at Paine Webber. I went, and I also went for an interview at Kidder Peabody. Of the two, I liked Paine Webber and contacted the woman who had conducted the open interview. She said, 'I had you in the 'maybe' pile. You went to Furman, didn't you?'"

Rob acknowledged that he did. She said that she too went to Furman.

"Being at the right place at the right time has its advantages," Rob said.

Rob turned down Kidder Peabody's better offer, and went with Paine Webber where he stayed for three years. From Paine Webber, he went to Merrill Lynch for five years, Smith Barney for seven, Morgan Stanley for seven and back with Merrill Lynch, working in Wealth Management: high net worth, endowments and pensions.

Susan Lascori and Rob Labriola were married in April of 1994. About this time, when Rob was 35, Lasik eye surgery had been perfected and was readily available.

"The doctors said they could fix the left eye and 'tweak' the right. The surgery was painless, and the next day as I rode the train to work I could read the *Wall Street Journal* without glasses. I was ecstatic. I thought, too, this would help my tennis. You never see tennis players wearing glasses. Why? Because they fog up, or you drip sweat into the eye and need constant toweling. And, when you are serving or hitting an overhead, the ball goes out of the range of the glasses which can be disconcerting.

"When I was 45, I had to have the right eye redone, and now I can wear contacts, which I never could before. With all the improvements in contacts, I can keep them in for three or four days without changing them. It's amazing."

"When did you get back into tennis?"

"Robbie, my son, was born in 1997 when we were living in New Jersey, and we decided we wanted to go back to Westchester County. We didn't want to go back to Armonk - too nouveau riche - and in 1999 we bought a house in Cross River, New York, not far from Katonah and in the John Jay School district - John Dokken's old haunt. I was back with my old tennis friends again. I joined Saw Mill, where a lot of them played in a 5.0 league, and I played at Chestnut Ridge in another good league. Also, I wanted to teach Robbie my favorite sport.

"But I wanted to spend more time with my Dad too. He didn't play tennis. He played golf and cards. In 2001, I joined Whipporwill Country Club, the club my family had belonged to for years, and took up golf. When I take up a sport, I'm serious about it. I was playing 40, 50, 60 rounds a year. I'm glad I did that, because my Dad died not long after, but I had some quality time with him doing what he loved.

"The tennis program at Whipporwill was hurting then. One of the members of the tennis committee asked if I would get involved to help revitalize the program. We hired a new pro, Adam Kework, 11 years ago and he's still with us doing a terrific job.

"When I turned 45, I wanted to compete again in USTA sanctioned national tournaments," Rob continued. "In 2011, I played in Park City, Utah in the 45 Indoor Hard Courts. Mario Tabares, a Cuban, who in his 20's was playing great tennis when Castro pulled him back into Cuba and didn't let him leave for nine years, beat me in the main draw. But Tabares had a win over Patrick Rafter, the great Australian player, so that wasn't a bad loss. I then went into the back draw and lost in the finals.

"I played in 2012 on the grass at Germantown," he continued. "I was unseeded and beat five seeds to reach the finals, where I met Gary Nadelbaum, an Aussie, now living in Texas. It rained the day of the finals, and we had to play indoors. I pulled a groin muscle and lost 7-5, 6-3. Of course, I was disappointed, but in the next tournament, also in Germantown, I was seeded. I was to play Jeff Layman, who played No. 3 at Clemson when I was at Furman. I called my old coach, Paul Scarpa, who had retired a few years before, and asked if he remembered Layman because I wanted some insight into his game. Scarpa never forgets a thing. He said 'Good serve and backhand slice.' Scarpa remembered correctly. I lost 6-4, 6-4 in the semis, but that was still pretty good.

"Even though I'm only playing for the gold, silver is OK," he said. "Also at Germantown, Dokken and I teamed up in doubles where we lost to Nadelman, my nemesis, and his partner in the finals. And we won our first silver ball together.

"In 2015, the 45s were in Cincinnati, and again I played doubles with Dokken. We had a great win in the semis against Ellis Ferreira, the big lefty South African who had won the Australian Open in 2000 and was ranked as high as No. 2 in the world in doubles with Rick Leach. Dokken and I lost to Nadelbaum and Brooks in the final 7-6, 7-6. Again, a loss to Nadelbaum, but we won another silver."

"Why do you like playing in the senior tennis tournaments?"

"You have a different perspective about competing at this age," he said. "It was your life when you were younger, but now it's extra special. I'm doing pretty well in my career, I have a great family, and believe it or not, I'm more relaxed."

Rob noticed my smile. "You relax?" I said. "I think your 'On/Off' switch is always 'On.'"

Rob told more stories of the camaraderie and satisfaction that tennis provides for him and confessed that he is playing more tennis now than he had in 24 years.

"There are moments on the tennis court I can't replace in my life," he said. "I get such a high - pulling your opponent out of the court..." and Rob's voice trailed off as he imagined himself doing that.

"What tips do you have for seniors?"

"Try to play as many days, consecutively, before a match. You'll know your optimum. It could be four days, five days. For me it's seven. Then it feels as though the racquet is an extension of my hand. Then I know I'm ready.

"Play with your friends; have a beer after and tell your favorite stories. Tennis can be a lonely sport as kids but not for seniors. As a kid you're trying to beat each other. In college, you're so stressed for time. It's different as a senior.

"Last year the 50s draws were full: 128 entrants in each tournament. Every year the draw is full. By the time you're 50, the kids are out of the house, your careers are going well and you have the time. It *is* a life-long sport that you can enjoy."

Rob was a good candidate to interview. He was not shy and gave good, complete and thoughtful answers. I've known him through my husband Gordon as they've played together for many years. But, more recently, I got to know Rob through a project that would likely overwhelm less committed, determined, passionate individuals.

Our local high school, John Jay, nurtures excellent high school players like John Dokken, the No. 1 at the University of Virginia in his day, Nick Crystal of the University of Southern California, and James Aronson, from the University of Richmond. But, the school did not have its own tennis courts -

one of the few in the area that does not. The players and their coaches had to take buses to town courts, often not in good shape, to practice and to play their home matches. Rob, as the high school coach, had had enough. John Jay needed to have its own courts.

Rob spearheaded a drive to raise over $500,000 to build six courts, to maneuver through all the State Education Department, the DEP [Department of Environmental Protection] the DEC [Department of Conservation] and other rules and regulations, to build a community effort now known as the Katonah Lewisboro Community Tennis Association, to promote tennis not only for the school physical education classes but also for the school teams and the entire community.

On September 18, 2015, the KLCTA gifted six beautiful hard courts to the Katonah Lewisboro School District and to the Town of Lewisboro. Today, the courts are used for tennis instruction during gym classes, for the boys' and girls' junior and varsity tennis teams, for the residents of the Town of Lewisboro and all the students and their families in the school district. That is giving back to tennis and making sure the popularity of tennis continues to grow.

Rob Labriola is devoted to the youth in his community. His boundless enthusiasm will surely keep him in the sport for a very long time.

CHAPTER 27:

JOHN NEWCOMBE, ROY EMERSON, OWEN DAVIDSON and COMPANY

S teve Flink, the well-known tennis historian, journalist and author of the book *The Greatest Tennis Matches of All Time*, gave me contact information to reach out to John Newcombe at his home in Sydney, Australia. This was a rare opportunity. I had watched Newcombe play many times on TV and at the U.S. Open. And like many women, I had a secret crush on him with his good looks, his Aussie accent, his unassuming charm, and, of course, his spectacular tennis.

He was at the top of his game just as I was becoming interested in and learning tennis in the 1960's and '70's. In singles, he won Wimbledon three times, the Australian twice and the U.S. singles title twice. When he won Wimbledon for the first time in 1967, he described it as "a dream of a 10-year old kid come true." When he defeated Jimmy Connors at the Australian Open in 1975, the whole tennis world loved him. In doubles, he won 17 major championships, 12 with Tony Roche and five more with other partners, among them Owen Davidson and Tom Okker of the Netherlands.

He was the top-ranked player in the world in 1967 and in 1974 and helped Australia to Davis Cup titles in 1964, 1965, 1966, 1967 and 1973. He also captained the Aussie Davis Cup team from 1994 until 2000, capturing the Davis Cup title in 1999, the first time his country won since 1986. In 1986, John received the ultimate tennis honor - being inducted into the International Hall of Fame.

John's game was exciting to watch, featuring a powerful forehand and big first serve that allowed him to get to the net quickly to hit winning volleys. He was also known for hitting second serve aces. Just as important were his mental toughness and strategy skills.

I was scheduled to meet "Newk" at his Texas tennis ranch in the town of New Braunfels in March, 2016 where he was hosting his annual "Tennis Fantasies with John Newcombe and The Legends" for senior men and women.

As I got on the highway, leaving the Austin airport and heading to his tennis ranch, I was assaulted by 18 wheelers and pick-ups flying past me at what seemed like 100 miles per hour. Then I saw a speed limit sign - '85'. That's when I knew I was in Texas.

Newk's ranch is another world - a cozy ranch house with western-style sofas facing a stone fireplace topped by a picture of John Newcombe in his prime. A movable partition with photos and memorabilia of John's earlier years and of his family separated the living room from the lounge.

I was to meet John at the ranch lounge at 7 pm, and there he was with his good friend and fellow Aussie tennis legend Owen Davidson, nicknamed "Davo," and other good friends Tex and Gayle from Stratton, Vermont. He asked me to join

John Newcombe

them, so I sat next to Gayle at the bar, and learned that she, Tex and John had been friends ever since John had his tennis camp in Stratton back in the 70's.

"We still get to see John occasionally and he asked us to come to the Ranch this week, so here we are," explained Gayle in her Georgia accent.

"John is a good loyal friend," I ventured.

"Oh yes. He doesn't have any airs and if you're his friend you're his friend forever."

After hearing about Tex and Gayle's years together, John asked us to follow him into the dining room for dinner. We joined Jeremy Friedland, the ranch CEO, and his wife, Debbie, at their table, filled our plates at the buffet table and then the stories began.

"Well, 1963 was a good year for me," began John. "I played for the Australian Davis Cup for the first time when I was 19. And, when I was playing in a tournament that year in Hamburg, Germany, I met a young German girl, the No. 2 junior tennis player in Germany."

When John returned to his hotel room after his date, he announced to Davo, his roommate that week, "I just met the girl I'm going to marry." And indeed he had. He and Angie Pfannenburg were married on February 2, 1966 in Sydney, Australia and raised a son Clint and two daughters, Tanya and Gigi. The Newcombes now have six grandchildren, two girls and four boys ages two to 11, all living in Sydney. Angie and

John celebrated their 50th wedding anniversary in February of 2016 and now split their time between a home in Sydney and a 200-acre farm an hour and a half away.

"We have a couple horses, a couple cows, some chickens, that's it," John said. "The grandkids love their time there. It's very relaxing, and I get to play my new game, golf.

"After 50 years, Angie's still my best friend," he continued. "Being married to me when I was on the tour and we had little children was hard on her, but we stuck together and now can enjoy our family and being together."

John said he spends about 10 weeks a year in Texas at the ranch, which he bought in 1968 at age 23.

"Traveling on the tour was tough on the family, and I thought a place in Texas would ease some of that," he said. "And I thought, too, that sometime in the future the ranch could be developed into something big. Over the years, I added an additional two hundred acres with the intention of building a country club and upscale houses. But when I was ready to do that, my timing couldn't have been worse. It was 2007. We all know what happened to the real estate market after 2007. But, we hung on, and now the development under the experienced eye of Jeremy is thriving. I'm only here 10 weeks a year, but Jeremy is my watch dog and CEO."

A native of Rhodesia, now Zimbabwe, Jeremy has been with John for 35 years. Nevertheless, John is a "hands on" businessman who runs the ranch, the tennis academy, the camps and the new country club with the assistance of a loyal, dedicated staff. The staff loyalty, I think, comes from John's fair, level-headed, unassuming, "no ego" but creative style of management. Turnover is non-existent; the friendships are solid.

If you want to play tennis or learn to play tennis, this is the place to be. With four clay courts, 20 hard courts and four indoor courts, a cadre of pros, you're set.

"We also have another 13 courts at the Country Club, three of which are owned by the ranch if we need more."

Phil Hendrie, a member of the Newcombe tennis family for 20 years, is the director of the Newcombe Tennis Academy and his staff work to train young players who hope to earn scholarships to play top college tennis and beyond. The program is harsh: up at 5 a.m. for running at 5:30, weight training, conditioning and grinding out hours and hours of tennis. Phil said that you have to feel the pain; you have to be an animal. But, everyone in the academy is part of the family and all are treated with respect. Phil knows what he is doing. He coached Lleyton Hewitt and Li Na among others and builds character as much as he builds tennis players.

"It's not just your strokes that are important; it's yourself," said Newk. "By becoming better tennis players, you become better people."

"When did you start playing tennis?" I asked John.

"Everybody played tennis in Australia. Every little town in Australia had tennis courts. This was just after World War II. Australia lost many men during the war, but, of course, we didn't have a war-torn country. Every house remained intact and most had a tennis court in the back yard. They were made out of ant bed."

I interrupted, "Ant bed?"

"Yes. We'd knock down these ant beds. They could be two, three feet high. And they were everywhere. Then we'd smooth the beds into a flat surface with a tractor, water them, put down lines, put up a net, maybe some fencing, and we had our courts. In every country town, tennis was the No. 1 activity for families - parents, kids, aunts and uncles, cousins. There was no TV, and every weekend we'd go to someone's house and play. So many future champions came out of these little towns. Tennis became the most popular sport in the country.

"When I grew up, tennis was a big thing - tennis and cricket. I was a good cricketer too. We kids with good hand/eye coordination gravitated toward certain sports: soccer, rugby, cricket and tennis. I had to make a choice because I enjoyed them all. At 11 and a half at the school I went to, I was selected for cricket. I told them I couldn't do cricket. I was going to play tennis.

"I had a dream to play at Wimbledon," he continued. "The school was very unhappy. They said I had to be a team player, but I stuck to my guns and that was it. When I was 13, the headmaster said I was wasting my life and I got 'Six on the bum.'"

"Six on the bum? What's that?" I asked.

"That's Australia's version of corporal punishment."

"I went to a big private school in Sydney and we had a Sargent Major. Anyway that's what he was called. Every Friday afternoon I was a regular on his drill squad."

"His drill squad?

"Well, that's what we called it, but it was actually detention. If we misbehaved in school, we'd get detention, and I was a regular. The Sargent Major had us go through drills and 'doubles' around the quad. We had to march in double time in formation for 40 minutes.

"Several years later I was asked to come back to the school and speak to the students. One of the first people I saw was the Sargent Major. I went up to him.

"'Sargeant Major, Sir!' I shouted out as was the custom.'Newcombe,' responded the Sargent Major.

"'Yes sir. Sir, thank you, Sir, for getting me through the tough five-set tennis matches.'

"The Sargent Major knew what I meant. The military training he taught made me fit and tough enough to win the long matches.

"I remember when I was seven" continued Newk. "It was 1951 and Frank Sedgman was playing the Davis Cup finals in Sydney against Ted Schroeder. My Dad and I went to White City where the matches were being played. The stadium was packed, and we had seats way up at the top of the stands. I remember watching and dreaming about playing in Davis Cup matches for Australia. Years later, I was talking to a good friend who was also at that match. He grew up in a tiny town, Tarcutta, a tiny town of 200 or 300 people in New South Wales. His father was the town butcher and they drove almost 300 miles to get to Sydney for the matches. And he told me he was thinking the same thing. Do you know who it was?"

None of us had a clue.

"Tony Roche."

Mouths dropped.

"Tony and I won 12 Grand Slam doubles tournaments. We played on several Australian Davis Cup teams and we worked together as captain and coach of the Australian Davis Cup teams in the 1990's."

I said, "Tell us about the U.S. Open doubles in 1973."

Davidson was delighted to hear that question and jumped in.

"That was the best. Newk and I are playing doubles together and we get to the finals. And who do we play?" he asked looking at Newcombe with a broad smile.

"Laver and Rosewall."

"Right. Laver and Rosewall, a tough team. But not too tough for us," stated Davidson, with pride. "Remember, it's best-of-five sets. We win the first set 7-5, lose the second 2-6, win the third 7-5. We're up in the fourth. At match point, Laver serves to my backhand. I didn't choke. I went for a big one, but Laver wins the point. Then we get another match point, and I'm thinking 'don't try to get a great shot. Just get the ball back.' Rosewall is at net, the ball comes to him - a sitter - and I'm thinking we're toast, but he dumped the ball into the net. I couldn't believe it. No one could believe it. We beat Laver and Rosewall in the finals of the U.S. Open!"

John smiled, relishing the memory and added, "How about the Australian Championship in 1965? My partner in the mixed doubles is Margaret Court - one of the greatest women players ever by the way - and we get to the finals. I'm staying in Melbourne in Owen's home, which I always do when I'm in Melbourne, and Owen gets to the finals too, with Robyn Ebbern. Now there's no way Robyn and Davo are going to beat Margaret and me. Just no way."

"Not so fast, mate," interjected Davo.

"So we're all in the finals and the rains came. And it rained and rained. At the same time Robyn and Davo were having a royal argument that went on for two days. Well, the finals were cancelled. Cancelled! They were never played and both teams were declared the winner. So, even though I knew without a doubt that Margaret and I would be the winners, we had to share the glory with Davo and Robyn. Lucky!"

Davo smiled broadly and sipped his wine. "Tell the story about the faith healer," he suggested.

"I had had a bad elbow for two or three months – since Wimbledon," Newk said. "This is 1974 and I'm playing in Manila. I get to the finals and think I've got to do something about my elbow. So the morning of the finals – at 6 a.m. – Mal Anderson, Bob Carmichael and another mate, Reed Witt, go with me to this faith healer. His name was Juan Blanche. He made an incision in my arm and took all this goo out. The swelling went down immediately and later that day I won the finals. The next week I'm playing in Japan, won the tournament and beat the shit out of everybody."

"Did you ever go to the faith healer again," I asked.

"I did. About a year later I was having trouble with my right knee, was in Manila again and I went to him, but he couldn't help me this time. So, he had a 50-50 record. I had to have surgery to remove the cartilage later when in San Antonio."

After some laughter and colorful comments from Davo, I asked, "What made the Aussies so strong in the '50's, '60s and '70s? You guys were invincible not only in the major tournaments but also in Davis Cup play. And you all still remain close friends. What do you attribute that to?"

Newcombe thought a minute, and said, "We've got to take you back to the beginning. Back to 1909, Australia and New Zealand teamed up to form the team, 'Australasia.' Everything was so remote for us and both countries were young. But, we can thank Norman Brookes and Anthony Wilding, who put us on the map and started it all. Wilding, from Christchurch, New Zealand, and Norman Brookes, an Aussie, were both great athletes, cricketers and footballers in addition to being tennis players. Cricket and football were the big sports in Australia then, but tennis was becoming more popular. Wilding and Brookes became serious tennis players, so serious that they were both ranked No. 1 in the world and had many victories at Wimbledon, the Australian Open and at the Davis Cup. From the early 1900's until 1914, Wilding brought us Australasia Davis Cup victories. Then he served in World War I and, tragically, was killed in May of 1915 in France. But, Brookes took his place as best he could and brought back many more Davis Cup victories after that. Wilding and Brookes were our inspiration. It's because of them that we developed such a strong Davis Cup tradition.

Davo joined in, "After World War II, Harry Hopman took over Australian tennis. He developed players who became the best - Sedgman, McGregor, Rosewall, Hoad, Laver, Fraser,

Stolle, Roche, Newcombe and me too. We were players under his regime."

Newcombe added, "Owen, Tony Roche and I were the 'Last of the Mohicans' - the end of his proteges in Australia. We learned from the great Aussies before us - Laver, Rosewall, Emerson, Stolle - all of them. Another piece of our long history: in 1939 the U.S. held the Davis Cup final round at the Merion Cricket Club outside of Philadelphia. We had John Bromwich and Adrian Quist on our team. We were down love two in matches and came back to win the Cup 3-2. I remember thinking, 'Here we are so far away from the rest of the world, and we're able to dominate.' And we Aussies were always gentlemen on the court, but we would fight to the death because we weren't representing ourselves. We were representing our history - the Australian Davis Cup history - and our country. Those of us who came later kept the tradition going. We gave 100 percent. We'd leave Australia and be away for eight months at a time. Our teammates became our family. Our motto was 'All for one and one for all.' But when we played against each other we'd spill our blood to win."

John continued, "My first contact with Hopman was when I was nine years old and I got a letter from him. I had been on holiday with my parents at Portsea, a coastal resort an hour from Melbourne. I was playing tennis against my father, and for the first time ever I beat him. A gentleman, Mr. Schrader, was watching the match and he happened to be a good friend of Mr. Hopman's. He wrote to Hopman telling him about this kid he had seen playing tennis. Not much later, I got a letter from Hopman, and at the end of the year – in December – after I turned ten, he invited me to watch a Davis Cup match at White City. It was 1954, and my father and I went to White City again for the Cup finals. A record number of people were in the audience – 26,000 – and stands had to be added to accommodate the crowd.

"Harry Hopman was our coach for many years," Newk continued. "I don't think he was a great tennis coach, but he was a great trainer of young men to get them to play at the top of their games. He trained us hard. He was a disciplinarian who demanded total concentration and commitment in such a way that when we played we were at our best. Hopman didn't like us amateurs to turn pro, but we had to make a living. Frank Sedgman was one of the first to turn, and Hopman was furious. He was almost a father to us. And then he was gone."

For personal reasons, Hopman went to the U.S. in 1969, where he started a tennis academy on Long Island and developed John McEnroe, Peter Fleming, Vitas Gerulaitis and others into top players.

"I don't think there's ever been such a long and strong bond among fellow Aussie tennis players, has there?" I asked.

Newcombe said without hesitation, "That's 100 percent true."

"A watershed moment in tennis came in 1968," said John. "That's when the Open era began, but for many years after there were problems. In late 1967, I, and seven others, signed five-year contracts to join Lamar Hunt's World Championship Tennis [WCT]. Lamar Hunt stepped up and did more than anyone to keep professional tennis secure and to get good prize money."

Lamar Hunt, the son of a wealthy oilman, H.L. Hunt, loved his sports and, with his vast inherited wealth, promoted football, basketball, tennis, ice hockey and soccer. In October of 1967 the "Handsome Eight" – John Newcombe, Tony Roche, Dennis Ralston, Cliff Drysdale, Butch Buchholz, Nikki Pilic, Roger Taylor and Pierre Barthes - signed on, and the first WCT tournament was held in January of 1968 in Sydney.

John explained, "The organizations that controlled tennis, the ITF [International Federation of Tennis] and the USLTA [United States Lawn Tennis Association] and the other countries' lawn tennis associations, were all run by amateur officials and had been for a hundred years. Letting go of that power was difficult and led to many heated disputes. The amateur officials decided that the WCT players could enter the majors, but they couldn't play on their Davis Cup teams. We thought the U.S. was behind this scheme. Not to play for our Davis Cup - that was a blow. We had had a winning team in 1967 with Emerson, Tony Roche and me, but then the juniors, John Alexander and Phil Dent, had to step in and take our places. We hadn't passed on the secrets of playing Davis Cup, but they had Neale Fraser as their coach. Fraser was a great player but he was older and the team lost five years in a row to the U.S.

"In 1973, our contracts with Hunt had ended, and we were free to play Davis Cup again. Fraser came to me and asked if I would play. 'There's no money,' he lamented. That didn't matter to me. 'Yes, of course, I'll play' I told him.

"Look out Americans! We played the finals in Cleveland that year. Laver was 35 then. He and I won our singles matches against Stan Smith and Tom Gorman and we won the doubles as well. The team won the Cup 5-0."

Davo added, "Just ask Stan Smith about Newk's mental toughness. You know there are hitters and there are players. There's a big difference between them. The players know the mental part of the game. The hitters don't. Newk was the toughest player."

John, cutting in, went back to the story of the turmoil after 1968 for the professional players.

"In 1969, I was the runner up to Laver at Wimbledon. In 1970, I beat Rosewall to win the tournament. Rosewall was my childhood hero, but I went into a zone and played the best tennis of my life to win the Wimbledon singles championship. In 1971, I won again, beating Stan Smith. In 1972, I was ready to defend the title that I had won two years in a row, but I received a letter from Wimbledon saying that all WCT players were ineligible to play in the coming year. That didn't make sense. We had been playing for Hunt since 1968. Why disqualify us now? I sent in my entry form anyway. I knew the contract with Hunt had only six months to go. That didn't matter to Wimbledon. We were banned.

"Then another controversy was brewing," he continued. "It's 1973, and we're free to play Davis Cup again. But Nikki Pilic from Yugoslavia didn't want to play on Yugoslavia's Davis Cup team. Yugoslavia and the ITF retaliated and suspended him, which meant he couldn't play at Wimbledon or at any of the other Grand Slam tournaments. We had just formed the ATP [Association of Tennis Professionals] with Jack Kramer as President to replace Hunt's WCT. We, the members of the ATP, declared our support of Pilic. We thought it was Pilic's choice to make. We claimed Pilic was an independent professional and should be allowed to play wherever he wishes. The ITF was testing us, and when we stated our case, the ITF said that they couldn't allow Nikki Pilic to play. We said, 'If you don't let him play we're pulling out.'

"Wimbledon and the ITF said 'We've got to stop this revolt.' They thought that Wimbledon was a good test because it was so important that the players would never boycott. And 84 of 87 ATP players pulled out, including 13 of the 16 top players. The boycott really made the ATP. We had power by sticking together and from then on the professional tour grew and prospered."

I said, "But that was a bitter pill for you not to play Wimbledon and defend your title twice, in 1972 and 1973."

"Things happen in life," he said. "Strangely, because I wasn't playing in the tournament in 1973, I was asked by NBC and the BBC to broadcast it live. That was the start of my TV career. I watched and reported on Jan Kodes' win over Alex Metreveli in the finals."

"John, what, for you, were some other memorable matches?" I asked.

"On January 1, 1975, I was 30 years old. I met Jimmy Connors in the finals of the Australian Open, played at Kooyong in Melbourne. Connors was much younger and was, of course, the favorite. We had a long four-set match. I won the first set. Jimmy won the second. I won the third, and the crowd was wild. The fourth set went to a tie-breaker. I won it 9-7, and when it was over I jumped the net to shake Jimmy's hand."

"You could do that at 30 after a long four-set match?" I joked.

John just smiled.

"Another very satisfying match was at the 1981 U.S. Open. Fred Stolle, then 42, and I, then 37, were playing John McEnroe and Peter Fleming in the semifinals. We lost 7-6 in the fifth, but they knew they had been in a battle."

The left-handed "Davo" was born in Melbourne, Australia in 1943 and was inducted into the International Tennis Hall of Fame in 2010. He is best known for his winning the Grand Slam in mixed doubles in 1967. He won the Australian title with Lesley Turner Bowrey and then won the French, Wimbledon and U.S. titles with Billie Jean King. In all, he won eight majors in mixed doubles with King and ten in all. In men's doubles, he won the Australian Open in 1972 with Rosewall and his aforementioned title at the U.S. Open with Newcombe in 1973.

"Being a lefty is an advantage, and I have a big wing span that helped my net game," he said of one of the attributes that

Owen "Davo" Davidson organizing matches
for John Newcombe's camp

allowed him to succeed in the highest level of tennis. And with some laughter, Newcombe kidded with his mate that Billie Jean King could more than hold her own, "though she didn't have success with other partners. I think you were the only one who could handle her."

We finished our conversation well after dessert had been served and left for a restful night before all the "Fantasy" players arrived.

The Fantasy players weren't due until the afternoon, but John, the Legends, Davo and Roy Emerson, nicknamed, "Emo," who had arrived late the night before, and his staff were busy making last minute plans for their arrival. After breakfast I wandered into the living room and met Steve and Debbie Contardi manning the table of souvenir tennis bags and other paraphernalia.

Debbie and Steve Contardi are longtime friends of John's, from The Club at Harper's Point in Cincinnati, Ohio, where they run the tennis programs there, and, in particular, the Contardi Tennis Camp, a bastion of Cincinnati tennis instruction for 42 years. The Contardis have also been handling the merchandising aspect of John's "Tennis Fantasies with John Newcombe and The Legends" for many years.

Two "Fantasies" are held each year, one in March for men and women, and one in October for men only. They're both exceedingly popular, with many of the same "campers" coming back year after year. The men's camp in October, however, is larger and, therefore, the number of legends increases. For the October, 2016 camp, Emerson and Davidson returned as well as Laver, Rosewall, Stolle, Ross Case, Mark Woodforde, Marty Riessen, Dick Stockton, Brian Gottfried, Charlie Pasarell, Rick Leach, and brothers, Murphy and Luke Jensen.

"What an array of talent and the men can't get enough of it," Contari said. "Most of them are regulars, and it's all very competitive. These guys take this opportunity very seriously, and their games have improved enormously."

"So what's your overall impression of senior tennis?" I asked Steve.

"The future of senior tennis is excellent, no doubt about it. The older folks are in better shape now, and they're not stopped by aching hips or knees. They just get the surgery, and they're back on the courts with new enthusiasm.

"We've also developed new teaching techniques, and, of course, the new equipment helps. We were being invaded by 'pickle ball.' A lot of the older folks enjoy it, but we're coming up with ways to meet the competition. We're using low compression tennis balls - just like they're doing with the kids - and we have players in their 90's playing three times a week. We put them on a three-week program where we start with the lowest compression balls, the red ones. Then we move on to the middle compression balls, which are green and end with the highest - yellow. The new drills are age appropriate, so we may start with simple throwing and catching depending on the student's skill level.

"There was considerable fallout from the '70's boom in tennis because the game is so difficult to learn, but our new equipment and drills make learning the game easier. As a result, the older seniors are back, they love the social aspect, they love the exercise, and they're having fun and staying fit. You should see them! It's a joy to watch these folks in their 90's enjoying tennis."

I would have talked longer with Steve, but the Fantasy campers began to filter in, and he and Debbie were busy handing out the camp schedule, directions to their condos or conchitas, and telling them to meet at The Gazebo at 3 pm sharp.

"Newk and the Legends will be there to greet you."

The interruption gave me a chance to meet and talk with Roy Emerson. "Emo" was the first player to win 12 major singles titles, a record not broken until Pete Sampras did it in 2000; in all, he won 28 major titles, 16 in doubles; he was the only male player in history to win a career Grand Slam in singles and doubles and he was the first male player to win each major title - Wimbledon, French, U.S. Open and Australian - at least twice in his career. He dominated men's tennis in the 1960's, was ranked No. 1 in the world in 1964 and 1965; ranked in the top 10 nine times, and he helped his Australian Davis Cup team win an amazing eight Davis Cup victories: 1959, 1960, 1961, 1962, 1964, 1965, 1966 and 1967. What happened in 1963? The Aussies lost to the United States 3-2.

Emerson was born in November 1936 on a large dairy farm in Blackbutt, Queensland. He too started to play tennis on an ant bed tennis court. He was strong, some say from milking the Illawara cows on his farm, but I doubted that. I grew up on a farm with Holsteins, and I don't think you really get strong from milking. More likely, it was all the other farm work that got him in shape.

"I was very lucky," said Emerson. "I played and won for my country. I won Wimbledon. From 1954 on I played with all the Australian greats: Rosewall, Hoad, Laver, Stolle, Roche and

Roy Emerson

others. And I was coached by Harry Hopman.

"I remember going to the U.S. National Championship at Forest Hills in 1954 with Ken Rosewall, Lew Hoad, Rex Hartwig, Mervyn Rose, Neale Fraser, Rod Laver, Fred Stolle and Hopman. I was only 17, a promising junior, and I got to see Vic Seixas beat Rex in the finals and Seixas and Tony Trabert, both Americans, defeat Rosewall and Hoad in the doubles finals. This was inspiring tennis for a kid like me.

"Hopman was a tough disciplinarian," he continued. "I liked working with someone who demanded hard work. He wanted us fit and in shape to survive those five-set matches. That definitely made a difference. And he was a tactician too. You can't just play well. You have to know the game inside and out. You have to play smart to win."

Davo joined us and asked, "Did you tell Judy the story about our match at Wimbledon in 1966?"

"No," he replied.

"Well, then I'll tell it," Davo interjected. "It's 1966, and we're playing Wimbledon. To play at Wimbledon back then was the pinnacle of tennis. So I get to the quarters and I have to face Emo. The match goes like this. Emo wins the first set 6-1. Then it's 2-1, Emo's favor, and I hit a great drop volley. Emo runs for it, skids and crashes into the umpire's stand, hurting his shoulder. But Emo didn't retire or anything. He played till the end, and I beat the shit out of him."

Davo flashed a devious smile. Emo just smiled. The next day Davo went to the hospital to visit Emo.

"Emo was really hurt pretty badly, but he wouldn't quit. He finished the match without a complaint. That's my good friend, Emo. There's nobody quite like him."

"But I recovered," offered Emo.

"Thank God. Actually, I have to say, the odds makers had you winning Wimbledon that year. You had won the tournament the two years before, and you were the No. 1 player in the world. That was a safe bet."

Emo nodded and smiled.

Emo was known for his endurance, his backhand that dipped over the net bouncing at the server's feet as he moved to the net, his speed, his big serve and attacking game and stunning volleys that ended points quickly.

"Didn't you continue to play tennis into the late '70's?"

"Yes, Rod Laver and I joined the senior circuit and then we ran tennis camps together for a while. But in 1973, 43 years ago, I started the Roy Emerson Tennis Weeks in Gstaad, Switzerland. I had won the Swiss Open five times and thought Gstaad was the most beautiful place in the world. 'Wouldn't it make sense to run a tennis program there?' I thought. And we made it happen."

The tennis program is held at The Palace Hotel, one of the finest in the world, sitting high on a peak in the midst of the Swiss Alps. Players of different levels come from all over the world and often come back again and again. Since 2008, Emerson's Tennis Weeks have been voted the No. 1 tennis camp in the world. The sessions run from the middle of June to the middle of September, and, in addition to fine instruction from Roy and his staff, the campers enjoy elegant dining and old-world charm, as well as a chance to get to know Emerson. What could be better?

"Roy, can you comment on the future of tennis as you see it?"

"Well, I'm not a big endorser of the new game," he said. "I played when everyone relied on their classic strokes and varied strategies. We attacked the net much more. That's where we won the points – at the net. Now the game is fought from the baseline. Today, with the new equipment and training, it's a power game. Actually, the new equipment has improved the women's game. Footwork is key and the top players are masters. Roger Federer is my favorite. He has more finesse than the others - more cat and mouse, more variety to his game. It's difficult to play this baseline game of today when you're older. I suggest giving your opponent a little garbage if you have to and work on developing a terrific net game."

"Aside from teaching, are you playing much tennis today?" I asked.

"I play with my wife, Joy. She's my practice partner."

"How did you two meet?"

"It was on a tennis court in Brisbane, Australia in 1958. She was and still is a good player."

Roy and Joy raised two children, a daughter Heidi, and a son, Tony. Now, when not in Gstaad, Switzerland, Joy and Roy reside in Newport Beach, California.

At 3:00, the campers gathered around the Gazebo, anxious to be split up into groups for the beginning of their fantasy weekend.

John first welcomed them, with Emerson and Davidson at his side. Then Chris Jacques, another Australian and head pro of the adult tennis facility, introduced his staff, young men and women from New Zealand, the Philippines, Scotland, Australia and New Mexico. Chris had been at the ranch for 11 years, where he met his wife Annie, now the popular masseuse at the Ranch. Yes, it seems to be one big, happy family. Chris read out the lists of campers and what courts they were to go to. They grabbed their gear, laughing and chatting excitedly, anxious to meet their pro for the day and to start the drills and match play.

John had mentioned that I was "a visitor" writing a book on senior tennis. The campers were only too happy to answer questions. I had a chance to talk to a few before leaving the next day.

Judy Hart and her husband Michael moved from an almond ranch in Northern California to New Braunfels and were "locals."

"We wanted to be around good tennis," said Judy. "We had been campers here before and decided this was where we wanted to be. We made the right choice. We fit in immediately. I'm playing tennis all the time and loving it. My husband has to go back to Northern California now and then to take care of the ranch, but I'm here permanently."

"Judy, how old are you?"

"I'm 61, but I don't feel 61."

"And you certainly don't look it," I said.

"I think playing doubles in an 8.0 league helps."

Judy had been playing doubles on a far court and soon returned to the Gazebo with another camper, Lynba Levine.

"This is my third time at the fantasy camp, and I love it," Lynba said. "I live in Galveston so it's not hard to get here. I still work full time, but I'm managing to get in more tennis, but it's never enough.

"I guess I'm going to have to give up my day job," she said with a laugh.

Lynba, petite, pretty and frisky, had a foreign accent and I asked where she was from.

"Latvia."

"What is your day job?"

"I'm an oncological gynecologist at the University of Texas."

"Wow. Good for you! Did you get your medical degree in Latvia?"

"Yes and I took all the necessary exams to become certified in the U.S."

"When did you start playing tennis?"

"Five years ago. I had always loved tennis. It was my childhood dream to play. But as a young girl I only had a chance to play competitive table tennis. Then five years ago, I took up tennis very seriously. I've gone to Roy Emerson's Gstaad Tennis Camp three times already for a week each time. And now I'm coming here too."

"How old are you, Lynba?"

"Fifty."

"One would hardly know."

Then Judy and Lynba were on their way.

I cornered Dana Flynn, 47, and Teresa Riehn, 52, from Woodlands, Texas, a suburb of Houston.

"In 2001 everybody I knew was playing tennis, so I joined a tennis club with child care," said Dana. "I had played in Oregon where I grew up but with family I had to stop. Now Teresa and I play together. We're both 4.5s."

"But," added Teresa, "I can't keep up with the young girls who are 4.5s. They're too young and strong and fast. I'm in the 50's now and I'm liking senior tennis just fine."

Jeffrey Sands was sidelined with a bad knee. As I returned to the bleachers to watch the pros drilling the campers, I saw Jeffrey with a big ice bag on his left knee. He didn't seem like a tennis player to me - a bit overweight.

"Can't play?" I asked.

"Yeah. I aggravated my knee last night."

But Jeffrey didn't seem to be upset.

Jeffrey said he earned a scholarship to play tennis at Washington State. He graduated in 1985 and went east to Harbor Point to teach tennis for two years.

"I'd never played on clay before going east and my first time on a clay court I slid and slipped right over the net. But, I got to like it after a while. In 2006, I hated tennis. I had been teaching it and playing it for so long that I burned out. Then, eight years ago, I started coming to the Legends Fantasies and I've been playing ever since. My knee flares up from time to time, but I've got my wife Barbara playing too. She took it up ten years ago. She's now a 3.5 and loves the game."

"Is she here now?"

"Oh yeah. She wouldn't miss it."

Later that night as I was standing in the buffet line for the welcoming dinner, Steve Contardi came up and said, "Judy. I have someone here who wants to talk to you. He has a story to tell you."

There stood Mark.

"Your name is Judy Aydelott?"

"Right. How did you know?"

"After the clinic today I called my good friend Ian McFadzen from Sleepy Hollow to tell him about the fantasy camp. And I told him some woman was here writing a book about senior tennis and he said, 'Oh, That's Mrs. Aydelott.' I said 'You mean Debby Aydelott's mom?' He answered, 'Yes.' he answered.

"I remember when your daughter was a lifeguard at Sleepy. All the boys my age had a crush on her."

I smiled, "I think I remember hearing about that."

After filling my plate with healthy, delicious-looking food, I joined Mark and Paige Starcher at their table. Mark and Paige have been married 23 years and live in McLean, Virginia.

When Paige turned 60 - that was two years earlier and she looked to be 40 - she retired from her job in Washington D.C. as a U.S. tax attorney. Mark was still working in the computer science industry, but both are addicted senior tennis players.

Since Paige retired, she had more time to devote to tennis. "I was worried that I'd be bored when I retired, but with tennis I'm busy all the time," she said. "I've made new friends, my tennis has improved. I'm a 3.5/4.0 now."

"When I started playing as a kid in West Virginia, I got my first racquet from K-Mart - a pre-strung variety," she continued. "I was self-taught and didn't take any lessons until I was in my 40s. Now I'm making up for lost time."

Mark, originally from upstate New York, started playing tennis as a 10-year old and played on his college team for one year. Then studies interfered, but he continued to play and continued to love the game.

"I'm actually getting better, even though I'm 59," he said. "I love senior tennis. Everybody knows your name, it's very social, and it's good tennis."

The Legends, one by one, approached the podium at the dinner, and everyone knew that the team selections were about to be announced. But first, stories were told about past victories and losses. The most poignant was Davidson's story about his win over Emerson at Wimbledon. Although Davidson portrayed himself as the clear winner, there was a catch in his voice when he described the "never give up" attitude of his friend Emo.

I had to leave before the competition began and didn't get a chance to interview some of the other Legends, like Ross Case, another Australian who, while not as well known as Newcombe, Emerson and Davidson did win two major doubles titles.

I was also going to miss the battles between the Newcombe/Case team, the *Wallabies*, and the Davidson/Emerson team, the *Kookaburras*. But there is no doubt that the competition was going to be fierce.

The *Kookaburras* were called to the front of the dining room first to be taught their fight song. Emo mimicked the loud, laughing call of the kookaburra, a bird found commonly in Australia, and encouraged his team to join in. The team was definitely challenged – it needed a lot more practice.

John's team fight song was the war cry of the Huka Warriors from the Maori people of New Zealand meant to intimidate their rivals, also used by the modern-day New Zealand's rugby teams. John's rendition was priceless with the shouts, the stamping, the fierce intimidation.

Even though I missed the actual competition, I saw enough to be reassured that senior tennis is alive and well thanks, in part, to "Tennis Fantasies with John Newcombe and The Legends."

After I began writing Newcombe's chapter, I called him with two final questions.

"Do you think the future of senior tennis is strong or not?"

"It's very strong," said John. "People are taking better care of themselves these days and surgery is making a big impact. New knees and hips are available and the players are back out on the courts free of pain. And I see improvement in my fantasy campers who come back year after year."

"Do you have any tips for senior players?"

John's answer was simple. "Enjoy what you're doing. Nothing is better than a good game of tennis."

John Newcombe is an extraordinary person and I was privileged to have a chance to meet and interview him. He continues to be the charming, good looking Aussie I had a crush on years ago. He continues to cherish his days as a Davis Cup player and captain for his beloved Australia. His Davis Cup teammates continue to be his best friends: Emerson, Davidson, Laver, Rosewall, Stolle and others. Their friendship has been nourished by their lives together, their stories, their struggles during the change from amateur to professional tennis, their fun-loving good humor and their plain and simple decency. But beyond that, John has established himself as an outstanding businessman, sportscaster and tennis ambassador with no apparent ego. He is idolized in Australia and rightly so. John has lived his life well. We should all be as good at living as he is.

CHAPTER 28:

JUDY and GORDON AYDELOTT; JIMMY BIGGS and GORDON AYDELOTT

"I'm having as much fun now as I did when I was a kid."
–Jimmy Biggs

Tennis came into my life on Friday, May 11, 1962. Actually, it was probably three weeks before that, when a college friend at Smith, Joanie, asked if I would go on a blind date to Dartmouth's Green Key weekend.

A blind date for a whole weekend? Are you kidding me? This was my immediate thought.

"No thanks," I told her. "Not interested."

But a day or so later, she brought it up again. "No," I told her again. "Besides, it's the end of the semester and I have papers due and exams to study for."

Joanie was persistent and told me that I'd really like the guy. Gordy was his name. He was president of his fraternity, Kappa Sig. Again, I declined. A few days later, Joanie brought in reinforcements. Joanie, and our good friend, Mandy, worked me over some more. The latest enticement was that he was a really good tennis player. Tennis? The only tennis player I knew was my piano teacher, who talked often about his wins and losses during my lessons. He was a wonderful piano teacher, but he was a little guy, and I figured tennis was a wimpy sport. I was much more interested in muscle and brawn, preferably football players. Perhaps that had something to do with growing up on a farm and having an older brother who condescended into letting me be the center for his pickup football games with his friends. They needed somebody to hike the ball, and I loved it.

Not long after, I got a phone call from Ellie, another friend, who was going to Green Key. She gave me the hard sell. Green Key, she told me, is the best weekend of all Dartmouth weekends. The New England spring had arrived; the grass is green, the trees are in full bloom, the weather is generally warm and sunny, and the campus has shed its winter gloom, as have the students. For Dartmouth seniors, Green Key is especially memorable, as it is the last "college blast" before graduation. She assured me I, too, would have a "blast" as she knew Gordy and thought we would "enjoy each other's company," she added in her delicious Southern drawl. She suggested, too, that she and I could room together for the weekend. That wouldn't be so bad. I liked Ellie. She was from Little Rock, Arkansas and had all the charm of a Southern belle – and she knew her way around men too. I don't mean that in a derogatory way. She was very attractive, a great dresser, quite a dancer and lots of fun.

"I'll think about it," I responded. But the thought of spending a whole weekend on a blind date was still not appealing. Besides, I still had those papers due and finals to get through.

I really don't know what possessed me, but I gave in. I told Joanie I'd do it. And then a letter arrived signed by "Gordon Aydelott," saying he would meet me at the train station in White River Junction Friday afternoon. Now, I was having second thoughts. I was convinced disaster loomed. But I got my papers done, finished my exams and literally dumped some clothes into a suitcase before heading for the Northampton train station. It was Friday, May 11, 1962.

As I got off the train in White River Junction, I looked around for someone who might look like what I imagined Gordon Aydelott to look like. No such character in sight. But driving up to the station were Joanie and her boyfriend, John, in a hot little convertible. Joanie explained that Gordy had a tennis match that went into a third set, so he was delayed and couldn't meet me. They were taking me to the fraternity house, and I'd meet Gordy there. Fine with me. The longer it takes, the better.

I got to the fraternity house and it was not bad. A buffet was laid out in the big "living room," plainly furnished with large leather sofas, a worn out Oriental rug and a framed photograph of the house members in the place of honor over the large fire place. French doors led to an outside patio. I tried to inspect the photograph to see the head shots with the names underneath, but it was too high, and I didn't want to be too obvious. As I waited, the room filled up with dates and the brothers who were much better than I expected them to be. There were a lot of nicknames: Julio (as in Julio Basaha, a famous baseball player at the time), Goph, Hawk, J.C., RiRi, Cheeseman, Raybird, Cruiser and the Grand Gord. Remember, this was back in the days of the infamous "Animal House."

The brothers were engaging, friendly, funny and very curious about me and what I was doing there. Little did I know that they knew who I was. They knew that "Gordy" had a blind date and that he wasn't looking forward to it. They knew he thought the date would be a 'dog.' The only thing Joanie would tell him about me was that the girls liked me, which Gordon Aydelott took to mean, "Yeah, but the guys don't." Besides what girl would agree to go on a blind date for a weekend unless she were desperate?

As I grew more comfortable about what lay ahead, I didn't care when Gordon Aydelott showed up. It turns out, he was happily wiling away his time, getting a little 'buzz' on down in the basement playing beer-pong. What a wuss. He was too afraid to face the consequences. I learned later that he couldn't get to the train station on time because he had "tanked" in the second set to prolong the match. He then won easily in the third, had plenty of time to shower and get to the fraternity house before "the lovely date arrived."

Gordon Aydelott's cowardly behavior soon became obvious to one of his fraternity brothers, who went down to the basement to alert him that I was upstairs. "Gordy. You better get up there. She might get snaked away."

I saw "Gordy," as he was known by his friends, come through the basement door in his khaki Bermudas, a red polo shirt and loafers, wearing a sheepish grin. My first thought was, "Perhaps this is going to be fun." After a somewhat awkward introduction, we meandered into the living room, stopping at the buffet table for a snack and something to drink, and then out onto the patio, where we sat on the front step talking about family and hometowns. And that's how our weekend began.

Gordy, tall and surprisingly good looking, was from Waverly, a tiny town in northeastern Pennsylvania. He told me that the "town" consisted of the Community House, commonly known as The Comm, a large, rambling, red brick building housing the post office, the village library, snack bar, bowling alley, gymnasium and auditorium with an ample stage. The Comm sat at the edge of the village green, a gently sloping quadrangle, bordered by lovely white clapboard houses built in the early 1800's. Gordy lived in the one that stood proudly on the corner, directly across from two clay tennis courts nestled at the far end of the green. His family always knew they could find him on one of the courts if it wasn't freezing cold or if there wasn't snow on the ground.

Gordy spoke fondly of his Dad, Jack, and Mom, Marjorie, both from Ohio and proud graduates of Ohio State. A brother, Pete, 19 months older than Gordy, had recently graduated from Cornell and was an Ensign in the Navy. Bill, ten years younger, was still in grade school. Saint, an Airedale, made the family complete.

"My brother, Johnny, just graduated from Cornell too," I added. "But he joined the Army and is at Fort Rucker being trained to fly helicopters."

We were beginning to connect. Our stories of home and family continued throughout the weekend. I began by explaining that I grew up on a farm in Putnam County, 50 miles north of New York City. Actually, it wasn't a farm; it was a dude ranch owned and run by my parents, Jesse and Ruth.

"A dude ranch. Really? In New York?" asked Gordy.

"Yes. Echo Valley." It was given its name because when standing at the end of the long dirt driveway, looking down over a grassy valley with a stream passing through, you could call out and hear an echo.

I loved my home. An old farmhouse that had been in my father's family for several generations was converted into an inn with modest men's and women's dormitories, three or four private bedrooms and a large back bedroom with double-decker beds for the cowboys and kitchen staff on the second floor, a large living room with card tables and comfortable sofas and chairs, a dining room with fireplace for family style meals and a busy kitchen on the first floor. In the back of the house was my father's tiny office, a small bedroom for my brother and me – he, being four years older, slept on the top bunk – and my parents' bedroom, the only room providing them privacy and comfort.

"You know who lived there for a summer?" I asked.

Gordy looked at me, clueless. How would he know who lived there one summer?

"Do you know George Richey? "

"The tennis pro, George Richey?" asked Gordy.

"Yes. He was hired by a club in a nearby town to be the tennis pro for the summer season. Somehow, the club contacted my father and made arrangements for George Richey, his wife Betty and their two children Nancy and Cliff to rent the cabin for the summer," I explained.

"George Richey is one of the top tennis pros in the country. Nancy's one of the top U.S. players now and Cliff isn't far behind."

"Yes. We're still friends and keep in touch. When she lived in the cabin, she was seven and I was eight – we're exactly one year apart, minus two days. We were inseparable. A couple of times, Mr. Richey gave us a tennis lesson, but he thought we were too young to have a steady diet of tennis. I haven't held a racquet since."

"Too bad," commented Gordy.

"Over the years, Nancy would let me know when she was playing at Forest Hills and I'd go watch and visit. She always brought up the time the West Point cadets came to visit."

"The West Point cadets?" he asked.

"They came in late August after the freshmen, known as plebes, finished their eight weeks of beast barracks. Nancy spent the night with me before their arrival. We woke up even before sunrise to watch from my bedroom window the military supply trucks, filled with kitchen equipment and crates of food, bumping down our long, dirt driveway. By ten or so our front yard was the gathering place for friends, neighbors and ranch guests to greet the troops. Nancy and I got the best spot: sitting on the stone wall right next to the driveway. Soon we heard the plebes approaching on Hill Street, boots on blacktop, all in cadence. We wiggled with excitement. Then we saw the first company turn onto the driveway, sweating and tired from their 14-mile march with 60-pound packs on their backs, but always in formation. The other companies followed until all 1,000 plebes had marched right past Nancy and me on their way to the fields where they'd set up camp. Then, of course, Nancy and I skipped along behind to watch the pup tents go up. Finally, the plebes had a chance to relax with pick-up baseball and football games, and there we were, along the sidelines, taking it all in."

On Friday night of our Green Key weekend, we were off to a fraternity party at a cabin somewhere in the woods. Walking there was a challenge. I had only brought sandals, but a little mud on my feet didn't matter. The band was great and the dancing, just what I loved, was too. And Gordy seemed to be having a good time as well. Our low expectations were floating away as if they'd never existed. Saturday, sunny and warm even in New Hampshire, started with another trek through the woods to an open field and a small lake, perfect for a picnic, softball and swimming. That night a band treated us to the best of Elvis, early Beatles, Sam Cook, Three Dog Night and other favorites for more terrific dancing. Sunday featured an inter-fraternity water fight with fire hoses, pails, empty garbage cans, balloons and whatever held lots of water. I guess we were all in the mood to party and let off steam.

During the weekend, I, of course, met Jimmy Biggs, Gordy's best friend, roommate and doubles partner. Their stories of tennis wins, losses and related issues clearly piqued my interest in the game.

"We started playing tennis together when we were at the Hill School," Gordy said. "We met sophomore year on the tennis courts when our coach, Frank 'Chief' Bender, decided we would make a good doubles team. We played No. 3 doubles and didn't lose a match. During our junior and senior years, we were No. 1 doubles and had good solid records.

"Colleges didn't recruit back then, but I wanted to go to Dartmouth and applied there. Jimmy was going to Yale where his father, grandfather and brother went."

Jimmy then decided to cut in. "During Christmas break I visited my brother Whitney and spent time with his fraternity brothers," he said. "I thought they were all snobs. I quickly applied to Dartmouth sight unseen just before the deadline. Ned Hall, our headmaster, I think, wrote a really good letter of recommendation for both of us and we were both accepted.

"When we got there and tried out for the tennis team – as freshmen we couldn't play on the varsity - the coach, Red Hoehn, had a ready-made doubles team, and we've played as a team ever since."

Gordy asked, "How about our spring trips?"

Jimmy laughed.

Gordy continued, "Each spring our coach would arrange matches against the University of Miami, North Carolina, North Carolina State and Navy. With all the snow and cold weather, we hadn't touched a racquet in months. It took us 37 hours to drive down to Miami. We had four players in each car, two in the front, two in the back, with four hour shifts each. When the driver and co-pilot finished their four hours, we'd rotate. The driver and co-pilot got in the back seat, and the guys in the back took over the driving. The guys in the back slept – or at least tried to. When we finally got to Miami, we were pretty beat but

Gordon Aydelott teaching Judy Aydelott tennis

happy to see the warm weather and sunny skies. After a night's sleep, we faced Miami. They were formidable. We were not, and we got killed. We played them again the next day. Same thing happened – we got killed. That night before driving to North Carolina we bought some six packs, went to a bowling alley and tied one on. All the empty beer cans were on the floor in the back of the car.   The next day, Red Hoehn, our coach, wanted to ride in our car, and we kept saying, 'Red. Sit up here in the front,' but he kept heading for the back seat. When he opened the door he immediately saw the empty beer cans. His only comment was, 'Guess you boys had a pretty good time last night.' He settled himself in the seat and we were off."

'Red' was much loved by his team.

"Red may not have been the best coach of tennis, but he was patient, caring, fair and long suffering," said Jimmy. "He was old school, always a gentlemen and wanted his team to be gentlemen."

Gordy chimed in, "A friend of mine, Fred Hammer, remembers watching a match between Dartmouth and Colgate being played in Hanover. The team score was even at 3-3 and the final match was being played. Dartmouth spectators cheered their team and jeered Colgate's. Red went up to the crowd and said, 'If you don't stop this behavior, I'm taking my players off the court and we'll forfeit the match.' The crowd went silent. Colgate won."

Jimmy picked it up, "After Miami we did well against the other schools beating them all. On our way back, our last scheduled match was against the Marines at Quantico. Red Hoehn's son, after graduating from Dartmouth, entered the Marine Corps, and he was stationed at Quantico. There were no matches scheduled the next day, so that night we all went to Dick's 'Snake Ranch' and overindulged."

If you've never heard of a "Snake Ranch," you're not alone. Gordon explained that it is the name given to an apartment that Marine buddies rent where they can "entertain" friends and young ladies.

"Ron Pickett, a senior, drove the car back to the barracks where we were staying," Gordy said. "In the middle of the night, two MP's came into the barracks, woke up Red and said 'One of your boys left a car running. You gotta move it.' So Red got up and took on the task."

Jimmy continued, "As a lesson, the next day Red announced challenge matches. It was a brutally hot day, and I was supposed to play Jack Herrick. He was not feeling at all well and said, 'OK. The score will be 6-2, 6-1. You win and don't run me.'"

Dartmouth had the same trip during their junior year that proved more sobering.

"When we arrived in Miami, we went to a drug store to buy some sun tan lotion, and we overheard a news story on the radio – and I'll never forget it - the announcer said, 'The Yale tennis team was involved in an automobile accident in Fayetteville, North Carolina,'" Jimmy said. "One of the passengers died at the scene, and two were seriously injured and taken to the Fayetteville hospital. This was terrible, very sobering news. We knew all the guys on the team, and we knew the guys in the car: Sidney Wood, Craig Joiner, the team captain, and Stu Ludlum, believed to be the driver."

Gordy added, "On our way home we stopped at the hospital to visit Stu, who had gone to the Hill School with us and was on the tennis team there. Stu was recovering, though slowly; Sidney Wood died in the hospital and Craig had died at the scene. I think because of that incident colleges and universities changed their policies and provided the transportation for their students traveling to and from sanctioned events."

After a pause, Jimmy continued, "But later that year, Gordy and I, playing No. 1 doubles for Dartmouth, won the ECAC [Eastern College Athletic Conference] championship played at Colgate by beating another Dartmouth team, Ron Pickett and Larry Holden, in the finals. Our actual reward was a small medal on a ribbon, but the college wanted a photograph with a big silver trophy. The photographer borrowed a large silver bowl that he found in the trophy case, and if you look closely you can see that it was for a rowing victory sometime in the past."

Jimmy's greatest claim to fame was playing against Ramanathan Krishnan - who ranked as high as No. 6 in the world - in the first round of the U.S. Championships at Forest Hills in 1959. Jimmy had won several New England tournaments that summer and was able to get into the main draw.

"It was Labor Day weekend and the match was scheduled for the stadium court," Jimmy said. "There was a pretty good crowd in the stands. My family was there. Gordy was there. I was nervous as hell before the match, but as I walked on to the court I felt great. As we warmed up, the umpire announced the players. First, was Krishnan, seeded No. 3 in the tournament, an Indian Davis Cup player, semifinalist at Wimbledon and I don't remember what else. Then he announced me, 'Jim Biggs, captain of the Dartmouth freshman tennis team.' That was it. I served first and won. Then I had a break point on Krishnan's serve, and hit the best shot of my life. I'd been practicing it – a short cross-court backhand – and could never get it in, but on that day, at that time, it worked. But, Krishnan ran it down and won the point and held his serve. I served and held. At the changeover I was leading 2-1."

Gordy added, "We're in the stands and Jim's father leans over and says, 'Get a picture of the scoreboard while Jimmy's ahead. The lead may not last.' After that the match went very quickly. And it was Jimmy's last lead of the day.

"Then that same year we had a thrill. Jimmy and I played in the National Doubles Championship at the Longwood Cricket Club outside of Boston against Marty Mulligan from Australia and Bob Hewitt from South Africa. They were world class players, and, of course, the No. 1 seeds. We break Hewitt's serve, and I say to Jimmy 'If we can hold your serve we have a shot at winning this set. Jimmy is serving to Hewitt, I'm at net, and I hear Mulligan, also at net, saying 'Cross.' I think he thinks I'm going to cross, but instead after Hewitt returned serve, Mulligan crossed on Jimmy's first volley and hit a blistering shot down my alley. So much for holding serve. We lost in three straight sets."

There would be more tennis stories, but then the weekend came to an end after the huge inter-fraternity water fight. Gordy made arrangements to borrow a car to take me back to Smith, and Jimmy came along too. After we said our good-byes, I wondered if Gordy had had as much fun as I and if I would be hearing from him soon. Monday passed, no phone call; Tuesday passed, no phone call. Then, on Wednesday night, I was studying in my room when the hall phone rang. I rushed to answer it, and I wasn't disappointed. Gordy asked if I'd like to go out Friday night. He said Jimmy would be coming too, and could I get a date for him. I fixed Jimmy up with a friend, and the four of us went to the Satire Room, a hot spot among Smithies with a good band and dancing. It was then that I learned that Gordy and Jimmy were playing in a tournament at Wesleyan in Connecticut and were in the finals, but I didn't know any more details. We left the Satire Room very late – I had a key and could get into the dorm after 11 pm., our curfew. Gordy and Jimmy didn't get to Wesleyan until 3 a.m.

They were playing in the New England Intercollegiate Championships, seeded No. 1 because they had the best record in the Ivy League. I learned later that Gordy's parents had driven to Wesleyan from northeastern Pennsylvania to watch the match with high expectations. Little did they know that Gordy and Jimmy made a road trip to Northampton the night before. The next day, the boys didn't play up to their usual level and lost in three sets.

When explaining the outcome to his Dad after the match, Gordy said, "Well, sometimes there are more important things than tennis."

That statement stunned his father. Nothing in his son's life had ever been more important than tennis.

I missed Gordy's graduation ceremony from Dartmouth as I was due in Washington D.C. to begin a summer internship with Senator Jacob K. Javits of New York. I was one of six Smith students who was chosen to participate in a Smith-sponsored program organized in cooperation with Yale Law School. We rented a house in the Northwest section of Washington for the summer and interned in various capacities for Congressmen,

Gordon Aydelott, Dartmouth Coach "Red" Hoehn and Jim Biggs

Senators and the World Bank. Being a part of the Yale program gave us entrée too to private seminars with Yale alumni who were then leaders in Congress, the State Department and the West Wing. The experience was eye-opening, glamorous and wonderful.

Gordy, after graduation, went directly into the U.S. Navy, assigned to a destroyer, the USS Willard Keith, whose home port was Norfolk, Virginia. We saw each other a couple of times that summer since Norfolk wasn't too far from Washington. Then I returned to Northampton for my senior year at Smith. I hadn't been back a month when, in October, 1962, Washington was embroiled in one of the most stressful encounters with the Soviet Union in the history of the Cold War. It brought us closer to nuclear war than ever before or since. An American surveillance plane flying over Cuba had discovered and photographed Soviet missiles being installed on the island to effectuate a first strike position against the United States. President Kennedy's military advisors were recommending an air strike, whereas other advisors were considering a naval blockade to keep Soviet ships from delivering more arms and equipment to Cuba. Despite grave risks, President Kennedy opted for the naval blockade. Gordy's ship, the Willard Keith, a Sumner-class destroyer, was ordered to take its position in a heavily armed armada of destroyers, aircraft carriers, cruisers, oilers, tankers and submarines spread out across the Caribbean Ocean. Gordy, however, had been sent to Key West, Florida for anti-submarine warfare training. Key West, a short 90 miles from Cuba, fortified itself against a possible invasion. Barbed wire was erected around the utilities – water and fuel tanks – and jets were flying into and out of the airfield at all hours of the day and night in case an air strike was called. Machine guns were placed on the beaches.

The President demanded secrecy and did not inform the public of the proposed blockade until the order had been given. Despite the cry for transparency, it was probably a smart move. The public was spared a few days of anxiety. President Kennedy addressed the nation – and the world – from the Oval Office and explained the dire circumstances and his plan. Then the media began to speculate whether the blockade would hold and whether the Soviet ships would stop. The world was terrified that nuclear war was imminent. Rumors were spreading that Khrushchev, the Soviet Union's premier, had been deposed in a coup. With whom could the United States negotiate? Who among the Soviets was in control? Some news reports indicated the blockade had been broken and that the U.S. Navy had no choice but to fire on Soviet ships.

After a few days of heightened tension, it became clear that Khrushchev was in control and that he too understood the insanity of confrontation. The Soviet ships were ordered to stand down. Armageddon was avoided. The first strike missiles on Cuba were dismantled, but only after the United States secretly agreed to dismantle its missile site in Turkey. Kennedy insisted, however, that the dismantling of our missiles not occur for six months and that it not be linked to the agreement to end the blockade.

In the meantime, communication between Gordy and me was non-existent. I couldn't get through to him by phone and letters didn't arrive until well after the fact. I was somewhat comforted that he was in Key West and not on the Willard Keith in the middle of the blockade, but I didn't know about the heightened alert there, thankfully. Staying busy was the best remedy.

Soon after that crisis, Gordy was back on the ship and off on a Mediterranean cruise to the Middle East, the Red Sea and the Horn of Africa. The mission was to "show the flag." One of his letters described that, as they went through the Suez Canal, beggars clamored to get on board and had to be, literally, beaten back. Another letter told me he was in Djibouti, French Somaliland. I struggled to find it on a world map. Gordy wrote that he was the 'officer of the deck' the first night the ship was in port. Half of the crew was at liberty, giving them permission to leave the ship – and to get into trouble. They headed for the nearest bars, making up for months of abstinence and returned to the Willard Keith totally drunk and out of control. Actually, the shore patrol had to round up the motley crew. Out of uniform, they had replaced their hats with foreign legion souvenirs and even spears. Their return to quarters was far from orderly, and the other half of the crew did not appreciate being awakened. Fights broke out, and the Officer of the Deck, Gordy, with the help of the Bo'sun Mate of the Watch, well-respected by the crew, had to step in and restore order.

Reading his letter, I realized how much Gordy's life had changed. Where had the carefree days of tennis, fraternity parties and Dartmouth gone?

When Gordon got back from his Mediterranean mission shortly before the holidays I got a phone call from him. He was going to be home on leave and wondered if I could spend Christmas with him and his family in Pennsylvania. My parents were disappointed that I wouldn't be spending Christmas at home, but they consented. Gordy drove his pea green VW bug that he had purchased from his parents from Norfolk to my home in New York. He met my parents briefly though they had heard much about him and approved, in part, because he was a Dartmouth graduate like my mother's brother. A Dartmouth grad could do no wrong.

On Christmas Eve, after everyone had gone to bed, we were sitting on the floor in front of a roaring fire. And out of Gordon's mouth came, "Will you marry me?" I was shocked. But I guess not shocked enough not to say, 'Yes.' We hardly knew each other, but I was head over heels in love. From my first sighting of the guy who couldn't face his blind date, I liked him. I've never told him this, but he was considerate and almost gentle as we talked about our homes and families. I could tell from the good-natured fun and camaraderie displayed that he was well-liked and respected by his fraternity brothers. He was often called "The Grand Gord," their leader, and he wore his role well. We had such fun together; we seemed to have the same values. And, as I said before, he was very good looking, a quality which didn't hurt. He was tall - 6' 2" -

blue-eyed, square-jawed with dark hair. And he was in good shape. Gordy was the one, and thoughts of going to law school which I had planned to do after graduation, disappeared. It was an impulsive act for sure, but I wasn't concerned that I was making a mistake. I look back now and think how young and reckless we were, but we were married in September, 1963. Sometimes, recklessness with a touch of good instincts can be a good combination.

Immediately after our honeymoon, Gordy had a new assignment as an instructor at the Naval Officer Candidate School (OCS) in Newport, Rhode Island. We found a small, furnished apartment at 16 Mann Avenue and settled in. Newlywed life in Newport was blissful. We made friends quickly with other young Navy couples, some assigned to OCS, others on ships stationed in Newport. We were seeing the Navy from a new perspective – no more long cruises, blockades or anti-submarine warfare exercises. This was shore duty and being a part of OCS meant that the officers' social life was much improved.

Gordy's new job at OCS gave him lots of time to play tennis – and to get me playing too. Finally, it was time for me to start learning the game. I had always been active – horseback riding, softball, basketball, cheerleading - but back in the 1950's girls' sports were very limited. I was a willing and eager student, but a total beginner. Patiently, Gordy would go through the basics of hitting forehands and backhands with topspin. He has always been a stickler on form. And after 50 years, he hasn't changed a bit.

Gordy was an accomplished player when I met him, having started tennis when he was eight, thanks to his father. Jack Aydelott was devoted to tennis. In the early 1900's, Jack and his father built a tennis court out of dirt in their back yard in Cincinnati, Ohio. As a young father, Jack started his sons playing the game on a neighbor's concrete court. Then his family joined the Scranton Tennis Club, a very modest facility with six clay courts and a small, non-descript club house that needed a lot of work, but there was never any money to fix it up. But to the Aydelotts, that didn't matter. What they cared about was playing tennis. Gordy took lessons from the club pro, Eddie Klaus, and got games with his brother and some of the older players who were glad to have this young kid join in. But Jack thought Gordy needed a better teacher and made arrangements with Ed Faulkner, the pro at the nearby Buck Hill Falls Club in the Poconos, the former Swarthmore College tennis coach, and well-known coach for U.S. Davis Cuppers Vic Seixas and Straight Clark.

In addition to taking lessons from Faulkner, Gordy worked for Faulkner as one of his tennis boys the summer before he graduated from high school.

"There were four of us and we lived in Faulkner's cottage," Gordy said. "We had to get up early to roll the courts and get them ready for the day's play. Faulkner was an old-school teacher who used to stay on the same side of the court as his student to get a better view of the student's stroke and to give instructions. Sometimes he'd write diagrams on the court to help explain. We tennis boys would feed the balls during the lessons. Faulkner would yell, 'OK. Hit all forehands,' or 'Hit all backhands,' and we'd do as he said. It was a good way to teach. And Faulkner was one of the best.

"On Saturdays and Sundays, Faulkner would invite some of the top players from Philadelphia to come to Buck Hill to give exhibitions" Gordy continued. "Vic Seixas was one. Straight Clark, a former U.S. Davis Cupper and top U.S. player in the '50's, was another. We tennis boys would fill in for the doubles."

Faulkner, too, was a stickler for form, the classic stroke-making of tennis. In 1970, his book, *Ed Faulkner's Tennis: How to Play It; How to Teach It,* was published. It is still considered one of the most comprehensive and instructive books on learning to play the game.

"During that same summer I got some time off to play in the Pennsylvania Chamber of Commerce junior tournament," said Gordy, "The tournament was a qualifier for the Nationals being played in Santa Monica, California. Each state sent two players, the finalist and the winner, to the Nationals. Ralph Howe, who later went to Yale, and I were the two top players and qualified. At the Nationals I won singles in the first round but lost in the second round 6-1, 6-4 to Allen Fox, then at UCLA and playing for California, the ultimate winner of the tournament. Fox went on to be on the U.S. Davis Cup team, the tennis coach at Pepperdine for many years and an author of several books on sports psychology.

"In doubles, Ralph and I beat Tom Richardson, Ham's brother, and Alby Stark from New Jersey in the first round but lost to a team from Indiana in the second. Jimmy was also in the tournament representing Connecticut and met a fate similar to mine."

There was not much competitive summer tennis for Gordy after this. His subsequent summers were spent re-paving roads in Scranton and Wilkes-Barre, including running a 60-pound or 90-pound jackhammer and also working on a local farm. Between his junior and senior years, he started his obligations with the U.S. Navy, going on missions in the North Atlantic.

While we lived in Newport, Gordy didn't just work on my game in his free time. He entered the Base and North Atlantic Regional tournaments, conveniently held at Newport, and won them both. They were followed by the All Navy Tournament.

Richard Raskind, a big left-hander and Yale graduate who was in the Navy finishing his residency in ophthalmology, wanted to play doubles in the All Navy, but only with the player who won the regional tournament. That player was Gordy. He and Richard won. Shortly after the win, Gordy got a call from someone in Navy personnel. A certain Admiral who had played tennis was looking for a new aide. Gordy didn't want to be an admiral's aide playing tennis with some bumbler, so he asked if he could know the name of the Admiral. "Farrin." Admiral James Farrin, with his son, Jimmy, the No. 1 player at Princeton, had been three-time runners-up in the National Father-Son tournaments. In that case, Gordy would be happy to be Admiral Farrin's aide.

I was fine with the idea too. But, nine days before leaving Newport for Norfolk, I gave birth to our first baby girl, Deb. Gordy and I were parental neophytes and I remember saying to Deb before leaving the hospital as I struggled to put on her little outfit, "OK Deb. This is the first time for you and it's the first time for me. But we'll get through it." We did.

One of Gordy's responsibilities was to manage the Admiral's schedule and tennis matches were always an important part of the Admiral's routine. Gordy set up the matches with top players from the Norfolk area. Not bad duty….

We were housed in the Marine officers' quarters and started making friends with the Marines and their young families. When Deb was only four weeks old, she watched her new mom and dad play tennis from the sidelines, cozily wrapped in a soft blanket in her 'carry bag.'

The most exciting event that Admiral Farrin hosted was the commissioning of the new aircraft carrier, the USS America. A motorcade of black limousines with motorcycle police escorts, flashing lights and occasional sirens, carried the dignitaries, including Dean Rusk, then Secretary of State and the principal speaker, from the Naval station to the port where the America was docked. I was in the limousine with Mrs. Farrin; Gordy was in the limousine with Admiral Farrin. I was twenty-three and felt like a celebrity.

Gordy was honorably discharged from the Navy in the summer of 1965. We both left behind good friends, many of whom were Marines heading to Vietnam; some never returned. We harbored some guilt that we were fortunate to go on with our lives. But I have to say that the Marines we got to know in Virginia were the most devoted, driven warriors and proud Americans, anxious to test their mettle in combat. *Semper fi* to country, fellow Marines and family.

Amy, our second daughter, arrived in March, 1967, shortly before Gordon heard that he had been accepted to join the Class of 1970 at Villanova University School of Law. We were thrilled on both counts and didn't question the challenges of no income and two little girls to care for.

We started our new life in Bryn Mawr, Pennsylvania, in a family-friendly area known as Cooperstown. Money was tight, of course, but we had the G.I. Bill, 100 dollars per month from Gordy's Dad, and I gave piano lessons, though that was hardly enough to scrape by. The solution was Gordy's mother's real estate business. By this time, Gordy's father Jack had retired from his work at International Salt and joined his wife Marj at Aydelott Associates. They had more free time to travel and suggested I get my real estate license which I did. What would we have done without their help? So, when they went away for however long, I handled the business, together with one or two other agents. And, much to my surprise - and theirs too - I was a pretty good saleswoman!

Meanwhile, Gordon did well in law school, becoming an editor of *Law Review*, and I helped by typing all his class notes. Reading his notes and becoming familiar with the legal concepts rekindled my passion to go to law school myself. I decided to see if Villanova would consider taking me as a part-time student. After some meetings with the Dean of the law school, Dean Reuschlein, and re-taking the LSATs, I was allowed to take three courses - Contracts, Torts and Property - and join the class of 1972.

Gordy and I juggled the girls, play dates, class schedules and grocery shopping. Our little VW Squareback was often filled with neighborhood playmates when Gordy and I switched roles, with me going to class and him doing the babysitting.

Seeing the crowded car, one of my friends said, "Judy. I knew you had kids, but I didn't know you had *that* many!"

But, Gordy graduated in 1970 and decided to take a position in New York, which meant no more Villanova for me. But I was able to finish law school a few years later while we lived in Mahopac, New York, when Deb started fourth grade, and Amy went into the first grade.

In time, we had moved to Katonah, New York, closer to Manhattan, so I went on interviews in the city and surprisingly received an offer from a firm in Manhattan, Cravath, Swaine & Moore, but after contemplating a daily 90-minute to two-hour commute with a young family, I declined the offer, choosing to seek an opportunity closer to home. White Plains, Westchester's county seat, was my target, but the firms that I was interested in didn't hire women. But my timing was right. The managing partner at the leading litigation firm in White Plains, Henry Miller, had decided it was time to hire a female attorney. I joined Clark, Gagliardi and Miller a couple months later. I could not have been happier, though some of my colleagues in this 12-man law firm weren't quite so excited. I stayed there for five years, when Gordy and I opened our own firm, Aydelott & Aydelott in Mount Kisco, New York, which grew and was later moved to White Plains.

When we moved to Katonah, Jimmy was living nearby in Fairfield, Connecticut, and the Biggs/Aydelott doubles team came back to life.

What happened to the Biggs/Aydelott team after Dartmouth, the Navy and law school? They picked up right where they had left off. As durable as the partnership is between Gordon and me, the partnership of Biggs and Aydelott is even more so – now 62 years! That has to be some kind of a record.

By this time Jimmy had graduated from Columbia Business School with an MBA and was working for People's Bank, a career that led him to the bank presidency in 1997. He and his family were members of the Fairfield Beach Club, where an annual member-guest tennis tournament was played. The competition was strong and the Biggs / Aydelott team triumphed for many years.

"There were several weekend tournaments in the area that we entered," said Jimmy. "In our early 30s, we won most of them. In our later 30s, we would win or lose in the finals; in the 40s, we could count on playing on Saturday and going into the 'consies' – or consolation rounds - on Sunday. The younger guys were getting too good. We were playing in the finals of a tournament at the New Canaan Field Club against Joe Fahey and his partner, whom I don't remember. But this was when the nine-point tiebreaker was played to end a third set tied at six all. It was called 'sudden death' because if reaching a score of 4-4, each team had match point. At 4-4, Fahey was serving. I hit a clean return, Fahey hit a good shot from the back court while I charged the net and hit a good volley. Fahey took a big swing, and the ball hit the back fence. Game, set, match to Biggs and Aydelott."

Gordy remembered another interesting tale with the mercurial former U.S. Davis Cupper Whitney Reed.

"We started entering the national tournaments in the 35s played at Shelter Rock on Long Island and we got to the quarters and were to play Don Kirkbow and Whitney Reed," he said. "The time to start the match came and went. Whitney Reed didn't appear. The umpire said that we were entitled to a default, but we said we wanted to play. Reed was found at the bar with quite a buzz on. We got him out to the court and he and Kirkbow killed us. Reed can play sober or drunk."

Gordy and Jimmy had many other senior tennis adventures of victory and defeat, even having the opportunity to play on the famous Grandstand court at the USTA National Tennis Center in Flushing Meadows, where many great U.S. Open matches were played, during the USTA National 40s. They won a silver ball together at the USTA National 60's grass courts. By virtue of playing matches for the United States against other countries, Gordy and Jimmy are also members of the International Club or the "IC." I was fortunate to become a member too, when Gordy was the chair of the nominating committee. I had some 'insider' help.

"The I.C. combines playing tennis with men and women from all over the world, visiting them in their countries, hosting them in the US and fostering good will," Jimmy said. "The trips since have been amazing. One of my favorites was when we played the French at Roland Garros in Paris. Our first match was against Monsieur Clement, the uncle of Arnaud Clement, a former top French player, and Monsieur LeClerc. They were favored to win, and it looked like they would after they came out strong in the first set, but we got our 'mo' going and won in two."

"They weren't too happy," Gordy chimed in. "But by lunch time, they were fine. We ate under center court at Roland Garros and were treated to fine French wines and a great lunch. Then we went up into the stadium and watched Todd Martin and James Blake win their US Davis Cup doubles match in five sets against the French."

"The I.C. trips are remarkable," Gordy continued. "We travel all over the world – Australia during the Australian Open, New Zealand, Argentina, Russia, Cuba and most of Europe. I think my favorite was Australia, where Jimmy and I got to play at Kooyong against Ken Rosewall and John – I can't remember his last name who had won the Wimbledon juniors years before. That's when both of us knew not to hit to Rosewall's backhand, but you had to test it just once. And that ball came back so fast and out of reach, I yelled to Rosewall, 'If you keep practicing that shot, you'll become a world class player someday.'"

We all agreed that the I.C. connected us with wonderful people and great players and made lasting friendships. It is an integral part of our "senior" tennis experience.

"I enjoy the competition, the chase," Jimmy said of senior tennis. "I enjoy seeing the people I've played with and against for decades. And then there are a lot of players who are good now who never even played before. They took up the game later, took lessons, entered clinics, practiced hard and became good players in their later years. I've had a ton of injuries – 12 surgeries on my hip, neck, knees, shoulder, you name it. One of our good tennis friends Clyde Barker who is a kidney transplant physician in Philadelphia and also a member of the USIC, told me not long ago, 'Hip and knee replacements are the greatest medical advance of the 20th century. I can give someone a new liver or kidney, but you can't do that very often. Hip and knee replacements are done routinely and change people's lives.'

"Gordy and I have both had hip and knee replacements that let us go back on the court without pain," he continued. "And tennis is great therapy, a stress reliever. I don't think of anything when I'm on the court except my tennis."

Jimmy wrote an article for the *Super Senior Newsletter* and described his and Gordon's enduring friendship this way.

"What keeps a doubles team together for over 60 years? First and foremost, we have been fortunate to have a strong and enduring friendship, sharing values that place a premium on honesty, integrity, loyalty and perseverance, and perhaps the most important, a sense of humor. We take our tennis seriously, but we don't take ourselves too seriously. In fact, through all these years we have never had an argument on or off the court. We just choose to enjoy the game for what it is.... We both share a love and passion for this wonderful game of tennis. We have never forgotten that tennis is a game and games are meant to be fun. Hopefully we will be able to enjoy the game and savor the competition for many more years... the '75s, the 80? Who knows. But we are at 62 years and counting. Here's hoping!"

Gordon added, "For me, I like to compete and in competing I have to exert physical effort. I enjoy the results of that. I always played sports, not just tennis. In high school, I played basketball, football and tennis; at Dartmouth I played rugby and tennis, plus some intramural wrestling. But tennis endures. Except for an occasional pick-up basketball game or touch football at Thanksgiving when family and friends come for the 'Turkey Bowl,' you can't play those sports as you age. But, with tennis you can. Strategy becomes more important as you get older. You can't move as well or hit the ball as hard, so you have to think your way through your matches. It's a complete game for not only your body but also for your mind. And, if you want to play competitive senior tennis, you benefit from the age categories that are established. Actually from the time you start playing competitively at age eight or under until you hang up the racquet in your 90's, or maybe even later, you're playing with people your own age. Outside tournament play you can play with whomever you want – younger or older – depending on your skill level or who your tennis buddies are.

"I like myself better if I'm fit, keep my weight in check and get good exercise," he continued. "Tennis helps me get where I want to be. If you don't like the way you feel it comes through in your personality, and you won't be a 'can do' person. You don't have to play matches all the time either. I just like hitting the ball; striking it well; having a good practice session. It feels so good after a strenuous workout."

Both Gordon and Jimmy have given back to the game that has provided them so much. After he retired, Jimmy volunteered to coach the men's tennis team at Sacred Heart University for 13 years, taking the team twice to the NCAAs. When he stopped coaching, Jimmy became very involved in Bridgeport Community Tennis, a grassroots program for elementary school children in Bridgeport, Connecticut. With a federal grant and a $45,000 grant from the USTA, old public courts were reconditioned, racquets for ten-and-under kids were purchased, and teachers were hired providing tennis instruction in 23 of the 26 elementary schools in Bridgeport.

Meanwhile, Gordon, while still practicing law part-time, volunteered to give clinics over the years at town parks and became the volunteer assistant coach for the John Jay High School tennis team for several years. Both Gordon and I were very involved in the building of the six tennis courts at the high school.

As for me, once my trial work lightened a bit, I had more time to concentrate on tennis and improving my skills. I began playing more competitive tennis, both singles and doubles, usually with younger women, took lessons and practiced. I love to practice tennis. I get 'highs' when a new shot I'm working on begins to click. The trick is to translate those good practice sessions into match play. A book that has helped me tremendously is *The Best Tennis of Your Life: 50*

Mental Strategies for Fearless Performance by Jeff Greenwald, a sports psychologist. The title sounds daunting, but it's a little, tiny book of 150 pages and each of the 50 chapters is only two or three pages, but the book is filled with common sense ideas that I have underlined. When a big tournament is coming up, I review the underlined portions, and it puts me in the right frame of mind, basically: play with gratitude, enjoy the moment and focus.

For years Gordon and I had a regular Friday night game with our good friends Nancy Coates, now McKinney, and Jack McGinty. We also played on a regular basis against a Saw Mill pro, Miguel, and his wife, Barbara. Our matches were always competitive, and we'd end the evenings with dinner out. This prompted us to enter some mixed doubles tournaments in our area and in Nantucket where we did well, often getting to the finals and winning it once. As long as I stayed healthy and without injury except for some pesky tendonitis, I was actually playing my best tennis.

The ultimate thrill was getting a national ranking in husband/wife mixed doubles in the 140 age category. True, there are not many husbands and wives who play mixed doubles together as a team. And husbands and wives in our age category who play mixed doubles are rare, but you'd be surprised that many of these old timers who enter the 140's are pretty darn good. And they're having fun too – good matches, good exercise, positive attitudes and new friends. Fifty years of tennis has brought me even more - fabulous trips, tough competition, wonderful lifelong friends, opportunities, and good health. Tennis is the sport of a lifetime. Try it. You'll be glad you did!

ACKNOWLEDGMENTS

Nancy Geary knew of the idea floated by Mary Pat, the tennis player mentioned in the Introduction, to interview famous septuagenarians. Nancy suggested, however, that I concentrate on tennis-playing seniors. She planted the seed, but this book never would have happened had it not been for Steve Flink, the Hall of Fame tennis writer, author and historian. Steve advised and encouraged me, led me to my publisher New Chapter Press, edited tirelessly, opened the door for me to meet and interview the legendary John Newcombe, and, in the process, he and I became good friends. For that, I am very grateful.

I am also thankful for the patience, candor, good humor and editing skills of my publisher Randy Walker of New Chapter Press and for all the outstanding people who allowed me to spend time with them, to learn of their lives before, during and after tennis and how the game of tennis has enriched their lives.

Thank you too to my family, who read drafts and made valuable suggestions, and to my granddaughter Kiley who guided me through the mystery of modern technology and to many friends who encouraged me throughout this journey.

Last but certainly not least, to my husband Gordon, who introduced me to tennis…The Sport of a Lifetime.

ALSO FROM NEW CHAPTER PRESS

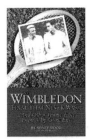

The Wimbledon Final That Never Was... And Other Tennis Tales From A Bygone Era

By Sidney Wood with David Wood

The only time in the history of Wimbledon that the men's singles final was not played is told in detail by the crowned champion in this illuminating tennis biography. Sidney Wood won the 1931 Wimbledon title by default over Frank Shields—his school buddy, doubles partner, roommate, and Davis Cup teammate—in one of the most curious episodes in sports history. Wood tells the tale of how Shields was ordered by the U.S. Tennis Association not to compete in the championship match so that he could rest his injured knee in preparation for an upcoming Davis Cup match. Three years later the story continues when he and Shields played a match at the Queen's Club for the Wimbledon trophy. Also included are a compilation of short stories that deliver fascinating anecdotes of the 1930s and a signature document of the play and styles of 20th-century tennis legends.

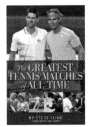

The Greatest Tennis Matches of All Time

By Steve Flink

Tennis historian Steve Flink profiles and ranks the greatest tennis matches in the history of the sport. Roger Federer, Billie Jean King, Rafael Nadal, Bjorn Borg, John McEnroe, Martina Navratilova, Rod Laver, and Chris Evert are all featured in this book that breaks down, analyzes, and puts into historical context the most memorable matches ever played.

The Greatest Jewish Tennis Players of All Time

By Sandra Harwitt

Unique among other books on tennis, this guide to the best and most influential Jewish tennis players in the history of the sport includes features and biographies of the greatest players, stories of both break- out success , anti-Semitism and famous players with partial Jewish heritage.

A Backhanded Gift

By Marshall Jon Fisher

It's the late 1980s, just before the fall of the Berlin Wall, and Robert Cherney, a 30-year-old aspiring writer, has left New York City for a job teaching tennis in Munich. Love, tennis, sex, frustrated artistic ambition, and the dilemma of being a German Jew are all ingredients of this literary delight that is at turns serious and comedic.